4 x 8/10 ✓ 12/10

D0398853

fP

VELOCITY

Combining Lean, Six Sigma, and the Theory of Constraints
to Achieve Breakthrough Performance

— A BUSINESS NOVEL

DEE JACOB, SUZAN BERGLAND, AND JEFF COX

FREE PRESS

New York   London   Toronto   Sydney

To those who began this journey before us.
And to those who will continue it.

FREE PRESS
A Division of Simon & Schuster, Inc.
1230 Avenue of the Americas
New York, NY 10020

First Free Press hardcover edition January 2010

FREE PRESS and colophon are trademarks of Simon & Schuster, Inc.

For information about special discounts for bulk purchases,
please contact Simon & Schuster Special Sales at 1-866-506-1949
or business@simonandschuster.com

The Simon & Schuster Speakers Bureau can bring authors to your live event.
For more information or to book an event contact the Simon & Schuster Speakers
Bureau at 1-866-248-3049 or visit our website at www.simonspeakers.com.

Manufactured in the United States of America

1 2 3 4 5 6 7 8 9 10

Library of Congress Cataloging-in-Publication Data

Jacob, Dee.
Velocity : combining lean, six sigma, and the theory of constraints to achieve
breakthrough performance: a business novel / Dee Jacob, Suzan Bergland,
and Jeff Cox.—1st Free Press hbk. ed.
p. cm.
1. Industrial management. 2. Industrial efficiency. 3. Organizational
effectiveness. I. Bergland, Suzan. II. Cox, Jeff. III. Title.
HD31.J2338 2010
658.4'013—dc22   2009031900

ISBN 978-1-4391-5892-0
ISBN 978-1-4391-8121-8 (ebook)

Introduction

Experienced managers know that nothing is static in the operating environment; over time there is change. The rate of change may be slow. It may be alarmingly fast (or seem that way to those caught by surprise). But change is forever occurring in markets, in technology, in methods, in processes, in skills, in regulations, and in everything else, including the art and practice of management itself. To cope with unending change – and indeed to make the most of it – the effective manager understands that the long-term success of the organization depends upon ongoing, progressive, positive adaptation – what has come to be called "continuous improvement."

Over recent decades, going back to the 1980s and earlier, there have been a number of organized efforts aimed at achieving continuous improvement, many of them becoming known by a three-letter acronym. There were TPS (Toyota Production System), TQM (Total Quality Management), SPC (Statistical Process Control), JIT (Just in Time), as well as many others. All of these, even those that fell by the wayside or were absorbed into other disciplines, had elements of value, with important concepts and useful tools and methods. Unfortunately, there were also flaws in the thinking that went into the implementation of these efforts, and sometimes in the very assumptions on which they were founded. As a result, most organizations, though they learned from these programs and disciplines, were never able to achieve the degree of sustained performance they expected.

When we talk about continuous improvement, a number of essential questions arise. For instance, *what* should be improved? Everything? That is, should we seek to improve *everything* throughout the entire organization? Many well-intentioned program managers, executives, and consultants would, indeed, say, "Yes, we must improve everything, every function, every aspect of operations, from A to Z!" As if to say, "We must focus everywhere!"

Yet it's a serious question: should the management team seek to improve *everything*? All at once? Simultaneously? *And* continuously? What should be the scope of the improvement effort? Do you include every function? Every customer service and supplier interaction? What about housekeeping, accounting, and maintenance? And which resources do you include? If you include *everything* and *everybody* in any but the smallest of companies, you're into a massive undertaking. How do you organize it? More important, how do you make it effective?

Conversely, perhaps for obvious reasons of practicality and budget, suppose you do not seek to improve everything all at once. Then you're back to the original question: *what* do you improve? *Where* do you focus? By what criteria do you select your improvement initiatives and assign resources and tasks? Can you know in advance whether there is really going to be a bottom-line gain for all your trouble and investment?

What people tend to mean when they say, "We must improve everything," is that they want "everything" to improve. In other words, they want *everything* – the entire organization – to achieve a significant, overall performance gain that increases year after year. They want to improve the *total system* that is producing whatever output it was created to produce, and they want over time real bottom-line results to show for it. However, "improving everything" is not the same as "everything improving." If you doubt this, by all means please do keep reading this book.

Both in the past as well as today, many organizations have invested in large-scale improvement efforts, with lots of training and internal meetings and so on, with sincere conviction. The assumption typically was (and is) that many, many small improvements will accrue in terms of "savings" or efficiency gains or waste reduction or even employee morale – and ultimately the sum of these improvements will yield major gains in profitability, competitiveness, and customer satisfaction. In fact, what occurs is a number of local-area improvements, i.e., less waste in Function B, fewer defects in Function M, less variation in such-and-such a process, shorter processing time within Function T. But many of the supposed gains *never* actually accrue to the bottom line.

These very same issues as above confront and challenge Amy

Cieolara and her colleagues who populate the following business novel, *VELOCITY*, just as they do a vast number of managers and executives in all types of companies and organizations around the world. These issues are vital, because the need for continuous improvement is truly urgent. There are business and economic realities that are demanding advances in organizational performance – and while crucial in normal times, they never have been more so than in our current times. Yet what are managers, as well as professional practitioners of improvement disciplines such as Lean and Six Sigma, supposed to do? So many companies and other organizations have made major investments in Lean and Six Sigma and other improvement concepts, as well as in plant and equipment and technology, but the yield on these investments is not providing the expected return. What is the answer? What should be done?

This is why we wrote *VELOCITY*. This book is concerned with three major continuous-improvement disciplines – Lean, Six Sigma, and the Theory of Constraints – and how to combine them so that the organization does achieve systemic gains that yield improved bottom-line performance. Many if not most readers will be familiar with one or more of those three. For the uninitiated, very briefly, Lean was founded upon concepts established in the Toyota Production System (TPS) and emphasizes elimination of waste in its many forms. Six Sigma was derived from Total Quality Management and other quality improvement methods, and its strength is in reducing variation. And the Theory of Constraints (TOC) was created by Dr. Eliyahu Goldratt, the founder of our organization, the AGI-Goldratt Institute. TOC holds that a system constraint is the most practical way to reliably manage a complex system, and once the system is stable and predictable, provides the focus for systemic improvement. And *VELOCITY* – as a concept – is the means by which the organization orchestrates all of its resources, as well as all three improvement disciplines, and achieves both speed and direction toward its strategic goals. We believe that this is a very powerful approach to organizational improvement. As you read, you might keep in mind that *VELOCITY* consists of three pillars: Theory of Constraints – TOC – as the system architecture; TOC, Lean, and Six Sigma disciplines – TOCLSS – together as the focused improvement process; and Strategy, Design, Activate, Improve, Sustain – SDAIS – as the deployment framework. We have confidence that, if it is properly applied, you and your company or organization can achieve major benefits using this approach.

One final question: why write about this subject by way of a business novel? For one reason, we have a strong precedent. *The Goal*, which is now considered a classic in business literature and has sold millions of copies globally, was a novel created by our founder, Dr. Goldratt, working in association with creative writer Jeff Cox. Mr. Cox now returns to the subject matter and style of that now-famous book by working with AGI to write *VELOCITY*.

However, it should also be noted that fiction provides some significant advantages over a conventional business text. Strategy, technology, tangible assets, material resources – all of these and more are essential for a functioning business. But it can be said, with no sentimentality, that human beings are really at the core of every organization. A novel allows readers to experience business concepts as actual people might. We can reveal with fairly good accuracy where conflicts can develop, and the resolution of those conflicts. The story becomes a way to better engage the reader, and to explore the ideas as they actually might play out in the readers' own environments. And, aside from all that, a novel can make the reading of the book a heck of a lot more interesting to anyone in your organization.

So we hope you enjoy *VELOCITY* – and that you gain practical insights to make you and your organization more successful.

1

The news spread by way of hushed murmurs in hallways, muffled conversations behind closed doors, mutterings over the tops of cubicle walls, quiet phone calls with hands covering the mouthpieces. However, one poor chump was stupid enough to broadcast it in an email – and he eventually got the blame and was canned, although he in fact had not been the one initially to leak the word. In any case, within hours – and a good two days before the official announcement – practically everyone at the headquarters of Hi-T Composites knew what was only supposed to be known by certain boards of directors, key executives, and a few trusted subordinates.

Amy Cieolara, who was not one of those privileged few, had just got back to her office after her regular Wednesday meeting with her marketing and salespeople. She was a slim woman, age forty-one at the time, with sandy brown hair cut midlength that she wore either pulled back or in long, flowing curls framing her rather angular chinline. This was a curls day, and she was having trouble keeping them out of her face as she walked briskly through the offices while thumbing a text message at the same time. Almost in lockstep behind her as she went into her office came Linda, her assistant, who closed Amy's door and held it shut, leaning against it lest some intruder should come barging in and hear her speak of the appalling secret.

"Have you heard?" Linda asked.

"What? About Elaine and Bill? Well, everyone said it was never going to last, and guess what, it didn't."

"No!" said Linda in an exclamatory whisper. "We're getting sold to some huge company!"

Amy's green eyes sharpened their focus on the younger woman's worried face.

"Well? Is it true?"

"Linda, if I knew, which I don't, I wouldn't be allowed to say anything to anybody. By the way, who told you?"

"Nobody. There's an email floating around. I'll forward it to you."

"No!" said Amy. "I don't want it on my computer. Print a copy for me."

Linda slipped out the door, back to her desk. When she returned a few minutes later, sheet of paper in hand, Amy took the email printout and read it quickly, then blew a soft whistle from between her lips.

"Wow, is this guy in trouble," Amy said under her breath. Then, to Linda: "Look, it's probably just one of those rumors that gets started. Don't get yourself in a tizzy."

"But Bobby just got laid off and I'm five-and-a-half-months pregnant! What if we have to go through all that downsizing stuff again?"

"If it ever happens, it's a long way off. All right? Anyway, Bobby is smart; he'll find something else. You'll both be fine – I mean, all three of you, you'll be just fine. Now, I need you to make some travel reservations for me . . ."

With Linda calmed down and returning to her normal high-level competency, buzzing away at task after task and all but leaping tall buildings, even in her pregnant state, Amy whisked herself down the hall. Email printout in hand, she hurried into the corner office of Hi-T Composites Company President B. Donald Williams. She shut B. Don's door behind her and leaned her slim frame against it, almost exactly as Linda had done.

"What's up?" asked B. Don.

"Have you heard?"

He blinked his eyes as if feigning ignorance, then relented. "Well, yes, I have heard. I have to say, I am not shocked."

"You're not?"

"No, I'm not."

Amy's mouth dropped open.

"Anyone could have seen it coming," he said.

"Well, I couldn't."

"Come on, Amy! Everyone knows Bill is a jerk – and Elaine, much as I appreciate her professionally, would just be impossible to live with."

"No! Not them. This!"

She handed the sheet of paper across the desk to B. Don and sat down in one of his well-worn, sun-faded chairs. The business unit president put on his glasses and then scrutinized the words, his eyes widening as he read.

"Oh . . . ! Oh snap!" he said. "Where the snappin' hell did this come from?"

"According to Linda – who had nothing to do with this – everyone knows. Or thinks they know. Anyway, everyone is talking about it. By the way, is it true?"

B. Don leaned back, removed his glasses, and gave them a toss, such that the glasses spun across the leather blotter on his desk. He then shut his eyes and pinched the bridge of his nose with his thumb and forefinger.

"Can you tell me . . . or not?" Amy asked.

"You," he said with emphasis, "cannot tell anyone."

"But everyone knows."

"But you cannot talk about it. Okay?"

"Okay."

"To anyone. Understood?"

"Well, sure. But according to Linda, it's all over the place."

"Most of what's in this moron's email is pure crap. However . . . and unfortunately . . . the basic story is true. We are being sold. That's why I've been going to St. Louis so often the past few months. I've been at headquarters meeting with the board and the new buyer."

"Who's buying?"

B. Don leaned over his desk and whispered the name.

"Really?"

"Yes," he said. "Now, what I've just told you could probably get me fired . . . or, these days, even get me sent to jail. So –"

"I won't breathe a word, you know that."

The president tipped back in his chair, shook his head, and exhaled, making a sound somewhere between a chuckle and a sigh.

"Amy, I hate to swear in front of you –"

"B. Don, it's fine. I'm sure I know all the words."

"But what really pisses me off is . . . we finally got it right. We got our production issues sorted out. And we nailed the Herbie."

"Excuse me?"

"We nailed the Herbie."

"The what?"

"The . . . the bottleneck. The system constraint. We nailed it, and it's not movin'. And these guys are going to come in and screw it up. I just know it's going to happen. They are going to come in high and mighty and they are going to screw it all up."

"Don, I'm sorry, but I don't know what you're talking about."

"Well . . . you're marketing. What I'm talking about is a supply chain issue –"

"Which does affect marketing. Not to mention sales."

"Anyway . . . so be it. One does what one can do," said Don. "Now, Amy, you're a far better wordsmith than I am. Help me write something I can send out to the general world countering the so-called rumor, especially the piece of it that's true. In other words, help me lie through my teeth and yet not seem to be completely evil or stupid in a few days' time."

Five months later, the shareholders and the various regulatory bodies gave their approvals and the deal closed. Hi-T Composites became a subsidiary of Winner, Inc., a global corporation headquartered in New York City. Meanwhile, Linda and Bobby had had a baby girl – Holly – and Bobby did find a job, though at a much lower wage than he had previously earned, and he was looking for another. And, to everyone's amazement, Bill and Elaine patched things up and even went on a second honeymoon (their first honeymoon having been a mere two years prior), although upon her return Elaine complained that she and Bill were arguing even before they got on the plane to Costa Rica.

With the transfer of ownership accomplished, B. Donald Williams went to New York to present Hi-T's business strategy and otherwise become better acquainted with Winner's top management. Upon his return, B. Don conducted a series of meetings with employees talking up all the wonderful advantages of being part of the Winner family and downplaying the many concerns over what the future might hold. But Amy Cieolara, who could always read him, discerned that there was much that B. Don was not saying publicly.

Late one afternoon, after most people had left for the day, Amy was still in her office and B. Don came by, pausing in her doorway.

"You got a minute?" he asked.

"Sure. Come on in."

He did so and closed the door behind him.

"This is in confidence."

"Understood," Amy said.

"There are some things I want you to know about. You and a few others. The good people. Things I can't say to everybody."

B. Don hesitated then. He stared out her window for a moment, collecting his thoughts, then pulled a chair next to her desk and sat down.

"Amy, this transition is going to be worse than what I first thought. These guys at Winner . . ." He shook his head slowly. "They've got a very different culture from what we're used to. Very competitive. Way, way, way more competitive than what the St. Louis management set as the overall tone. In fact, I would go so far as to say that inside Winner it's a survival of the fittest mentality."

"Oh. Gee! That's great!" she said. "In fact, this really sounds like fun!"

"Yeah. Well, it's going to be a different ball game. For instance, every manufacturing plant will be competing with every other manufacturing plant on the same metrics. And the same goes for every function. Your marketing and sales team will be competing with every other marketing and sales team across the board inside Winner."

"Competing for what?"

"Resources. Talent. Bonus money. Stock options. Perks. Promotions. Recognition. And there are sticks to go along with the carrots. Those who lag in performance will be weeded out. Weakness will not be tolerated."

"Well, I'd like to think we can hold our own," she said. "I'm not afraid of a little competition. Just tell me what the rules are, and I'll deliver whatever is required."

"That, Amy, is a big part of the problem."

"What, you mean there are no rules? It's like a bar fight or something?"

"Oh, they've got plenty of rules, all right!" he said with a chuckle. "Plenty of policies – both written and unwritten – and you must abide by them. Listen, Amy, I'm not afraid of a little competition either. Our team at Hi-T can go head to head with anyone, and there's a time and place for everything."

Amy leaned back in her chair. She could sense a "but" coming, and she was not disappointed.

"But on the other hand, I have seen the metrics that Winner uses for manufacturing, for service functions, for administrative, you name it. And I am not at all convinced that most of what they're measuring really contributes to the bottom line. In fact, I don't think what they're mandating actually makes money – and I suspect a lot of it gets in the way of making money. You go read their annual reports, Amy. Not many of their divisions are actually growing their businesses – not by very much, and they're not throwing off a lot of cash either. Some are getting the tar kicked out of them. You look at Winner's corporate numbers – revenue growth, increasing earnings per share, and so on – and they seem impressive. But drill down and it soon becomes obvious that Winner is mostly growing only by way of acquisition. That's why they have to keep buying businesses like ours, using leverage and driving up their debt, by the way, because what they have going internally is really not getting it done. For all their vaunting of the virtues of competition, Winner is really not very competitive!"

Amy was listening closely but fidgeting, shifting in her seat, playing with her pen, which was what she did when she was nervous or unsettled.

"So," Don continued, "it's going to be tough."

She flashed an uncomfortable little smile and said, "You know what they say, Don: When the going gets tough, the tough get going."

"Yes, and that's my plan," said Don.

"Excuse me?"

"I am going. Leaving. Bugging out. Hitting the bricks."

"When?"

"No definite date. But I'm pretty dang sure Winner does not want me for the long term. If I hang around I can probably haggle for a supergood package from them. But I don't know if I even want to endure the aggravation. I'm fifty-nine; I've got enough money to retire now if I want to. And if I get tired of sailing my boat or playing golf or cruising the world, that's what headhunters are for."

Amy's eyes had watered just slightly. She sighed.

"I'm really going to miss you, B. Don."

He nodded. "Well . . . thanks. We've done a few good deeds together, haven't we. Saved the business and got it growing again after some bad times. Kept a lot of jobs right here in Highboro. Not all of them, but we're still a major employer. Helped keep the big ones flying with replacement parts . . . and that's the truth. Made nice profits, even as we brought prices down and grew our market share. And now we've got new generations of composites coming on, and the wind turbine segment shows some real promise on the energy front. I'll miss it. I'll miss you and a lot of the others. I'll miss the challenges. But when it's time to go . . . ."

Don leaned forward. Amy thought he was going to stand up and do just that, but he didn't. Instead he looked straight at her and lowered his voice.

"Amy, this conversation, of course, never took place, but if I were you, and I hate to say it, you might want to bring your résumé up to date and have a look around yourself."

She shook her head. "I can't. Not unless the job is here in town or pretty close by. Not with my parents the way they are."

"They are up there in age, aren't they. You were the change-of-life baby, I believe," he said with a smile.

"Yep, I was the surprise. But, Don, you know the situation. Dad's got Alzheimer's. If he moves to a new place, he'll never figure it out. Mom's finally got a good set of doctors here for all her problems. I can't just uproot them and take them with me, and they really need somebody to look in on them every few days. Then there are my kids . . . they'd lose all their friends. I can't bring myself to say the hell with everybody and go look for the perfect job. So I'm kind of stuck here."

"I understand. But, Amy, there is one last thing I feel I need to warn you about, in case you do stay. In the past, you have complained to me privately about a perceived glass ceiling in place at the St. Louis headquarters."

"And you always insisted it wasn't there."

"Well . . . I'm not saying it wasn't there, but I always figured the right woman, the right anybody, could punch through it. In St. Louis. But these guys . . . I heard in New York a few things said, never mind what, things you yourself will never hear. And at Winner, that glass ceiling, sorry to say, is in place. Try not to be too harsh in your opinions; I think it's just part of their competitive thing."

Amy sat stoically for a second, then snapped her lips together to form a happy idiot's grin.

"Well . . . B. Don! You sure have cheered me up! I am so glad you stopped by!"

He laughed and stood to leave her. He extended his hand. Amy shook his hand, but then came around the corner of her desk and hugged him.

"Amy," he said, "you take care of yourself, you hear?"

Within months B. Don was gone, retired. He and his wife, Daisy, soon booked a year-long world cruise and sailed off from Miami into the sunrise.

Taking B. Don's place was a man said to be one of Winner's up-and-comers, a man on the fast track to the top: Randal Touran-dos, more colorfully known behind his back as Random Tornado.

Indeed, he was a whirling dervish of managerial energy, often arriving at Hi-T's downtown Highboro offices at four thirty in the morning to review in detail the metrics from the previous day, which had been prepared by his own dedicated IT squad – soon unofficially called the Microbursts – who worked in shifts to compile the latest data for him. Before long, it became common for Amy and everyone else to arrive at work to find as many as five or six emails demanding immediate attention to whatever the Tornado had happened to notice in the metrics that morning. Even worse was to walk in and find one of Randal's outsize Post-it notes adhered to the seat of one's chair, the messages almost unreadable in Randal's speed-written scrawl. But if you got one, all other responsibilities had to be postponed until you had addressed the Tornado's concerns – and correctly discerning what those were was often the biggest challenge.

Key to everything, as far as Randal was concerned, was WING3.2 – or Winner Information Network, Generation 3.2 – sometimes just called "WING." This network was used throughout the corporation, and it had software designed to monitor every function in every business unit at a level of detail that was mind-boggling. Well, it was mind-boggling to many, but not to the Tornado, who was a computer whiz. In fact, as Randal himself was proud to tell everyone, he had been one of the software engineers on WING1.0, the first generation of the network. He had *written* some of the original code back in the day. And he still tinkered with it, adding or refining drill-down techniques and data-comparison features whenever the network was not doing something he thought it ought to do. He boasted that WING3.2 could tell you how many boxes of paper clips and pens were supposed to be in the supply closet at any location, based on purchases and estimated consumption rates. Future generations of WING, he claimed, would add what he termed "robust artificial intelligence" with queries and alerts to individual workers regarding what each one was supposed to be doing at any given moment. Amy Cieolara found it all to be rather Orwellian, but Randal was the boss and there was nothing she could do except go along.

Although full implementation of WING would take years, Randal and his IT techies, with the help of platoons of consultants, was able to get an essential implementation up and running in a matter of months. Almost as soon as it was in place, the Tornado began making his moves.

He started by mandating a 10 percent across-the-board staff cut in all functions, no exceptions. Amy almost lost Linda, who was one of

the higher-paid assistants, but was able to save her in the end by fir-
ing two other assistants who were caught stealing laptops and toner
cartridges. Even with such a legitimate excuse for termination, the
whole process was exceedingly painful – for everyone.

Next, the Tornado closed and sold off what he called a "job shop"
in northern Virginia that did small-lot and single-piece custom work,
mostly for Hi-T's Formulation & Design unit, which was based in
Rockville, Maryland. He consolidated all production at the Oakton
plant, located about twenty miles outside Highboro. He then introduced incentive pay at Oakton – over the protests of plant manager
Murphy Maguire – in order to increase productivity. And there were
a multitude of new policies and work rules, such as the directive that
each and every function at Oakton would only process its work in the
batch sizes that WING had calculated to be economically optimum.

Then there were the rather screwy and mean-spirited new policies upon which he insisted. For instance, he banned all coffeemak-
ers from company offices and got rid of the little refrigerators where
employees could keep soft drinks and store their lunches, claiming
that it was not the company's responsibility to provide space or electricity for these. More seriously, he began pressuring managers to
keep coming up with new ways to reduce expenses in every conceiv-
able way.

In his first year, Random Tornado reported to Winner's corporate management an 11 percent increase in Hi-T's net income, and a
17 percent increase in productivity. Amy, for one, was not sure how
"productivity" was calculated, but that was the number that WING
printed and so it was taken as gospel. For this marvelous first-year
performance, the Tornado was given a tremendous bonus, rumored
to be in the range of millions of dollars. He then put himself and all
the Highboro managers on one of Winner's corporate jets and flew
them to a resort in Jamaica for three days of work, surf, and frolic.

On a personal level, Randal could actually be a fun guy to be
around. He was very work-hard, play-hard. Amy, almost against
her will, found herself liking the Tornado in Jamaica. When she returned, nicely tanned, to the office, she showed Linda pictures of
Randal wearing a dreadlocks wig, doing a cannonball dive into the
resort pool, and pretending to bite the dorsal fin off a shark he had
hooked on an afternoon fishing charter.

"And, Linda, you should see him dance," Amy said. "He just needs
a couple of Cuba libres to get him going. You'd never know he was the
same . . . well, you-know-what from here in the office."

Then, eighteen months after he arrived, the Tornado was gone. He was hired away from Winner to run a semiconductor company in Silicon Valley that had survived the tech-bubble crash only to stagnate and decline in the marketplace. The Tornado was certain that he could turn the company around in a matter of a few years, and that disciplined cost-cutting was the foundation on which he would build. For accomplishing this, his total take from the company – mostly in stock options – was said to be potentially enormous, perhaps even beyond millions.

The Microbursts threw a wild good-bye party for the Tornado. Oddly, no one else was invited to attend. Amy got Randal a bottle of good champagne and attached ribbons and a card wishing him well. But the first morning after the Tornado's departure, when she arrived at her office and found no emails on what WING had ferreted out of the metrics and no Post-it note on her chair, she breathed a deep sigh of relief. Within days, the coffeepots reappeared.

That relief, however, was short-lived. Well before the Tornado went off to California, even before he had collected his enormous first-year bonus at Hi-T, Amy could sense that things were not going as swimmingly as a 17 percent jump in productivity suggested.

In the beginning, right after Winner acquired Hi-T, Amy had tried to make the best of it. She had some slick presentations and brochures created to cast the best light on the change of ownership. She briefed the sales force. She herself met with key customers and spoke to them reassuringly of the exciting times that lay ahead. Yet as WING3.2 came online and Randal mandated his changes, Amy had a feeling that maybe she should have been less enthusiastic in her assurances to everybody.

There was a vague sense in the air of Hi-T losing altitude, of a loss of momentum, of a rudderless yaw. The decay in performance was gradual and hardly detectable at first. Amy first noticed it in the faces of her fellow managers, the frowns when the Winner policy changes were handed down, the faces filled with stress as the Tornado turned up the pressure. There were several good managers who, like B. Don, either retired or moved on during this time. Amy herself, for a brief period, had her résumé out, but the only position in the Highboro area that she found even slightly appealing would have entailed a precipitous drop in pay. So, like everyone else who stayed, she hung on.

As the end of Randal's first year had approached, Elaine – Hi-T finance manager, also the Elaine of Bill and Elaine – began making noises about dwindling cash and dramatically increasing inventories at Oakton. The Tornado had told her that as WING continued to optimize all functions and to reduce costs, these issues would melt away. Anyway, Elaine often made noise about lots of things. It was her nature to fuss and complain and predict dire consequences if her warnings were ignored. Under B. Don, her drama-queen theatrics often *were* ignored or played down, and nothing very bad ever happened.

Then Amy noticed an increase in service-related complaints. When she spoke of these matters to Randal, he told her much the same thing he told Elaine, that these were "teething problems" that were somewhat inevitable with changes going on, and that as WING became more fully implemented, these would go away over time. When the teething problems then began to grow fangs, the Tornado threw it all right back at her, insisting that the service complaints were Amy's to solve. At one point he accused her salespeople of promising unrealistic delivery dates, when in fact the lead times being quoted were exactly what Hi-T had been working within for quite some time.

There were quality problems as well. The Tornado first said they didn't exist, then asserted that they must be the result of the aforementioned unrealistic delivery dates – again, Amy's fault – which rushed suppliers and workers so much that they could not always get it right the first time. In any case, he told her, the most important objective was to boost productivity, and to bring down costs.

"Quality," he actually told her, "is secondary."

The Tornado had said that about a month before announcing that he was leaving Winner. He left, but WING stayed. So did the problems that WING was supposed to solve.

2

At the end of a trying day, having stayed late to talk to a major customer who yelled at her over the phone, Amy left work in a state of utter dejection. She got into her BMW and drove listlessly home.

Her house was in a quiet neighborhood of tree-lined streets and older wood and brick homes that had been sumptuous in their day, decades ago. Amy and her two kids had lived there for one of those decades. She had bought the place with Aaron just after Michelle was born, and although her current salary would have allowed her to buy something newer and larger, this house always felt like home to her – cozy, familiar, safe. Besides, after Aaron's death, she and the kids needed a sense of stability and continuity, and the house gave them that.

Her parents' huge Ford was parked out front as usual when Amy drove into the driveway. Harry and Zelda lived about a mile away, and every afternoon Zelda would drive them over to Amy's to be there when Ben and Michelle got home from school. On most days, unless Amy was bringing home takeout, Zelda would start making dinner, and the five of them would eat dinner together, after which Amy would drive her parents home in their Ford – Zelda didn't drive after dark – and then jog back to the house. It was a comfortable routine, one that Amy enjoyed on most days. Tonight, though, Amy was beat; she just wanted to be left alone. But it was not in the cards.

Ben and Michelle were in the living room fighting over the remote control to the television as Amy walked through the front door. Ben was thirteen and had just gone through a growth spurt. He had the remote and was holding it high over his head where it was impossible for ten-year-old Michelle to grab it away from him – though she was jumping up and down, trying any way to get it. Whether by strategy or by accident, she countered her brother's height advantage by stomping on one of his bare feet, causing him to howl in pain and lower his arm to where Michelle could latch her little fingers around both ends of the prize.

"Hey!" said Amy. "Stop that!"

When their tug-of-war continued, Amy held out her hand, palm up.

"Give it to me," she said. "If you can't share it, it's mine."

"But Mom!" they both whined.

Amy shot the look that they knew meant business. Michelle immediately let go of the remote, and Ben sullenly handed it over.

"Is your homework done?"

"I don't have any," said Michelle with a bratty, sweet smile.

"Then go read a book. Ben? Is your homework done?"

"No."

"Go to your room and get started on it."

"But Grandma says dinner is almost ready!"

"You heard me."

He slinked toward the stairs. On the sofa, her father, Harry, was napping, oblivious to the chaos. Amy set her briefcase down, and went to the kitchen. White-haired and rather frail, her mother stood at the sink methodically washing lettuce.

"There you are!" said Zelda. "You're really late today."

"Yes. It was a long day – and not a very good one."

"You don't seem to be too happy with your work lately."

"I'm not."

"Why? What's wrong?"

"Oh . . . I don't know." Amy opened the refrigerator to find something to nibble. "I mean, that's just it. I don't know what's wrong. But something is, and nobody seems to be fixing it."

Her mom, who was eighty-four years old, shrugged her stooped, bony shoulders.

"Well, you're a smart girl. I'm sure you'll figure it all out at some point."

Amy ignored the "girl" reference, knowing that it was impossible to change her mother's mind that she was not, and began stuffing green grapes into her mouth as if she hadn't eaten in days. Even as she did this, she recognized it as a bad sign; she always overate when she was stressed from work. After the first few dozen, she made herself shut the refrigerator door and pulled up a stool to sit at the counter next to Zelda.

"I really miss B. Don," said Amy.

"Who?"

"Don, my old boss. We used to call him 'B. Don.' His first name was Bartholomew, which he hated, so he just shortened it and used his first initial. Anyway, I miss him. He would know what to do. The only trouble with B. Don was that he always kept everybody slotted."

"Slotted? What do you mean?"

"Kept us in our silos."

"What?"

"In our separate functions. He liked people to stick to what they knew best. There wasn't a lot of crossover. That was just his style. He was a good manager, but if he had a shortcoming that was it. I never got to learn much about a lot of the other areas – the whole supply chain part of the business, and a lot of other things as well."

"Have I ever met him?"

"Yes, Mom, you met him several times."

Zelda clucked at herself. "My memory anymore . . . not what it used to be."

"Please, Mom, let's not go there. One parent with Alzheimer's is bad enough."

At that moment, her father shuffled into the kitchen with a bewildered look on his face.

"Where am I?" he asked.

"You are in Amy's house," Zelda patiently explained.

"Who?"

"Amy. Your daughter."

"Hi, Dad!"

"Oh. Amy. Right, right, right. Well, what are we doing here?"

"We come here almost every day," said Zelda, "to watch our grandchildren when they come home from school and to have dinner together."

"Amy lives down south somewhere," he muttered. "Somewhere in Carolina or someplace."

"That's right, Dad. And so do you and Mom. You moved here to the city of Highboro, North Carolina, just about eight years ago, after my husband passed away. But you're just visiting at my house right now. You and Mom live in your own house not far from here."

"I thought we lived in Cleveland."

"We did once," said Zelda. "But that was a long time ago."

"Right, right, right," said Harry, waving his hand, pretending all the shards of his mind had just fallen into place. And he shuffled off, back to the living room.

Amy just looked at her mom and sadly shook her head.

"It's always the worst when he first wakes up," said Zelda.

"I don't know how you do it, Mom. How you put up with him."

"Because I have to," she said. "And because I still love him."

In the morning, when her alarm clock began to chime, Amy struggled to wake up. The very thought of going to work made her groan. Only a few times in her career had that sort of dread come over her.

She finally got both of the kids out the door and off to school and was gathering her things to go to work, when it suddenly occurred to her that this was one of those rare days when she had absolutely no meetings scheduled all morning. The realization was so inspiring that she ran up the stairs into her bedroom, unplugged the phone, flung off her clothes, dived onto the mattress, pulled the covers over her head, and went back to sleep.

Two hours later she awoke refreshed, dressed and did her hair for the second time that day, went downstairs, poured a glass of orange juice, and switched on her cell phone – only to discover that Linda had called five times. Without even checking Linda's voice mails, Amy called her office.

"Where are you?" asked Linda.

"At home. Playing hooky."

"You've got to get moving right away."

"Why? Did the building burst into flames because I'm late to work?"

"No, you got a call from the Winner headquarters in New York City."

"Me? About what?"

"The executive assistant to a Mr. Peter Winn, who's –"

"The founder, chairman and CEO of Winner," Amy said, her green eyes popping.

"Right, he wants you in his office in Manhattan for a meeting at three o'clock this afternoon."

"What for? Was there a reason given?"

"No, but his assistant said to tell you that it's extremely urgent."

"Oh, crap. Is anyone else from Hi-T going?"

"No, just you. Now, I could not get you on a commercial flight, but I've chartered a private plane to fly you to New York, and there will be a driver to take you into the city. But you're still going to have to hurry. Do you have something to write with? Here's where the plane is waiting for you . . ."

The airplane had propellers – two of them, Amy noted – but it possessed sleek, rather handsome lines. As did the pilot. He was slim, but built, she also noted. Not especially tall. His hair was buzz-cut short on the sides, but longer on top. He had an older, lined face, his cheeks a bit hollow, eyes covered by classic wraparound Ray-Ban sunglasses. He stood waiting next to the plane, which was bright red with gold detailing. He had the doors already opened for her.

"Hi, I'm Tom Dawson," he said in introduction, taking her briefcase. "I'll be your pilot today, as well as your copilot and flight attendant, no extra charge."

"I'm really in a hurry," said Amy. "Could we –"

"Absolutely, ma'am. We will be wheels up in just a few minutes."

He settled her into a passenger seat behind the cockpit, shut the doors with a reassuring thunk, strapped in, did his preflight checks. The twin engines came to life, and the plane began to move. Dawson taxied onto the runway, and throttled up. Amy felt herself pressed back into her seat, and she shut her eyes for a moment. When she opened them again, they were airborne, angling skyward – all in less than five minutes, probably closer to four.

Once Dawson had trimmed the plane and set the autopilot, he turned to look at her, and gave her the thumbs up. Amy nodded and waved. *Just leave me alone*, she thought.

And he did. She leaned her head back and tried to fathom why she was being called to New York on such short notice. The conclusions she reached as to the possibilities were not happy ones.

After a while the pilot turned to check on her again and apparently was uncomfortable with what he saw.

"Excuse me, ma'am. Are you all right? You're looking a little green around the edges."

"I'm fine. I mean, I've been better, but . . ."

"There's an airsickness bag –"

"No, nothing like that, Mr. Dawson. I'm okay. I'm just very nervous."

"If it makes you feel any better, ma'am, I have flown a plane once or twice before. At least twice, maybe even three times."

"Are you counting the crashes?"

He grinned. "The crashes? Well, ah . . . I'd rather not talk about those."

"Seriously, have you ever crashed your plane?"

"Not this one. This one's been lucky for me. It was the other one." Then his face lost the grin and became serious. "No, it was quite a while back. Had a little problem on a mission and had to eject. It wasn't a good day."

"You're ex-military?"

"United States Marine Corps, retired."

"Is that why your airplane is painted red and gold?"

"Yes, scarlet and gold. You are very perceptive, ma'am."

"Thank you. By the way, how fast are we going?"

"We are currently cruising at approximately one hundred ninety knots."

"Can we go any faster?"

"Well, yes. A little. May I ask why the need for speed?"

"I'm being called on the carpet, if you know what I mean. The parent corporation of my company is, I think, displeased about something. And . . . well, there's a possibility that I might be fired. So I don't want to make them angrier than they already might be by being late."

"What time is your meeting?"

"Three o'clock."

He waved, as in nothing to worry about. "Our ETA into Teterboro, New Jersey, is roughly one p.m. Now I can't predict traffic in Manhattan, but two hours . . . well, then again, let me see what I can do. Might be bumpier, but if they'll let us fly higher, I think I might just find us a nice tailwind."

Dawson turned his attention to the controls.

An hour and a half later, he turned to her again.

"Excuse me, ma'am, but thar she blows. You can see Manhattan now. Let me give you a little better view."

He expertly crabbed the plane to turn it a bit sideways, then dipped the right wing so that Amy could look out her side window and see the skyline – a dense and intricate forest of steel, glass, and stone needling from a hazy gray smudge.

By 12:49 p.m., they were wheels down and taxiing across the tarmac toward the car that would take Amy into the city.

"Good luck in your meeting, ma'am," said Dawson as he took her hand to help her step down. "Hope it goes well, but if it goes for worse, I do offer flying lessons at reasonable rates. You never know; I might even be able to work you in as a copilot."

Amy smirked. She took her briefcase from his hand and walked to the car, which drove her away. Minutes later, creeping along in traffic, she wondered: had he actually been flirting with her? Yes, she decided, he had been, and for a split second she was annoyed. But for all her anxieties, somehow the whole thing made her feel . . . like laughing. Midway through the Lincoln Tunnel, she did. Much to the confusion of her Pakistani driver.

Winner, Inc. was headquartered in an elegant black building a few blocks from Rockefeller Center in midtown Manhattan. Amy Cieolara, wearing a navy blue skirt and jacket over a white silk blouse, stepped off the elevator onto the plush carpeting of the fifty-ninth floor at 2:53 p.m. She had spent most of those past two hours in traffic moving at maddening snail-paced speed, inching toward the city and through it. But she'd made it. The receptionist, who looked as though she had walked out of a page in *Vogue* magazine, took her name, made a call, and cordially invited Amy to have a seat.

At 3:22 p.m. a silver-haired woman briskly walked up to Amy, smiled rather mechanically, and informed her that Mr. Winn would now see her. The silver-haired woman then led the way through a dizzying succession of hallways, antechambers, and outer offices, ultimately to the double black-walnut doors that opened into the seemingly vast corner office of Peter Winn, chairman and chief executive officer.

She walked across the largest oriental carpet she had ever seen, her footsteps nearly silent on the luxurious pile with its jewel-tone patterns. On the far end of the carpet was a desk table of dark wood with legs intricately carved to suggest a grape vineyard. Behind it sat Mr. Winn – Amy recognizing his face from photos in the annual report. He had the aura of an aging movie star – thin and tall, ruggedly handsome, reddish blond hair, bushy eyebrows, a narrow and rather pointy nose, and intense hazel eyes that peered out from a classic chiseled brow. He had taken off his suit jacket and was in his shirtsleeves – a buttery cream-colored, hand-sewn shirt with a tie of red, black, and silver diagonal stripes.

In front of the desk, to either side, were two low-back chairs upholstered in oxblood leather. Both chairs were occupied. In one sat Nigel Furst, a European of English and German upbringing; his title was "group president" and the group over which he presided had three separate business units, one of which was Hi-T Composites. Nigel favored London suits, was lanky and athletic-looking with long legs and a narrow waist, had pale and almost colorless blond hair, and a thin, long face with large gray eyes that always looked dead serious even when he smiled or laughed.

Amy had met Nigel and had been in meetings with him during the tenure of the Tornado. But the man seated in the other chair in front of Peter Winn's desk, she had never seen before. He was large boned, yet slim – his face somewhat hollow cheeked, and his head was shaved like that of a pro basketball player or a Tibetan monk. His eyes were large, dark, and had a shining intensity. His skin was pale white, causing his face at first glance to seem rather skullish, though his features on the whole were quite handsome.

The stranger rose partially from his chair to greet her, smiling to welcome her, but when neither of the others made any attempt to rise, he sat back down. Indeed, neither of the other two acknowledged in any way her entry into the room. They simply continued their conversation as if she were not there. They were talking about golf, about the challenges of a particular course somewhere in Bavaria, Germany. They went on and on, Peter doing most of the talking with Nigel adding insightful comments, and the third man chiming in when he could, just so as not to be left out.

As there was no chair for her within casual reach, Amy just stood there awkwardly and silently, trying to size up what was going on. One minute, then another passed.

They are giving you a stress test, she finally told herself. *Do not show your anger. Do not show impatience or any particular emotion. At some point, hopefully before dinnertime, they themselves will run out of patience and speak to you.*

An instant later:

"Do you golf?" Peter asked.

Amy realized the question was directed at her.

"Yes, as often as I can."

"Do you use the women's tees? Or the men's?"

"The women's," she said, straightening herself. "But with course ratings and a properly calculated handicap –"

"What is your handicap?" he asked, cutting her off.

"What would you like it to be?" she asked, not batting an eye.

The third man chuckled. Peter and Nigel seemed less amused.

Pulling back the cuff on his shirtsleeve, Peter checked his watch and said, "Well, better late than never. At least you got here."

"Sir, I was told the meeting was three p.m. Eastern time; I was on here on the floor before two fifty-three," said Amy.

Nigel grinned like a shark. "There you have it, Peter; I told you she could stand up for herself."

The three men forced a brief laugh. Peter then stood, as did the others. And they were giants, all of them: Peter a good six foot five, Nigel six foot six, and the third man only a hair shorter. Amy stood five foot six in heels.

"Let's go over here," Peter said, gesturing to an elegant sofa and chairs with ample seating capacity for all.

On the way over, the third man leaned down and quietly introduced himself. "Miz See-o-lawra, my name is Wayne Reese. Pleased to meet you."

"Very pleased to meet you as well, Wayne," she said, shaking his enormous hand. "By the way, my name is pronounced 'Kee-o-lara.' The *C* is hard like a *K*."

"Oh, sorry about that."

"Not a problem, and please feel free to call me Amy. Do I detect a slight New England accent in your voice?"

"Born in Boston," he said, deliberately letting his native tongue say it as, *Bawn in Bawstin*. Then he added, "But I've moved around a lot since then. Most people don't notice that once in a while my *awhs* just don't come out the way *othah* people's do."

As Wayne smiled a bit sheepishly, they sat down and faced Nigel and Peter.

"So, now that we have the geolinguistics out of the way," said Peter, "why don't you tell me a little bit about yourself, Amy?"

"Well, I'm not sure what you know or don't know, but I was born in Shaker Heights, Ohio, near Cleveland. I've spent most of my career in sales and marketing, first with a steel company – for a while my sales region was New England, which is how I noticed Wayne's very slight accent. And then my husband changed jobs, we moved to North Carolina, and I joined Hi-T Composites as a sales rep, and . . . well, here I am today as Hi-T's vice president of marketing and sales."

"So you're married?" asked Peter.

"I'm widowed. My husband died a few years ago."

"Kids?"

"Two. Boy and a girl. May I please ask why you sent for me?"

"We'll get to that soon enough," said Peter. "Since we've never met, I'd just like to get a sense of who you are."

"Sure, Mr. Winn. Ask whatever you'd like," she said.

"Any plans to remarry?"

She hesitated; the question seemed too personal, but she answered it anyway.

"No. None."

"Have you had any operations experience, Amy?" Peter asked. "Any experience managing production?"

"Not really. Briefly, I worked in production planning at the steel company." She chuckled. "And I've taken plenty of customers through our Oakton plant on tours – prior to playing golf – but that's about the extent of it."

"Tell me, are you familiar with Lean manufacturing?" asked Nigel.

"Yes – I mean, I've heard of it," said Amy. "I think it has to do with eliminating waste, doesn't it?"

"Yes, but more exactly, it's about creating value for customers by *means* of eliminating waste," said Nigel.

"In fact, Amy," said Wayne, "anything that does not create value in the customer's eyes is considered to be waste in the Lean view of things. It's a long-term, evolving process of continuous improvement. Eliminate the waste, focus on increasing value, do it all faster, and keep striving to please your customers – that's the essence of Lean."

"I see," said Amy, looking at Wayne and wondering what his role here was.

"How about Six Sigma?" Peter asked her. "Are you familiar with that?"

"Again, yes, I've heard of it. Six Sigma was, I think, originally developed by Motorola, wasn't it? It's a quality . . . thing."

"Six Sigma is one of the best quality management and improvement programs that's ever been developed," Wayne chipped in. "In a nutshell, it's about reduction in variation – and through that reduction, the elimination of errors and defects."

Amy nodded slowly and solemnly.

"You see, the Greek letter *sigma*," Wayne continued, "is used in mathematical notation to represent a standard deviation within a statistical population – in simple terms, a spread of values, or numbers. By applying Six Sigma techniques, the spread becomes tighter and tighter, meaning that the process is coming under closer control, and the results of the process more predictable. When a process reaches the sixth sigma, it is thought to be just about as close to perfection as it possibly can be."

Nigel cleared his throat.

"Sorry," said Wayne. "Didn't mean to lecture."

"That's fine," said Amy. "I always wondered where the name came from."

"In any case," said Nigel, "Winner has made a major corporate commitment to both of these programs . . . these methodologies, if you will. And in recent years Lean and Six Sigma have been conceptually and synergistically combined to create what is known as Lean Six Sigma or LSS. Over the years, we have invested millions of dollars –"

Peter Winn grunted and muttered, "You bet we have."

"– in the training and education of our employees, process and equipment changes, and so on. And we fully intend to bring Hi-T up to speed on both these initiatives, but so far we've held off due to the need to stabilize the personnel issues and, shall we say, digest the acquisition."

"I see. Well, if there is anything I can do to help –"

"Are you aware of the delivery and quality problems that have been happening of late?" asked Nigel.

"Yes, I am. I've been getting calls and emails from our salespeople, and I've been on the phone myself talking to customers."

"What have you been telling them?"

"Mostly I've been apologizing . . . and doing what I can within my limited power to expedite whatever the people yelling the loudest say they need the most. And, I have to say, it's frustrating, because I'm not getting a lot of cooperation in many cases. I was on the phone a few days ago talking to Murphy Maguire –"

"Who?" asked Peter.

"He's their production manager," said Nigel. "Randal Tourandos was telling me he's a . . . well, a very colorful chap."

"Yes, he is that," said Amy. "Murphy has managed our Oakton plant for many years. Anyway, a few weeks ago, I was trying to run interference for one of our best customers, and I got no cooperation from him. He told me, no, he would not expedite, I guess because it would screw up his schedule. I mean, he was polite, but he just flat out told me, no. He said, and I quote, 'Y'all got too dang many cooks a-messin' with the soup.' "

Peter blinked his eyes several times in confusion.

"He talks like that," said Amy. "Especially when he's excited."

"But what did he mean?" asked Nigel.

"I have no idea. He seems to know what he's doing, but how and why he does things is anybody's guess. What I do know is that last night I had one of our most important customers on the phone yelling at me, threatening to pull a contract because our delay is causing some serious issues –"

"This customer you spoke to last night," Peter interrupted, "didn't happen to be an admiral in the United States Navy, did he?"

Amy felt a chill wash over her.

"Yes. Admiral Jones, as a matter of fact."

"Admiral Jones was put through to me late last evening at my home," said Peter.

"I am deeply sorry, Mr. Winn. I truly did the best I could," said Amy. "Sir, I spoke with the Admiral for over an hour –"

Peter raised his hand for her to say no more.

"And apparently you said the right things," said Peter. "Because the Admiral told me that in the end he regretted raising his voice to you, as he put it, and he praised you highly for both your can-do spirit and your common sense."

Amy breathed in relief.

"But that does not get you or us off the hook, Amy. There is a certain series of parts called, I believe, the V-Range Series?"

"Yes, sir, and I am told that some of these parts are very time-consuming to manufacture."

"Whatever the difficulty factor, Admiral Jones told me that their short supply was affecting the combat readiness of certain Navy and Marine aircraft. This is, to the military, a very serious matter."

"Yes, and with all due respect, it would seem that the matter should be taken seriously by all of us. We never know what may happen tomorrow. What state of the world we may wake up to."

Peter Winn scrutinized Amy's face. She was not posturing; she was sincere.

"In any case, the Admiral was extremely serious. He said that if the situation was not rectified quickly – and I could not pin him down on what exactly he meant by 'quickly' – that not only could the contract be rescinded, but there could be a congressional investigation."

Amy tried to swallow, and found her mouth was so dry, she coughed nervously instead.

"Now, I think – at least I hope – that the Admiral was bluffing with respect to the congressional investigation," said Peter. "But he did get my attention, I have to admit. This thing has to be turned around."

"Mr. Winn, as I think I said earlier, anything that I can do from a sales or marketing perspective –"

"Let us cut to the chase, Amy," said Nigel, as if taking a cue. "As you know, Randal Tourandos has departed for what he perceives to be greener pastures. Frankly, we are quite upset that he has decided to go. He made a great start and seemed to have matters well in hand. But he left us in a bit of a lurch, especially given the rather surprising mess he seems to have left behind. Not at all what we would have expected from Randal. In any event, we have a talent search for a replacement in progress. But that could take some time, and clearly we need someone to step in now and get things under control."

"Come on, Nigel, we want someone to do more than just put the current fires out," said Peter, saying it with a sense of sparks flying from his jaws. "We want to get from Hi-T the results that would justify our paying the premium for them!"

"Yes, exactly!" said Nigel. "But for now . . . Amy, I have spoken personally to a number people, including a number of customers – indeed, I too have fielded a few calls from the influential among Hi-T's customer base – and the one common thread is that your name keeps coming up in a positive way. People, especially customers . . . they respect you, they like you, they seem to trust you. Admiral Jones himself said that he would feel very comfortable with you in charge. So, Peter and I, brilliant as we so often are –"

"Actually, it was my idea," said Peter, "unless she screws up."

Nigel made an attempt to wink.

"Amy, we would like to offer you," said Peter, "the position of interim president."

"Really? President? Of Hi-T?"

"Yes," said Nigel.

Within Amy, time and space seemed to expand, and bounds became boundless.

"President . . ." she murmured. "Of everything . . ."

"Well, no, just of Hi-T," said Nigel. "We shall hold off for now on 'president of everything' for perhaps another day, another time. You would be interim president of Hi-T, although if you did well, it could become permanent. Now . . . Amy, are you listening?"

"Yes, I certainly am."

"You would keep your current salary, of course. But there would be, in addition, significant performance bonuses that could possibly double your total compensation."

Amy frowned.

"Is there a problem?" asked Nigel.

"Well, I'm not complaining about my current salary," said Amy, "but I just think that if you're going to make me president, even on an interim basis, that's a lot more responsibility, and usually an increase in responsibility is accompanied by an increase in salary."

Peter and Nigel exchanged glances.

"Amy, if you want the position, we'll make it work as far as the money," said Peter. "But we need someone *now*. Do you want the position?"

"Yes," said Amy. "Yes, I do want it. Provided I have your word that you won't bring in someone else in a few months. I'd like enough time to show what I can do."

"All right. Good. And while I am not going to commit to any specific time period, I think that it's not unreasonable to allow a year or so. Do you agree, Nigel?"

"Yes, but there's one more thing," said Nigel. "We feel you're going to need someone very strong on the operations end – because of your limited experience in that realm."

"Oh, I agree," said Amy.

"So that is why we have here today – drum roll, please – the man on your right, who will be your right-hand man, Wayne Reese. We would like him to become Hi-T's operations manager. Wayne is an expert in Lean Six Sigma – a Master Black Belt, if I'm not mistaken. He does have manufacturing experience, and most recently has administered our corporate-wide LSS initiative. He has volunteered to jump into the trenches and even to get his fingernails dirty, if necessary! So, Peter and I are confident that the two of you will make an excellent combination, with you, Amy, knowing Hi-T's markets and customers, and Wayne using Lean and Six Sigma techniques to improve the operational end of things."

"That's absolutely great. Thank you," Amy said. "Wayne, I look forward to working with you."

Wayne nodded in a humble way, and said, "Same here."

"Now, I emphasize, Amy, that Lean Six Sigma is to be taken very seriously," said Nigel. "Admiral Jones is a keen proponent of LSS, and Peter and I made assurances to him that we – or, rather, you – would make every possible effort to accelerate the implementation of the LSS culture at Hi-T. Only with those assurances were we able to pacify the good Admiral. Therefore, Amy . . . you must move quickly and you must not fail. You must implement Lean Six Sigma without delay. We don't want any more evening phone calls from the Navy – ever!"

Amy nodded soberly and said, "Right. I understand. Believe me, I will do everything in my power to keep the Navy happy."

Peter Winn then stood and addressed Amy Cieolara as he extended his hand.

"Then do you accept the position, Amy?"

"Yes, Mr. Winn, I accept the position. Thank you again."

And thus the glass ceiling of Winner, Inc., though it did not shatter, cracked.

3

In high school and later as a University of North Carolina Tar Heel, C. "Murphy" Maguire had played football on the defensive squad, usually as a strong safety, blocking and tackling opponents who were often more gifted with athletic qualities than he was, and doing it through sheer tenacity, quickness, and grit. Wherever the other team ran the ball, wherever they threw, there was Maguire – ready to take it to them or take it away from them.

But the taut physique of his youth had expanded and slackened over the decades to a stocky roundness. The handsome good looks that had drawn the attentions of the cheerleaders – one of whom he had eventually married – were now lost in a rather meaty face with the trace of a double chin. In short, his appearance these days was unremarkable. Yet, still, when Murphy entered a place, he filled it. People always knew he was in the room. When Murphy entered the Oakton plant at 7:30 on a Monday morning, a wordless buzz passed down the aisles and just about every Hi-T employee could sense he was on the floor.

His first stop was the Cooler – the gigantic freezer where they kept the resins and certain other raw materials to make the composites. These were stored at 0°F to keep them chemically stable. Indeed, once a resin came out of the deep freeze and began to warm, the clock began to run. It would begin its "out-life." For at a normal room temperature, the chemistry within the resin would start to change, and the plant had a limited number of days to make products with it. The window of opportunity was typically about three weeks, sometimes less and sometimes more, depending on the resin. But beyond that time frame, the resin became unworkable. It was junk.

Just as Murphy approached, the access door to the Cooler opened.

From a swirling cloud of vapors came Jerome Pepps, materials manager. He was dressed as if he had just visited the North Pole – in a hooded parka and wearing heavy mittens.

"Well, well, you must be a man who's looking for trouble," he said to Murphy.

"Having found you, Jayro, I know I'm within farting distance of it."

"I am going to tell you 'good morning' right now," said Jayro, "because that's the last 'good' you're likely to hear all day. Would you like some coffee, sir?"

"I'm trying to cut back," said Murphy, "but somehow I think I had better."

Jerome – Jayro, as Murph and many others called him – stripped off his mittens, unzipped his parka, and poured coffee from a fresh pot into two mugs, then handed one to his boss.

"How bad?" asked Murphy.

"Well, first of all, there's the Navy job –"

"Don't start with the Navy job! Haven't even had my first sip yet!"

"All right. I'll start with the folks in Autoclave."

"What about 'em?"

"They're all fussed up again. Don't know what to do. The computer's telling them things that don't make sense."

"That's that goofball WING-ding software a-gummin' up everthang again," said Murphy. "You look up *gridlock* in the dictionary and you'll find a picture of a WING3.2 terminal. All right, I'll handle it."

"Then we got four – *four* – runs on the schedule that require a twenty-three-hour soak. And they're all due to ship on Friday."

"Ah, shoot! That's bad. That's *really* bad. Jayro, we absolutely have to spread those out. What lamebrain scheduled four of those in one week?"

Jayro put on a happy face and said, "Don't look at me, Murph! I don't make the schedule; I just read the schedule."

"We've got to get one of those shifted to a Monday ship date, and the rest moved to later in the month. Wait a minute. How big are the orders? Maybe we can get them all out on Monday – but it has to be Monday, not Friday."

"I'll print the specs for you," said Jayro.

"Fine. Now, that's it, right? Except for the Navy job? Can I sip my coffee in peace?"

"Um, I'm afraid not. We need WEX-457 big time. I just checked inside the Cooler, and we are way below minimum."

"What happened? Didn't you reorder when you were supposed to?"

"Yes, Murph, I *did* reorder when we hit the minimum, but the replenishment has not come in. Now we are down to the dregs. And I also know from phone calls last week that Mom and Dad are on vacation. They have told us to be good chill'uns and be quiet while the house is on fire."

By "Mom and Dad," he was referring to Hi-T's parent, to Winner, Inc. Since the acquisition, it was the Winner Chemicals Company that supplied WEX, and by policy mandate, Hi-T was forbidden to procure any resin produced by WinChem from any other supplier. In fact, Hi-T was now sometimes required to buy Winner Chemicals products when Hi-T did not need them. Sometimes at the end of the month, the trucks would just show up.

"How's our WEX-100? I bet we got a lifetime supply," said Murphy.

"Pretty close. And the max recommended cold storage is thirty-six months."

Murphy chuckled with disdain and said, "So we don't have what we do need, and we've got a multiyear inventory of what we don't. Dandy. Anything else?"

"Oh, I could go on and on," said Jayro, "but the big thing –"

"Is the Navy job. Just tell me."

"Hairline cracks."

Murphy wavered as if he had just been tagged by a left hook.

"All of it?" Murphy asked.

"Some of it," said Jayro. "Maybe less than four percent. But now we have to check every last one. Can't ship. Unless you want to . . . you know."

"No. Absolutely not. C'mon, Jayro! You know me better than that! I would never do that, especially not to the Navy."

"Well, that order is already a month late. There are rumors that phone calls have been made to and from high places. Admirals calling big muckety-mucks. And when big muckety-mucks get called –"

"Yes, Jayro, I am aware of all that. But I am not going to ship bad product. Shoot, if only they would offer me early retirement with full benefits. At least that would solve *my* problem. You know, it doesn't have to be a gold parachute; it could be a bronze parachute."

"It might be a lead parachute if you can't solve this," said Jayro.

"What we need – and what we can't get – is to have one of them Geniuses in Rockville come down here and help us figure this one out."

Murphy was referring of course to Hi-T's Formulation & Design unit, based in Rockville, Maryland, outside Washington, D.C. And "Geniuses" was an apt, yet derisive term for the chemists and other scientists who worked there, many of whom were, if not geniuses, extremely smart and well-educated. F&D, as it was often called, was a separate profit center for Hi-T – indeed, a separate business – working in the intellectual realm and performing very sophisticated materials research and engineering.

"I mean, this cracking problem has got me," Murphy went on. "Is it something in the specs they're giving us? Is it something we're doing? I don't know. But we're having to run those V-series jobs four and five times to get enough perfect ones to ship."

"Well, the Geniuses don't want to get their fingernails dirty. You know that."

Murphy nodded with grimness. He suddenly set down his coffee mug, turned away from Jayro, and began walking off.

"Yo, Murph!" called Jayro. "Lunch?"

"Eleven thirty. Usual place," said Murph. "And you better o' brought the good stuff!"

Jayro grinned, one side of his lips rising higher than the other, and the appearance of his teeth was not unlike a quarter moon shining bright in a midnight sky.

The Oakton Plant was generally laid out as a big U. Materials came in via one leg of the U – with resins going into the Cooler, and "dry" materials going into bins and onto shelves in various storerooms, where they waited until they were needed. When a work order was authorized, the materials were released – that is, taken by forklift or hand cart or, if in bulk liquid form, often by pipe and hose – to where they would begin the journey to being finished products. If all went well, and they didn't end up in the Dumpster outside as scrap, they would complete the journey in Shipping, which was at the far end of the other leg of the U.

Dead center between the uprights of the U was the mold-and-tool shop – known to everyone as the M/T Shop – which was a factory within a factory, with computer-controlled machines creating the molds and tooling that would shape or form whatever had to be made. From there were a number of stages and processes grouped in areas such as the M57 Line, Laminating, Autoclave, Coatings, Finishing, Packaging, each of these transforming the original materials into something of greater value that a customer would pay for. To the average person, practically none of the finished products coming out of Oakton would be identifiable as to what they were or even what function they might serve. Oakton's products almost always became parts used in some other product: an airplane, an automobile, an offshore oil rig, a pipeline, a ship, or any of dozens of types of industrial equipment from pumps to electrical generators. The range was vast, and the applications often were specialized – although about half the total volume coming from Oakton consisted of "stock" or "off the shelf" products, in a multitude of varieties.

One of the most important processes was curing, in which the resins would harden and become chemically stable. And for this to happen in a controlled manner required the plant's autoclave. The Autoclave area sat at the bottom of the U, and it mainly consisted of a single piece of equipment – the autoclave itself. This was not the sort of "desktop" autoclave found in a college chemistry lab. This autoclave had been custom engineered for the Oakton plant. It was a huge orange-painted cylinder with a big round door on one end that looked somewhat like the door to a bank vault. On the far end was a smaller access door, and it looked like it had come from a submarine, with a round wheel in the center that would activate a number of latches. In the middle was a long cylinder – fifty-two feet in length, and twenty-two feet in diameter. Inside, the chamber could be compartmentalized to precisely handle a variety of small batches, or the compartments could be opened up to accommodate some very large composites. It could operate at a wide range of temperatures and pressures, and a complex array of tubing could introduce specialized atmospheres, such as pure nitrogen or an exotic mix of gases. Six full-time, well-paid technicians, two per shift, were permanently assigned to it, in addition to a supervisor and sometimes as many as six to eight other workers who helped set up, load, and unload this monster, which indeed they had named Godzilla.

As Murphy reached the Autoclave area, he immediately spotted Richy, the day-turn supervisor, who was seated at a computer console near Godzilla. He had a telephone cradled on his shoulder as he tapped the keyboard and worked the mouse with his hands. In a semicircle behind him stood half a dozen Autoclave workers, all of whom seemed to be waiting for Richy to get off the phone. Their expressions ranged from bewildered to bored.

"Uh-huh. Yes, sir, we'll keep looking," Richy said into the phone – then saw Murphy approaching. "Oh, hold on one second."

"What's the matter?" asked Murphy.

Richy put his hand tight over the mouthpiece and said, "It's a guy in sales out on the West Coast. There's some order that was supposed to ship last week, and now it's late, and the customer's all over them. He's trying to track it down."

Murphy wiggled his fingers to have Richy give him the phone.

"This is Murph Maguire here; who's this, please? Oh! Hey, Garth! How come you're callin' so early? It must be the middle of the night out there in California. Uh-huh. Uh-huh. I hear ya. No, sir, shouldn't happen, but sometimes it does. Right. You gave the order number and whatnot to Richy? All right, sir, I'm on it. Someone will get back to you in about an hour with whatever we know. You take care, buddy."

He hung up, looked at Richy, and asked, "So where's his order number?"

"Right here," said Richy, handing over a slip of paper. "But I can't find what he needs. I don't even see it listed on the schedule. And why he called me, I have no clue."

"He's called us enough to know that work-in-process backs up in Autoclave, that's why," said Murphy, dialing Jayro Pepps's extension.

"Hey, Jayro, it's Murph. I need you to look into something right away. Garth Quincy, that sales manager out on the West Coast, you know him? Well, he's got red ants in the pants because of some order that's missing in action. Richy here says it's not even listed. I'll give you the tracking numbers. Find out what you can, then give Mr. Quincy a call with whatever you know within the hour, and let me know the status. You got a ink-pen to write with? All right, here you go . . ."

When he got off the phone, Murphy turned to the assembled workforce. "Don't y'all have setups to do? You know my rule. I do *not* want Godzilla down for even a minute more than necessary."

"Mr. Maguire," said one of them, "that's the problem. We don't know what we're supposed to set up next."

"Okay, just give us a minute," said Murphy, "and all will be made clear."

As the Autoclave workers dispersed, Murphy grabbed a swivel chair from nearby, rolled it into place next to Richy, and sat down. Using the mouse, Richy was scrolling through the open work orders.

"Hell of a Monday," Murphy muttered. "Now, what's the confusion here?"

"According to WING, we're supposed to be doing this series," said Richy, pointing to a range of orders on the computer screen, "but I know that doesn't make any sense. Our next soak, we'd be running Godzilla half empty. And then these later soaks, the quantities are too big. They're not all going to fit, and they won't reach Shipping in time to go on the truck."

"You're right," said Murphy. "I'm very glad you spotted that. All right, forget what this stupid WING software says we ought to be doing. We'll do a manual work-order entry, and you'll have to update the records. Now, how much time do we have?"

Richy glanced at the clock and said, "The current soak will end in thirty-six minutes."

"All right," said Murphy, "no time to waste. Let's have a look-see . . ."

He took the mouse from under Richy's hand and began to click and scroll and scrutinize what appeared on the screen. He did most of the math in his head, but from time to time reached for his pocket calculator to double-check it.

"Okay," Murph said finally, pointing to the screen. "Soon as you got the 'Zilla purged, you load in these four, then this one . . . and these two. Gang 'em all together. Got that? Then next soak, we'll do these five."

Richy was quickly scribbling the numbers and letters.

"Are you sure, Murph? Those five, they're all different specs," said Richy.

"Of course they're different! The specs were written by the Geniuses! They sit in their pretty glass tower up there on the Beltway and whatever number happens to pop up on their computer screens, that's what they specify! They don't even talk to themselves half the time, never mind the likes of us! Anyway, these four are similar enough that we can gang 'em. I know what we can get away with. It'll work."

"All right, you're the boss," said Richy, and he turned and fired off instructions to the setup workers. "Git on it! Y'all got thirty-one minutes to do these setups! Move!"

Murphy and Richy went over the rest of the day's schedule for Godzilla. Then, satisfied that Richy understood the priorities, he patted his supervisor on the shoulder and began to stroll at a pace neither fast nor slow back along the main aisle. At every work center there was a WING terminal, and on the screens of many of them flashed a big red triangle with a question mark in the middle. Murphy ignored all flashing triangles and simply looked at what the people and their equipment were actually doing. A firm believer in MBWA – Management By Walking Around – Murphy knew almost every worker on sight, but there was one worker, a machine operator, whom he did not recognize. Murphy walked over to him and read the name on the operator's badge.

"Bobby? Hi. I'm Mr. Maguire, the production manager."

"Pleased to meet you, sir."

"You're one of the new hires, aren't you?"

"Started last week."

"Uh-huh. What are you working on?"

Bobby pointed to a line on the screen of the WING terminal, and said, "This lot right here."

"And why is that?"

"Because, well, that's what the computer told me to do."

"Shut that machine down," said Murphy.

"Excuse me?"

"I said, *shut it down!*"

Bobby pressed a red button on the control panel and the machine stopped. Almost immediately, a red triangle with a question mark popped onto the screen of the WING terminal.

"Put in a five-twenty code," Murphy told the young operator.

"That's the code for preventive maintenance," said Bobby, doing as he was told. "You want me to do preventive maintenance on this machine? In the middle of a run?"

"No, I do not. But we have to tell the WING server something, or it sets off alarms. Now, what I really want to know is, where did you get this material?"

"From the storeroom," said Bobby.

"You just went and got it?"

"Well, yeah. The computer said I should. Did I do something wrong?"

"Now, now, relax," Murphy said reassuringly. "You're new. You'll learn. But from now on, you work only on the materials *delivered* to your station. You hear? You do not go get them yourself, unless your area manager specifically tells you to do so."

"But I came in, and I didn't have anything to work on. What was I supposed to do?"

"If you have no material, Bobby, you cannot produce. And that is exactly what you are supposed to be doing: *not* producing. It's kind of an unwritten rule around here. I'm sorry nobody seems to have explained that to you."

"But the computer –"

"If the computer – the WING terminal – gives you a work instruction, and you do not already have material, ignore it. Because the software is based on faulty assumptions. Much of the time, the instruction will be giving you 'make work' just to have you be productive."

"Mr. Maguire, I don't mean any disrespect, but isn't that what I'm supposed to be? Productive?"

Murphy struggled for a moment, trying to think of how to explain this to the young man.

"Bobby, in simplest terms, when you have material in front of you to work on, then yes. We want you to be *productive* – as in producing. And we want you to focus and do your part as fast as you can, but in accordance with all safety and quality requirements. Okay?

"Now, when you do *not* have material, then we want you to be *useful*. You see? They are two different states. *Productive* is obvious – you are running your equipment and processing material. *Useful* is a little harder to grasp. *Useful* means being ready to produce once the material does arrive. It means maintaining your equipment so it does not break and runs at peak efficiency when you are producing. It means checking your tolerances and calibrating your sensors so that your output quality is perfect. It means keeping everything neat and tidy – or even just sweeping the floor. You get my drift?"

"I think so," said Bobby. "But I'm still not sure why you want me to ignore the computer."

"Because, Bobby, if you did everything that WING told you to do, you would scarcely be able to walk through the aisles, there would be so much work-in-process inventory piled everywhere. Which was pretty much the way it was just six months ago, when we were required . . . well, never mind all that. Just follow my rules: material comes to you, then you produce. When you run out of material, you wait and do everything to be useful."

Just then the plant loudspeaker sounded, with Richy's voice saying, "Attention, attention! Godzilla is about to vent. Please synchronize. Please synchronize."

"Bobby, you hear that?"

"Sure, I hear it, every so often. Sometimes once an hour, or every couple of hours, sometimes not for a long time."

"That's coming from Autoclave," Murphy explained. "Every process, everything we do in this plant is timed so that materials will arrive next to that big orange thing down there. That's the autoclave, what we call Godzilla – just because it's big and ugly. We always want plenty of material sitting there, ready to go into Godzilla whenever it finishes a batch, or what we call a 'soak.' We do not want large quantities of material sitting here or anywhere else, except for two places: the setup area next to Godzilla, and the shipping dock, packaged and ready to go on the truck."

Bobby was nodding.

"Now, you heard the loudspeaker say, *synchronize*. That means more raw materials are to be what we call 'gated' into production. They will be coming onto the floor, and it means you should have material to work on very shortly. So you should get ready. When it arrives, you scan the bar code, and you do the setup that the computer tells you. That's when you *do* do what the computer says. Got that?"

"Yeah, I think I do," said Bobby. "Can't say I fully understand the reasons, but it's simple enough."

"I see material headed your way now," said Murphy. "So you get ready now. And next time you have a chance, take this other stuff back to where you got it. Hope you have a good career here at Oakton."

"Thank you, sir. I appreciate that," said Bobby.

And Murphy walked on, as behind him Bobby shook his head in puzzlement.

A little before ten o'clock, Murphy commandeered a college kid working an internship, gave the kid his car keys, and sent him to the parking lot. The kid returned with a Styrofoam ice chest and followed Murph to a particular compressor motor whose inefficiencies were known to generate a reliable and continuous 173°F to 186°F ambient temperature. Murph then relieved the kid of the burden, sent him on his way, and removed from the ice chest a black, covered, cast-iron kettle, which he then set next to the motor cover. He left with no explanation to anyone in the area, as everyone knew that the kettle was not to be touched.

When Murphy returned an hour and a half later to retrieve the kettle, it had been joined by something wrapped in multiple layers of aluminum foil. Murphy took the kettle to a windowless, out-of-the-way, unused toolroom that contained only some shelves with seldom-used tooling, a few file cabinets, and a steel table with two chairs. A few minutes later, in came Jayro carrying a cardboard box containing the aforementioned foil-wrapped object, as well as paper plates, cheap napkins, and various fixings.

"What you got for me, Jayro?"

"Got for you? What you got for me? That's what's important."

"Oh, I might have a little something – if you got anything good to trade."

"I always got good. Since when have I ever brought anything bad?"

"Well, there was that gumbo awhile back. Just about took the top of my head off."

"Nuthin' wrong with heat. It's good to sweat."

"Couldn't taste a thang for three days!"

Every Monday for the past seventeen years Murphy and Jayro had been having lunch in this toolroom, just the two of them. Several times over the years they had attempted to include a few others, but it had never worked out. The two of them could talk about anything – and did. With other people in the room, the chemistry was different. Certain subjects had to be avoided. So they tactfully went back to having their Monday lunches be a private matter.

"Got the good stuff today, Murph." Teasingly slowly, Jayro pulled back the foil to reveal a beautiful, dark, brownish red slab of ribs. "Got spares."

"Mmm-mmm," Murphy murmured, leaning close to inhale the scent.

"They got my special, secret rub. Smoked over apple wood five hours last night while my son and I watched the game. What's yours?"

Murphy lifted the lid of the kettle and another smoky, spicy aroma wafted into the room.

"Barbeque, Jayro. Picnic ham from my neighbor's hogs. Nine hours in the Lang with seasoned hickory from my own woods. Plus my wife's coleslaw, and a jug of sweet tea. Now, grab yourself a bun, tear me off some of them ribs, and let's have at it."

The two men ate in silence for a few minutes, both savoring the delectable feast.

"Hate to ruin a good meal and all," said Jayro, speaking at last. "But I spoke to that Garth Quincy in California."

"You track down what he needed?"

"Yes, and guess what? It just came on the schedule this morning. It's already a week late, and it just came on the schedule. The Geniuses in Rockville didn't give it the design review clearance until last Thursday."

"How long did they have it in their hands?"

"Over two months. I guess nobody got around to dealing with it. Slipped through the cracks or whatever. Now we're caught holding the hot potato. Now *we* are the ones who look bad, like it's our fault."

"Jayro, I have tried for years to solve this problem. And I have gotten nowhere. Those Geniuses at F&D, they are in their own world, and they do not care about ours. So I have given up. I run Oakton, and that's it. I do the best I can. There is nothing more I can do. The design review clearances come in dribbles and drips, in big bunches and little bunches, and then we scramble and produce whatever has to be made. But there is nothing we can do until we get the clearance from F&D."

"Well, brace yourself, Murph, because it gets worse," said Jayro.

Murphy tossed aside a perfectly clean rib bone and shook his head.

"All right, I'm braced," said Murphy. "Hit me."

"The order Quincy was calling about, it's got a spec that calls for one of those twenty-three-hour soaks in Godzilla."

"Oh, gosh *dang* it," said Murphy, along with a few other less printable expletives. "Jayro, did you make any promises?"

"You can bet my bottom I did not," said Jayro. "I told Quincy that it had just come onto the schedule and I would talk to you about it. I can tell you, he was not pleased."

Murphy shut his eyes briefly, then reached for another rib. He gnawed on that for a while.

Then he said, "I'll call him. He'll hate me, but I'll call him. We can't even think about shipping until late Monday, not with a long soak like that. We have to do that long-soak stuff on the weekend. If I move his order to the front of the queue, it's going to make fifty or a hundred other orders late. And that's all those other customers mad at us, instead of just one mad at us – who's already mad at us."

"Makes perfect sense," said Jayro. "Great pork butt, by the way."

Murphy nodded, appreciating the compliment, yet it did not lift his spirits.

"Hey, just to change the subject," Jayro said, "what do you think of this new lady, this Amy, comin' in as president?"

"As 'interim' president," said Murphy, "which suggests to me they don't want her to stay. But as for Amy herself, what I know of her I like. I think she's a straight shooter. And I think she knows her end of it, the marketing and customer end, pretty good. On the other hand . . . she don't know a dang thing about production. And she's got this new ops guy from New York, this Wayne Reese, telling her what's what – she won't know how to judge what he tells her. And then she's got the Geniuses in F&D, who are in their own world up there and out for themselves. I seriously doubt if Amy can handle them. B. Don Williams could barely keep them in check. But we shall see. We shall see."

"What about the new ops guy?" Jayro asked.

Murphy was carefully placing beautiful shreds of pork barbeque on a bun and did not answer at first. In fact, he took so long that Jayro thought he was ignoring the question. Then Murphy said:

"We have suffered, Jayro. We have suffered through the across-the-board cuts, although I was able by hook and crook to protect Godzilla. We have suffered through pay-by-the-piece incentives, which I have now canceled. We have suffered the WING terminals that tell people exactly the wrong thing to do. We have suffered grid-lock work-in-process inventory in the name of productivity. We have suffered Winner Chemicals, which makes us buy what we don't need and can't supply what we are out of. And we have *long* suffered the indifference of the Geniuses at F&D."

"Right on, Murph, right on."

"Now, finally, we see the rays of hope. The Tornado is gone."

"Yes, praise the Lord."

"And we are slowly clawing our way back. We can now walk the plant floor and not kill ourselves tripping over excess inventory. Godzilla has been re-established as the production constraint, and all production is keyed to Godzilla's actual output. We have hired back some of those the Tornado forced us to cut, as well as a few new hires, to give us the speed we need for more throughput. Despite the cases like today of Garth Quincy and his unfortunate customer, we are actually meeting most shipping commitments better than we were."

"I raise my cup of sweet tea in tribute," said Jayro.

"So, yes, we still have our problems – cracks in the Navy job, orders that are late before they even get into production. But Oakton is getting better. We are returning to sanity and to a level of performance at least equal to where we were B.W. – Before Winner. And then . . ."

"Then what?"

"Then, just as I think common sense might prevail, I find out that Wayne Reese is coming in over me."

Now it was Jayro's turn to revert to silence.

"This Wayne Reese, he's into Lean Six Sigma, you know. 'LSS' if you prefer the alphabet soup. Ran the Winner corporate LSS program."

"Okay, what's wrong with that?" asked Jayro.

"Do you remember Quality Circles?"

"Nah. Before my time."

"How about TQM? Total Quality Management?"

"I do remember that one a little bit. Didn't last at Hi-T very long."

"And that's what worries me. These programs, they come, they go, and in between they can take on a life of their own. Before anyone knows it, the program somehow becomes the end rather than the means. That's what happened here with TQM. Not that TQM didn't have good intentions and good ideas. But the program itself became a burden rather than a bridge to a better place."

"So you think that's going to happen again?"

"Here's the thing, Jayro. We at Oakton are at a crucial stage right now. The Tornado hit us hard with WING and all his tricks to make the short-term numbers pop. Now he's gone. But what are Wayne Reese and Lean Six Sigma going to do to us?"

"Murph, has it occurred to you that the LSS stuff might do us a lot of good?"

"Jayro, I am just a few years from retirement. I can't afford a religious experience – not at work. And I'm told that's what this Lean Six Sigma can become. Look, I am not going to rock the boat. But I do need the boat to float."

"Sorry, I'm not following you, Murph."

"What happens if Wayne Reese comes in and what he makes us do doesn't work? He's a younger guy; he can move on. But an old fart like me – or even you . . ."

"Then I guess we open up that roadside barbeque joint we've been talkin' about all these years," said Jayro.

"That's what I'm afraid of," said Murphy.

That evening Bobby, the machine operator that Murphy had talked to, would tell his wife Linda about his day at work. And Bobby would try to explain to her the crazy things that Mr. Maguire had said, such as to *not* produce when, after all, wasn't that what he was being paid to do?

A few weeks later Amy Cieolara would ask her assistant, Linda, how her husband Bobby was doing. Amy had played no direct role in his being hired at Oakton, but through Linda, she knew of course that Bobby's application had been accepted.

"He's doing fine," said Linda. "Only . . . well, maybe I shouldn't say anything."

"You have already," said Amy. "What is it?"

"Bobby says that a lot of times he doesn't have enough to do. You know what a hard worker he is. I've told you that. But he says there are times when he doesn't have any material to work on. And one time when he went and got some material on his own – which was what the computer told him to do – the production manager told him not to do that ever again."

"Who? Murphy Maguire?"

"Yes, I believe so," said Linda. "So Bobby, you know, likes to be busy, and a lot of the time he's just waiting for more material to show up, and cleaning his equipment and such."

"Well, that's disturbing," said Amy. "Here, we've got some orders shipping late, and yet there are people standing around with not enough to do."

"I probably shouldn't have said anything," said Linda. "I'm sorry."

"It's all right. Our new ops guy, Wayne Reese, will fix that, I can assure you."

4

"Ben and Michelle, eat your salads please," Amy told her kids one evening. "If we have to throw them away, they're *muda*."

"They're what?" asked her mom.

"*Muda*," said Amy. She had just returned from a three-day executive seminar on Lean Six Sigma, and she was all fired up. "*Muda* is a Japanese word for 'waste.'"

"What was it again? *Moolah?*" asked Zelda.

"No . . . moo-dah," said Amy.

"Hey! You watch what you're calling your mother, young lady!" said her father from across the dinner table.

"Harry, it's all right! She's just explaining something from work," Zelda said, then turned back to her daughter. "Now . . . what's it about?"

"*Muda* is bad. *Muda* is the enemy. *Muda* is anything that eats up resources – money, time, energy, materials – but creates no value. And it's often almost invisible, because we're so used to it. Mistakes and the need to do things over again – that's an obvious form of *muda*. Scrap is *muda*. Delays and late deliveries; those are *muda*. But so is waiting in line for something. Making customers pay for features that they really don't want, that they're never going to use, that have no value for the customer – that's *muda*."

"I see," said her mom.

"And it goes on and on," said Amy. "When materials are just sitting in a pile, waiting to be processed, that's *muda*. It's wasted time. Meetings that could be over in ten minutes, but they last hours because that's how they're scheduled – that's *muda*. Workers standing around with not enough to do . . . *muda!* Underutilized machines that consume energy and cost money to keep and maintain – more *muda*! It's everywhere!"

"What's she talking about?" Harry asked Zelda.

"Dad," said Amy very patiently, "at the company where I work, we've started something called Lean Six Sigma. The purpose of it is to reduce waste throughout the company and to increase value for customers. We just started the meetings this week, and I'm really pumped up about it."

Her father nodded. "Oh . . . well, good."

"So anyway, Mom, this new vice president of operations, Wayne Reese, is sensational. He's a Master Black Belt in LSS."

"Black belt? Are you teaching people karate?"

"Right, Mom. We haul everyone into these meetings and then we beat 'em up and say, 'Don't waste resources!' No, black belt refers to a level of skill. If you come into the program, you get a basic level of training in LSS and you become a white belt or a yellow belt. Then there's the green belt level, which involves in-depth training. And ultimately there are black belts and master black belts, which involve lots *more* training and experience. And you have to lead projects to get certified and pass tests and all kinds of things. Anyhow, Wayne is a Master Black Belt, and he knows this stuff backward and forward. I just love him."

"Is he married?"

"Mom . . . please. Yes, he is married. Three kids, two in college, and one still at home. He's waiting to buy a house here until the last one graduates from high school. What I meant was –"

"Moolah," said Harry, as if the word amused him.

Amy tried to ignore him.

"What I meant was that Wayne has really shown me the light. I think the potential is huge. He says that every Winner business where he's implemented Lean has saved millions and millions of dollars – to one degree or another. Customer satisfaction has gone up. And the employees love it. Workplaces are neater and cleaner. People are involved in all these activities going on. Everybody's measuring everything to reduce defects and increase customer satisfaction. But Wayne also warned me that it takes a serious commitment to make it happen. Everybody has to be brought up to speed. There has to be what they call *cultural change* and for that to occur it's going to take a lot of –"

"Moolah!" Harry said again with a little chuckle.

"No, Dad, the word is *muda*," said Amy a bit testily. "It means –"

"I know what it means," said her father. "It means *waste* in Japanese. And do you know who taught me that?"

"Could it have been me?" suggested Amy.

"It was Taiichi Ohno."

Every once in a while, despite the ravages of the Alzheimer's disease, Harry would have these lucid moments. They tended to happen when something in conversation jogged his long-term memory and triggered his intellect. It was then that, for a few minutes, those around him could sense the remainders of the sharp, analytical mind that had once been.

"Who?" asked Ben. "Did you say the name was Oh-no? Like, 'Oh no, I forgot my lunch!' "

"Yes, Taiichi Ohno. Doctor Ohno to you, young man," said his grandfather. "And who else was there? I'm trying to remember . . . yes, it was Shigeo Shingo and Eiji Toyoda. Brilliant, all three of them."

"Mom, what's Grandpa talking about?" asked Michelle.

"I've heard of them," said Amy. "They were with Toyota."

"Yes, and they created the Toyota Production System," said Harry. "Elements of this became known, in English, as Just-In-Time production. Quite revolutionary. Low inventories. Better quality. Quick changeover of production, so you could make a small number of parts, then set up to make another part very quickly. We tried it at the company, but . . . it was too radical. The vendors, the lower management people . . . nobody understood it."

"Mom, is this true?" asked Amy.

"I don't really know. But, as I recall, back in the nineteen eighties, the company sent him to Japan –"

"Yes, that was the place!" said Harry. "I was in Japan!"

"Funny, but I do not remember this," said Amy.

"I think you were away at college, dear," her mother said.

"And we drank that . . . what was it?" asked Harry. "That clear, sort of sweet-tasting wine they have. What was the name?"

"*Sake*," said Zelda. "He came back from Japan and every Friday night he would have *sake* with dinner. And if it got cold – you're supposed to drink it warm – he wanted me to heat it up for him. Finally, I told him, warm it yourself, I'm not your geisha."

"Ah, but you are, my dear, you are," said Harry, a twinkle in his eye, and he leaned over the table and kissed her on the cheek.

"Grandma!" said Michelle. "You're blushing!"

Indeed she was. Zelda pulled back from him, smile on her face and a twinkle in her own eye.

"So, anyway, where were we?" asked Harry.

"Well, at one point, I was talking about *muda*," said Amy, "and you were talking about moolah."

"Right, right, right. And the question that occurs to me is, how are you going to get the moolah out of the *muda*?"

"Actually, Dad, that's a pretty good question."

"Of course it is. I asked it."

Amy turned to her children and said, "What your grandfather is asking is, how is my company going to use the opportunity of eliminating waste to make money?"

"Exactly," said Harry.

"Well, we're supposed to get some quick, early results. But it's a long-term proposition. We have to do the training. We have to form the teams. The teams analyze everything that's going on, and then they tell us in management where the opportunities are. You see, the people on the teams have to be motivated; they have to be involved and engaged. We can guide them – have to guide them – but we have to let them have a say in which projects to pursue."

"And so?"

"We urge them on, we encourage them, we recognize their efforts. We help them implement the solutions. And the results . . . happen."

"All right, but seriously," said her father, "how do you – as in your company – make money out of it?"

"Dad, I think that's obvious, isn't it? If we reduce *muda*, if we eliminate defects, then everyone can work faster."

"All right. Perhaps. But is that good?"

"Yes, of course it's good! Quality improves, everyone works faster, therefore, productivity increases, customer needs are met, and we make more money."

Her father listened to all of this sagely but then said, "I don't know. It just sounds to me like you're going to spend a lot of moolah, but I don't know if you know how you're going to get the moolah back. How you're going to make the moolah from the *muda*."

Amy nodded.

"Well, Dad, there are no guarantees. But I am committed. I am what they call the Champion, the executive who supports the Lean Six Sigma program. So I am going down this road and . . . I think it's going to work. In fact, I don't see how it can't work."

"Ice cream, anyone?" asked Zelda.

Both the kids perked up.

"After you finish your salads," Amy insisted.

"Oh, Mom!"

"So," said Harry, "where are we?"

"We were talking about –"

"No, I mean, where in the world are we?"

Amy slumped back in her chair.

Zelda put her hand atop Harry's on the tablecloth and repeated the litany:

"Harry, we are at Amy's house. Amy is your daughter. These are your grandchildren, Ben and Michelle. We live nearby, and we come here every day . . ."

Just that quickly, the moment had passed.

"Look at this," Wayne said in disgust, flinging his hand toward the seemingly endless line of orange barrels extending down the highway and a just as endless line of traffic creeping along. "There is *muda* here. Big-time *muda*. Miles of road blocked off where nothing is happening. All the gas being wasted in traffic. Once you begin to look at the world through Lean eyes, you see waste everywhere."

"You're probably right," said Amy. "I don't know why they have to shut down five miles of highway when they're only working on some little stretch – and half the time they're not even working."

"Exactly. The thing about Lean is that value is always defined from the customer's point of view. We, the motorists, are the ultimate customer, but the state highway departments and the contractors always seem to do things for their own efficiency, not ours. Anyway . . ."

The two of them were riding in Wayne's white SUV hybrid, Amy perched in the passenger seat catching up on email with her Black-Berry, while Wayne fumed in frustration as he drove. They were headed for the Oakton plant, about twenty miles from downtown Highboro, at the rate of about three miles per hour thanks to a construction zone that had narrowed two westbound highway lanes to one.

"Hey, on a brighter note," Wayne said, "I just want to say I'm really looking forward to introducing Lean and Six Sigma to Hi-T, especially at the Oakton plant. I really am a hands-on kind of guy. I love to immerse myself in the details, help figure out the value stream, get people turned on about LSS, get the projects going, all of that. And my goal for the implementation at Hi-T is for it to be worthy of a Lean case study – you know, pure and by the book."

"Well, great. Of course there are a lot of books out there, especially on Lean, as I'm finding out," said Amy.

"That's true. And there are a lot of different variations of Lean – including the one we developed for Winner, the one that I use. But what I mean is I'd love to see us achieve that cultural change that transforms the entire company into a Lean organization in every aspect, so that it's more than just a program . . . so that it's, you know, a mind-set."

"Hey, go for it," said Amy. "Wayne, you know you have my support, and that of Winner corporate. I'm really fired up about it myself. Just remember, you've got all of operations to manage, not just the Oakton LSS improvements. And of course we have to make some bucks, too. Nigel Furst is expecting growth from us, and Randal Tourandos set a pretty high bar."

"Amy, I'm going to stick my neck out here, because we don't have the projects defined or the potential savings or any of that – but my gut hunch is that, *if we do it right*, and keep striving for perfection, you won't have any trouble meeting your growth goals."

"Really? I mean, what makes you so sure?"

"Well, one of the first things I was taught when I was learning the Lean philosophy at Winner was that little improvements add up to big accomplishments. Every project we finish, while some of them may not seem that significant, will ultimately – maybe not immediately, but eventually – increase the success of the business. The gains we achieve with Lean Six Sigma are accretive – they can and should add up to big numbers over time. And the more we focus on customer value, the more the marketing side of things will flourish."

Inspired, Amy held up her hand with fingers splayed to do a high-five, and Wayne took his right hand off the steering wheel and their palms smacked. At the same time, as Wayne turned his body so his palm could reach hers, his left hand skewed the wheel and the SUV veered off the highway, grazing an orange barrel with the edge of his bumper and toppling it. Wayne recovered quickly, but Amy's eyes were wide as she watched the barrel roll into a gully.

"I hope that's not an omen," she joked.

"Nah!" said Wayne. "We're good. Probably not even any paint damage."

"No, I meant . . . never mind."

"Hey, more good news; I'm finding out, now that I've been longer in Highboro, that the ops administrative staff here is really strong. So of course I'll be keeping a firm hand on everything, but I should have ample time to make sure that we really do Lean Six Sigma *right*."

"What does doing it 'right' really mean?" asked Amy. "You know, by your definition?"

"Well, the big thing, I believe, is what I mentioned: doing enough of the right things right to achieve an organizational change in culture. You know, for instance, there's something I always taught my internal clients within Winner: it's the ratio of 'N over ten.' "

"What's that?"

" 'N over ten' means you take the number of employees and divide by ten, and that gives you the number of Lean and Six Sigma activities that should be taking place during the course of one year's time."

Amy quickly did the math in her head and decided it was a fairly large number.

"And what do you mean by 'activities'?" she asked.

"Well, by my definition, it's anything that promotes the Lean and Six Sigma mind-set. It's presentations, like the one we're giving today at Oakton, and in Rockville to F&D. By the way, I'm really glad we're extending LSS to a service organization – because the principles apply to services as well as manufacturing. Anyway, activities are presentations, improvement projects, events like what I call 'mixers,' where people come together to share their Lean experiences. Whatever promotes Lean and Six Sigma and ingrains it into organizational thinking."

Amy nodded, then said, "Well, you're talking about a lot of activities."

"Yes, I am. And that doesn't even include training, which is hugely important. I mean, it's expensive, sure, but you have to have enough people with the skills to actually do the improvements."

"Of course," said Amy.

"What I used to tell my internal clients was that you should be striving to achieve the correct green-belt to black-belt ratio. You know, you want your black belts to be about two percent of the employee population. Black belts are of course higher in skills, but you need enough green belts to stretch the Lean way of doing things into all parts of the organization."

Amy was not sure she wanted to have the correct black-belt to green-belt ratio further explained, so she asked the other question forming in the back of her mind:

"You say you had 'internal clients'?"

"Right. The past ten, eleven years or so my time at Winner has been entirely dedicated to Lean and Six Sigma. I became a corporate trainer in Six Sigma, then caught the Lean bug and became a Lean Six Sigma internal consultant. Winner businesses would pay for my time and experience, just as they would any other consultant, but at a somewhat lower rate. So I had clients and ran programs and so on. Finally, after doing that for some time, I moved up into LSS administration."

"Oh," said Amy. "But . . . I'm a little curious about this. I was glancing through your personnel file the other day, and . . . your actual operations experience? Where was it?"

"It was at Winner," said Wayne. "I was hired by Winner right out of college. I was a plant engineer for a year or so, and then they put me into a kind of fast-track training program where I learned a little bit of everything – purchasing, inventory control, plant management, maintenance, distribution, all of those. And then I moved into quality management – and that's where I really connected, first with Six Sigma, and then a year or so later with Lean manufacturing. Of course, my last job was administrative, coordinating all the LSS programs and activities throughout Winner, and it got old after a few years. Between you and me, I'm happy to be back here in the real world."

"Uh-huh. I see, but you've never actually managed operations?"

"Well, I've never had that exact title until now," said Wayne. "But I've dealt with all kinds of operational issues. As an internal consultant, I saw and dealt with everything. I mean, we all have to grow, don't we."

She felt the last comment was directed as much at her as himself. And she inwardly acknowledged he was right. What had she, Amy, done so far except manage marketing and sales? Yet Nigel and Peter, with a big nudge from a prominent customer, had trusted her, hadn't they. And they had chosen Wayne Reese. All right, she thought, maybe Wayne was a little light on direct experience, but if he had the confidence of the corporate hierarchy, how could she object?

"Yes, that's true," she agreed. "We all need to grow. And I'm excited about the year ahead. I really am."

Wayne smiled, as if they had a tacit partnership. Then he craned his head outside the SUV window to peer past traffic, which was now moving faster.

"All right, finally, here we go," said Wayne.

Just ahead, the orange barrels ceased and a sign announced the end of the construction zone; the westbound highway opened again to two lanes.

"Looks like we're going to be late," Amy said, glancing at her watch.

"That damn construction bottleneck," Wayne muttered as he zoomed into the left lane. He put the pedal to the metal. "We'll make up for lost time. Hope I don't get a ticket."

Meanwhile, at the Oakton plant, Murphy Maguire had called together all the plant-floor managers and was rehearsing the steps of the intricate dance that would allow production to proceed while Wayne Reese gave his presentation on Lean Six Sigma to employees who would assemble in the cafeteria. There would be two presentations so as to cover both day and evening turns, but to keep everything running would require some juggling.

"Where's Richy?" Murphy called out. "Richy, when does Godzilla vent?"

"Two fifty-six," said Richy.

"And we've got the next batch ready to go?"

"We're covered and set."

"And the next soak is how long?"

"Three hours and twenty-six minutes."

"All right, the downtown folks will be gone by then," said Murphy. "So, listen up, here are the groups who go to the first presentation . . ."

Less than an hour later, Wayne Reese was speaking to the first group of assembled plant workers, a wireless microphone clipped to his shirt, pacing slowly as he spoke to them. Behind him was a screen with computer-projected slides.

"What is this thing called Lean?" he asked rhetorically. "And what is Six Sigma? We often use the two names together as 'Lean Six Sigma' or by the initials, 'LSS,' but Lean and Six Sigma are two different things . . . two separate disciplines.

"Lean is a discipline for creating value for customers by way of products and services with minimum waste at optimal speed in perfect balance with market demand. And Six Sigma is a discipline for identifying and eliminating defects, errors, and anything quantifiable that is unwanted by customers. Those are the Winner definitions, the ones that I use. Really, though, Lean and Six Sigma are both about eliminating waste. Lean looks at eliminating waste throughout operations, in lots of different ways. Six Sigma reduces waste primarily by reducing variation and so improves quality. But they complement each other very well, and so we often pair the two and call them Lean Six Sigma.

"Today, I'm going to give you just a quick overview of Lean Six Sigma, because as a company, Hi-T Composites is beginning a very important journey to achieve LSS values in everything we do. And it's a journey that never really ends. It is continuous improvement that strives for perfection – knowing that perfection will never fully be reached. LSS is a philosophy in many ways. And yet, all of its tools and projects are practical. Its methods are structured and disciplined.

"I'm going to tell you a little bit about something called DMAIC: Define . . . Measure . . . Analyze . . . Improve . . . Control – which is a five-step process for solving problems. Today and in the future you'll be hearing about projects involving 'Five-S,' which is a method for reorganizing a workplace so that tools are within reach and equipment is well maintained. You'll also be seeing and hearing about a lot of these . . ."

He changed the slide and brought up something that looked like a graph with a lot of variable lines.

"This is a control chart, one of the key tools used in Six Sigma. And you'll be hearing about Lean projects to create 'one-piece flow,' and eliminate the traditional and wasteful batch-and-queue method. There will be projects for reducing scrap and for making processes mistake proof. And on and on. Those I've just mentioned barely scratch the surface.

"Before we get into all that, let me tell you why I personally think that Lean Six Sigma is meaningful. Lean, in particular, is about always looking for the better way. I'm sure that everyone here has at one time or another looked at the way things are being done – in the Oakton plant, or out in the community, or even in your own home – and wondered, 'Why are we doing it this way? It's dumb! It's wasteful! It doesn't make sense!' Or, as a customer, you buy something and you pay good money, probably more than you feel you ought to pay, and yet this thing you've bought is really not the way you want it. And if you dare to question the way things are done, you typically get an answer like, 'We've always done it this way,' or 'That's just the way it is,' or maybe even, 'We have to do it this way; it's policy; it's regulation; it's the law.' Whatever.

"Well, the Lean way of thinking is a challenge to all of that. Lean is about never being completely satisfied with the status quo. It's about continuous improvement. It's about always seeking the better way to do things. It's about identifying waste and eliminating it – or at least minimizing waste. Right now you probably think of waste as whatever is in the wastebasket. As trash, or scrap.

"But waste takes many forms – many of which are invisible to us. We just don't see them. A big stack of materials just sitting, sometimes for weeks or months, that is waste – not the materials themselves, but the fact that they are just sitting in a warehouse. The *waiting* is the waste, because there is money tied up in those materials, and we have to ask the question, why are there so many items in this pile made so far ahead of when they are needed?

"Lean is about delivering to the customer – be that customer the final customer, like a consumer in a grocery story, or be that customer the next workstation on the plant floor – delivering exactly what that customer needs and wants, right when the customer needs or wants it, and passing along *nothing* that the customer does *not* value.

"And we do that by getting rid of – or by not creating – the non-essential. What do you have after the *non*essential has been stripped away? You have . . . the *essential*. You have the essence. You have the essential, perfect thing delivered at the perfect moment for the perfect price. That does not happen often enough in our world. Yet that is what we are going to strive for here at Oakton and throughout Hi-T Composites."

Off to the side, Amy Cieolara, watching Wayne pace and gesture before the assembly, thought to herself, *Wow, he's good*.

And in the back of the cafeteria, Murphy Maguire nudged Jayro Pepps and whispered, "It's worse than I thought."

"What's the matter?" Jayro asked.

"He's an eye-dealist," Murphy said from the corner of his mouth. "Look out."

In his early childhood, Wayne had grown up in Fall River, Massachusetts, as the son of Edmundo Reis, an unskilled laborer of Portuguese descent who was quite intelligent despite having dropped out of high school in order to support his family, which at age seventeen was just beginning. Edmundo – Ed – had a passion for John Wayne movies, hence his insistence on the given name for his first son. After struggling a few years following Wayne's birth, Ed got a good job in a factory that made brass hardware.

But when Wayne was eight years old, the brass factory closed and his dad lost his job. Ed got another job, this time at a plant in Boston that made printed circuit boards. The family lived in what the locals called an "Irish battleship," a three-floor house on the fringes of South Boston. And to better fit in with the neighbors, Ed changed the spelling of the family name to the anglicized "Reese." For Wayne, the new spelling didn't help much; every day, it seemed, was a new fistfight as the kids he went to school with showed him that he, being an outsider, was nobody, or worse. After a couple of years, though, and a few lessons in karate, he showed them otherwise.

At the time, the future of printed circuit boards seemed bright, and in fact it was. The Reese family bought a little house in Medford and for a few years everything was fine. Wayne, now in high school, met Teresa, the young woman he would eventually marry. And then the plant where Ed worked shut down, continuing a painful pattern for Ed and his family. After many months of searching, Ed would eventually find other good employment, only to be among the first to be cut when times got tough. Ed ran machines making memory chips, assembled word processor terminals, and even shoes in factories in New Hampshire – and every few years, his job would disappear.

At every company, change worked against him. Competition, employee complacency, management lethargy, breakthrough technology, globalism – an entire range of factors undermined his security, singly or in concert. And there was not much that Ed as an individual could do about it.

"And, for me, that's where it comes from – this drive, this passion for continuous improvement. It came from my dad," Wayne told the employees of the Hi-T Oakton plant, wrapping up his presentation.

"I really think that every time my dad, Ed, took a new job, he expected to retire from that company. But it was never to be. Each company would have its time in the sun, but then would fall upon hard times, and everyone who worked for the company would suffer. There are many reasons why it happened, but the primary one, in my opinion, was inertia. None of the companies where my dad worked had a coherent system in place to bring about continuous improvement. They drifted along, pretending as if today was just like yesterday and tomorrow would be like today. When changes in the market, in technology, in global competition came, these companies could not adapt fast enough, and they could not survive and jobs went away."

Wayne paced in front of them – and everyone was listening.

"So . . . in conclusion, in the past forty-five minutes I've given you some idea of what Lean and Six Sigma are about and how we're going to be using them. Ultimately, our goal is to excite our customers with speed and quality. We want to blow them away. We want them to rave about us. And the way we're going to do that is through value – always seen from the customer's point of view. Whenever and wherever we can eliminate waste, we increase value. And we just keep improving and improving, striving to give the customer the perfect essence of what that customer really wants.

"But I wanted to end with that story about my dad, Ed, because right now, everyone working for Hi-T Composites has an opportunity that my dad never had. As hard as he worked at his various jobs, for all his loyalty to the various companies, he never had a chance to participate in a program that could really make a difference in the long-term success of the businesses where he earned his living. But *you* do. You have that opportunity with Lean Six Sigma.

"Look, I cannot predict the future, and I cannot make any guarantees or promises to you regarding what the future may or may not hold for any individual. But if you work with us to make this company the least wasteful, most flexible, fastest fulfillment, perfect quality, highest cost efficiency, precision composites provider on the planet . . . I think that future ought to be pretty darn good, don't you? I urge you to get involved in Lean Six Sigma and help us make Hi-T's future and your own a bright one. Thank you."

The applause began without prompting, and it was loud, long, and heartfelt. Wayne looked over at Amy, and Amy gave him a clear nod of approval.

Just after 5:00 p.m., Amy and Wayne were back downtown in Highboro, both agreeing that the day had gone well. Amy headed for her office, formerly the corner office of B. Donald Williams, which she had taken. The moment Amy plopped into her chair, Linda walked in.

"You're not going to like this," said Linda.

"Of course not. It's five o'clock. I'm ready to be done with making decisions and I'm actually in a good mood. What is it?"

"Your favorite airline –"

"Agony Airways. How have they screwed us now?"

"They just announced this afternoon that effective immediately they are canceling the last remaining direct-flight service between Highboro and Washington, D.C."

"No!" Amy shot to her feet and pounded her desk with her slim hand. "NO! They cannot do this!"

"Well, I'm sorry, but they did," said Linda.

"Effective immediately? What about tomorrow? We have to go to Rockville!"

"Here are the options: you can fly from here south to Atlanta and then take a flight north to Dulles or BWI. That's probably your best shot. Or, you can fly west to Nashville –"

"Linda, we need to fly north. Isn't there an option that flies north, not west or south or east?"

"Well, there is one, but you have to go to Pittsburgh first, and then it's a three-hour layover."

Amy slapped her forehead with the bottom of her palm.

"Wait a minute . . . who was that guy?" Amy asked. "That pilot?"

"Dawson. Dawson Aviation."

"Call him. See what he can do for us."

5

From a standing start, as the red light turned green, the silver Porsche Cayman S was doing eighty miles per hour through the apex of the curve down the on-ramp and was well over 100 mph and still accelerating as the car merged onto I-270. The hour was early; there was as yet very little traffic. And the driver, Dr. Viktor Kyzanski, from bitter experience, knew the location of every likely speed trap, as he drove this route almost every day. Where he could do so with reasonable "safety," Viktor pushed the car several times to 130 or so – two times the legal limit – streaking along under a beautiful blue summer sky through the green Maryland countryside. But within twenty miles, the joyride was over. He was slogging along, bumper to bumper, with all the other commuters, lucky that the traffic was moving at all.

Dr. Kyzanski, as he often introduced himself, was vice president and director of Hi-T Formulation & Design. He hated the "Hi-T" part of his title, despised the company logo, which he thought was ugly, but he could do nothing about those at present – someday, perhaps, but not now. He was relatively young – forty-seven – and extremely well paid, and he assumed he still had ample room to move if he so chose. (The acquisition by Winner delighted him.) Even so, he was in no hurry. For the most part he enjoyed his position and his work. He was very comfortable, and not about to leave.

The two glass-walled, multistoried buildings housing F&D were tucked away in a woods beside the interstate. Viktor made the most of a little S curve on the access road that meandered through the trees. He then parked the Porsche in his reserved spot next to Building One. Several spaces up from his in the empty parking lot, in the spot marked "Reserved for S. Schwick, Chief Chemist," was a bicycle.

Sarah Schwick was in her office near the chem lab, entering her comments into a spreadsheet containing test data. She was thin, almost bony, and just over five feet tall. Her hair was mousy brown and cropped short – she never paid much attention to it. Her face was dominated by thick glasses with icy-steel frames, but when she took them off, her face was very pretty. Beyond that, the best that could be said about her physically was that she was in shape. She jogged regularly and commuted on her bike – she didn't even own a car; she rented them when necessary, ordered almost everything over the internet, and had her groceries delivered.

Viktor came quietly into her office and stood behind her. He checked his Rolex; the time was not even seven o'clock. He then put his hands on her shoulders and began to massage them gently.

"You're here early," he said.

Without taking her eyes off the numbers on the screen, Sarah said distractedly, "The Highboro people are coming in today. I wanted to get through some of these lab reports before they show up."

"Was that the only reason?"

He began to kiss the back of her neck. She ignored him, or pretended to, until she had typed in the last of her comments. Then Sarah stood up, went to the door, and peeked both ways to be sure no one was around. She shut the door and pushed in the thumb lock. When she turned around Viktor was leering at her as he loosened his tie. Sarah leered back, unbuttoned her white lab coat, and let it drop from her shoulders as if it were a negligee.

A dozen minutes later they were dressed again. While their liaison had been inappropriate, it was not adulterous, and arguably not even immoral. Both of them were divorced – from each other. Sarah was not involved with anyone; she seldom was. Viktor was between girlfriends. He went through them the way he went through cars.

"What time are the Highboro people due to arrive?" asked Viktor.

"Late morning. Eleven, I think. We're supposed to have lunch with them before the meeting."

"The whole thing is so ridiculous. You'd think that even they would have enough sense not to bother us with this drivel."

Sarah, sitting next to him on her office sofa, her head lolled over onto his shoulder, said nothing.

"Don't you agree?" asked Viktor.

"I would like to hear what they have to say."

"Why? It's a program for factory people. For the drones. It just doesn't apply to what we do."

"Viktor, we are not as exemplary as you think we are. Believe it or not, we do have our problems."

"I never said we were perfect."

"Those reports I was working on, before I was so rudely interrupted –"

"How can you describe tender affection toward an ex-spouse as 'rude'?"

"– I am weeks behind. I don't know how I'm ever going to catch up. We can't keep expanding the testing loop!"

Viktor stood up and began to retuck his shirt.

"Are you listening to me, Vik?"

"We do important work, Sarah. When we give our word to a client, we have to be right. We may not be the quickest. We certainly are not cheap. But we do advanced, high-end work that is first-rate and technically brilliant. We are really good at what we do."

"I agree," she said. "And . . . so?"

"The last thing we need around here is some factory morale-booster program."

"I don't think that's what it's about!" Sarah protested.

"Factory productivity booster! Whatever! While I do not ignore efficiency, I am very aware that thoroughness and accuracy are far more important than speed. If we rush the work we do, things will slip through the cracks."

"Things are already slipping through the cracks. You just don't want to hear about it."

"Enough!" Viktor said. "I've wasted enough breath on this topic. Although I know I will have to waste even more later in the day paying lip service to it."

"It's a good thing for the company that you stop by every now and then," Sarah said, rebuttoning her lab coat. "Because I'm the only one who tells you the truth. Everyone else is afraid of your temper."

He put his arms around her and attempted to kiss her on the mouth. But Sarah pushed him away and pointed toward the door.

"I need to get back to work!" she insisted. "Out! Before I sue for sexual harassment!"

Viktor kissed her on the forehead, then quickly made for the door.

"If you ever did, I would have to counter-sue," he said over his shoulder. "And I would definitely have a case!"

At that moment, as Viktor and Sarah ended their tryst, Tom Dawson was taxiing his aircraft across the tarmac at Highboro Municipal

Airport. Seated behind him were Wayne Reese and one of his LSS Black Belts, and next to Dawson in the copilot's seat – for purposes of better weight distribution, he claimed – sat Amy Cieolara. They were headed for Rockville.

Ahead of them, a Cessna was preparing to take off. Tom idled the engines and waited.

"So," said Tom, just making conversation, "you folks are all from Hi-T?"

"Yep. All of us," said Amy.

"You know, there are a number of Hi-T parts in this very aircraft," said Tom.

"What sort of plane is this?" asked Wayne.

"It's an oldie but goody," said Tom. "A Beech Baron Fifty-Eight. A new one'll cost you a million bucks, but I got this one for a lot less and fixed her up a bit."

"Huh," said Amy. "Are you sure you have Hi-T components in this?"

"Yes, ma'am. They've got your logo on 'em."

"Funny, but I can't recall Beech as being one of our customers," said Amy. "And as former head of sales and now company president, you'd think I would know."

"Your products were part of a retrofit package," said Tom. "A performance upgrade that I had done. You see the leading edges of the wings? Those are Hi-T composites, made right here in Highboro."

Amy looked out her window at the curved front of the airplane's wings.

"Gee," she said, "I hope we did a quality job."

"Hope?" asked Tom. "You mean there's a possibility you didn't?"

Silence.

Tom checked that the runway was now clear, throttled up, and the engines came to a roar. He released the brakes.

"Well," Tom shouted as they hurtled down the runway, "I guess we're gonna find out if Hi-T makes a quality product or not!"

He pulled back on the yoke.

The wings held, as Tom Dawson knew they would, and the plane did not crash. No more was said about quality – although no one forgot about it either. They arrived safely in Rockville, Maryland, a few minutes ahead of schedule, and were soon at Formulation & Design being greeted by a smiling and hospitable Viktor Kyzanski.

Viktor that day was everything that had gotten him to where he was: sharp-minded yet charming, in command of all technical issues, tossing off brilliant-sounding insights about science and business as they went along. He personally conducted the tour of the F&D facilities, leading them through the various labs and showing them a number of "wow" demonstrations that had been set up: a polymer that could be deformed – bent, crumpled, folded – and yet would "remember" its original shape and slowly unfold, uncrumple, unbend itself to become almost flat again in a matter of minutes. A carbon-fiber material that could be heated to 1,000°F, yet would be cool to the touch within moments of being removed from the test oven. A sheet of a composite material called BL-726 that was as thin as a business card and light as a feather, yet so strong that Viktor himself could stand in the center of it when it was placed between two benches, and it would not break or bend.

"Unfortunately, it costs about five hundred dollars per square centimeter to produce it," Viktor remarked.

The tour took them through all kinds of equipment, most of it boring to look at, but some of it rather exotic in a techy sort of way. And Viktor made a point of introducing a number of his star chemists and engineers. At last, as it seemed the tour was approaching an end, Amy intervened.

"Viktor, thank you, this has been very good," she said, "but I think what Wayne – and all of us, for that matter – would really like to get a grip on is, what is the overall process? What is the business model here?"

"Right, we need to know what the flow is," added Wayne.

"The flow?" asked Viktor.

"The flow of a project from start to finish. Just for the heck of it, let's say that I am the project and I come into F&D . . . where would I go? In what sequence?"

"Well . . ." said Viktor. "It would depend. It would depend upon what was being investigated and so on. And the journey could be quite convoluted."

"Uh-huh, right," said Wayne. "One of the things that Lean Six Sigma can do is to reduce the convolutions – reduce the distances between processing steps. And when we reduce distances, we can reduce waste and make things happen faster."

"I see," said Viktor. "But . . . if you, Wayne, were the project, you or most of you would be traveling via Ethernet, which is to say electronically. That's how we move things around here. You won't find many forklifts in the corridors here."

"Right. I understand that," said Wayne, "But the number of convolutions . . . the number of steps and stages . . . I'd just like to know what goes on."

"Of course, and I'd be very happy to explain it," said Viktor. "And let's do it over lunch . . . which is right this way."

A luncheon of corned beef, turkey, cheeses, various breads, a number of salads, and so on had been brought in from a local delicatessen. This was set up in a first-floor conference room that had window walls looking out upon the woodsy surroundings. Amy took a moment to stare into those woods, and it struck her how insular it was here, nestled away from the rest of the world. She wondered if this was a good thing or not.

Sarah Schwick and several other higher-level F&D managers joined them there.

It took some doing, but with urging from Wayne and Amy, Viktor and his people did gradually lay out the essential stages of a typical F&D project progressing from the first meeting with a client through the ultimate release of final design and documentation, along with material samples and sometimes a prototype. In between were a dozen or so major and distinct steps that had to be accomplished – and Wayne Reese, on a legal pad next to his plate, patiently diagrammed the flow and the various branches of inputs, labeling each box in neat block letters. This was what Wayne called "the value stream."

At the core of it was a series of steps mainly consisting of testing and analysis that the F&D people referred to as "the loop."

"Or sometimes 'the infinite loop,' " Sarah quipped. "At least that's the way it feels."

"Why?" asked Amy. "I'm curious. Why do you call it 'the loop'?"

"Because it's a cycle," said Viktor. "A project may go through the loop multiple iterations – testing, retesting . . . analysis, reanalysis . . . query, requery, and so on. It cycles through until we have the results the client contracted us to achieve and – or – until we know everything we need to know."

"So it's not a straight progression," said Wayne. "I'm just wondering what the reason is. Why does the flow have to be cyclical? Why a loop?"

"Why not a loop?" asked Viktor.

"I don't know. It just seems that if you're going through all these iterations, you're not moving forward."

"But we are moving forward! With each cycle of hypothesis, testing, and analysis, we are learning more than we did on the previous cycle!"

Amy could sense that Wayne and Viktor were about to butt heads. She put her hand on Wayne's sleeve before he could respond.

"Viktor, I don't at all think that Wayne is questioning the validity or the wisdom of your 'loop.' He's simply trying to better understand your system."

"Absolutely," said Wayne. "It's just . . . why this configuration, as opposed to something else?"

"All I can say," said Viktor, "is that over the years – over the decades at this point – we have found that this is what works. You have to understand that we are not doing repetitive, mass production kinds of things here at F&D."

"I do understand that," Wayne asserted.

"Nothing here is cut and dried. It's cutting edge, not cut and dried. It's development. It's working with the unknown."

"Right, and I am not saying anything against that," said Wayne, "but the word you yourself used when I asked about the work flow was 'convoluted.' To me, 'convoluted' suggests opportunities for improvement . . . for greater value, faster speed, higher quality, and lower cost."

"Perhaps the word was ill-chosen," Viktor conceded with a smile. "Perhaps a more accurate word would be 'complex.' "

"Or flexible," said Sarah, chiming in. "What is going to happen during the course of a given project can't always be mapped out at the beginning. We go down one path . . . maybe we get what we started out to get, and maybe we don't! So we have to start over, try a new direction, go down a different path."

"Exactly," Viktor agreed. "And, Wayne, I mean no disrespect whatsoever, but here you have plotted out a nice set of boxes on a sheet of paper with arrows and labels and so on, and this is supposed to represent what goes on here. But please let me tell you something."

Viktor spread his fingers and placed his fingertips on Wayne's sheet of paper.

"You call this a value stream. But this does not depict the value we deliver to our clients. The value we deliver is in the thinking, which can't be mapped on a whiteboard or a piece of paper, because it is multidimensional! Within these walls, there is scientific and technical creativity at work! It's not a matter of 'move data-set one from station A to station B, process three iterations, and spit it out.' We are searching for solutions to very difficult and challenging problems. That is why they pay us the hundreds of thousands and sometimes millions of dollars every year for the work that we do. It's not just a stack of discs and a binder with an executive summary and a box of pieces of plastic. It's what's on the discs and between the covers and what the pieces of plastic will do. That's the value."

A brief silence followed Viktor's diatribe.

"Well, I am glad that's understood," said Amy. "And I'm very glad you made those points. Because we are not here to tell you how to do something when you clearly know better than we do, or how to go about it. That said, can you tell me, Viktor, that everything in F&D is perfect? Can you tell me that there is nothing here that could be improved?"

"Of course not!" said Viktor in a sort of merry thunder – changing instantly from argumentative to conciliatory. "No, I do not mean to suggest that everything here is perfect or that . . . some aspects of what we do could not be improved upon."

Amy nodded. "Good. Then we have a basis for understanding each other. Because the intent of Lean Six Sigma is continuous improvement. And LSS has been endorsed and has the full support of everyone within our organization, from our chairman and CEO Peter Winn to our group president Nigel Furst to . . . yours truly."

"And improvement . . . whatever its flavor . . . has my hearty endorsement as well," said Viktor. "I can assure you that Formulation and Design will cooperate fully with your LSS program in every practical way."

"Great," said Amy. "Then let's go make the presentation and get the ball rolling!"

After they had set up their laptops for the LSS presentation, Amy observed that Viktor was well out of earshot and nudged Wayne.

"What do you think of him?" she murmured, meaning Viktor.

"To say the least, I don't think he gets it," Wayne quietly replied.

"I suspect he might say the same about us."

Wayne raised his eyebrows. "Well . . . possibly. But despite whatever he says, and I'm not discounting the points he made, the operation here does have similarities to a factory. They don't make widgets, but they do produce a product. An intellectual product, consisting of information . . . knowledge of considerable value. To make that product, there are processes, just like in a manufacturing plant. Even the creative aspects he talked about – those are processes. There may be a lot of variation; there may be unpredictable events. Still, it stands to reason that if you optimize each and every one of those processes along the value stream, you're going to get better results."

Amy, as she thought about this, heard her name said aloud. Viktor was about to introduce her.

"We'll discuss this later," she whispered.

After it was over, Amy was not sure what impact the presentation had had. For one thing, there were a lot of vacant seats. In his email to F&D, Viktor had said to staff that attendance was suggested and requested, but was not mandatory. Then, right in the middle of Wayne's talk, one of the star chemists had abruptly grunted, stood up, and walked out. Half a dozen others in the auditorium also departed at various points. Amy knew that, as a matter of culture, F&D tolerated and even respected a degree of free-spiritedness, so she said nothing. But the walkouts were hardly encouraging.

On the other hand, there was a core group who sat in the front rows and who paid close attention. Appearances suggested that by and large they were über-geeks. When the time for questions came, this group kept Wayne and his Black-Belt associate on their feet for nearly an hour after the formal presentation had finished. Viktor, in fact, had to cut them off. Most of their questions had to do with the statistical tools of Six Sigma and Lean – and a number of the questions were not just asking for clarification, they were outright challenges. Yet Wayne and the Black Belt held their own, and the group even seemed enthusiastic at the end. One of that group was Sarah Schwick.

After a long afternoon, Amy felt the call of nature and visited the women's room, where she encountered Sarah. The two of them got to talking about one thing and then another, and Amy remembered a rumor she had heard some time ago.

"Is it true that you and Viktor were once married?"

"Yes, we were in fact. Years ago," said Sarah – then quickly added, "Actually, we're still very good friends. And we work well together. We just can't stand to be married to one another."

Both of them smiled at this.

"But it doesn't bother you that he's your boss?" asked Amy.

"No. He doesn't intimidate me. I can tell him anything – and I do."

Well, all right then, Amy thought.

They left the women's room and began walking back to the auditorium.

"So what do you think of LSS?" asked Amy.

"I'm still forming an opinion."

"Let me just say this: I would be delighted, Sarah, if you would get involved and go through the training. And it's certainly not going to hurt your career any if you do."

Sarah considered that and said, "Thank you. But I'd like to talk it over with Viktor."

"Understood. No problem."

Late in the day, after the Highboro contingent had left, Sarah went to Viktor's office. He was tidying up, getting ready to leave.

"Before you go," she said.

"Yes?"

"I want to be involved in LSS. I want to be a part of it."

Viktor fluttered his eyelids and regarded her with a most puzzled expression.

"Really, I want this," said Sarah.

"Do you have the time for it?"

"I'll make the time."

He plopped down and slumped back in his office chair, stroking his chin and thinking about the ramifications.

"All right," he said at last. "By all means, get involved. In fact, I like the idea of you being a part of it. Yes, go for it! I think it might give us an edge, maybe even some leverage."

"An edge? Leverage? What are you talking about?"

"Just that it's always a good idea to know what one's competitors are up to."

Sarah, who had been standing in the doorframe, came more into the office and folded her arms, even as she smirked in disbelief.

"Is that really how you see them?" she asked. "As competitors? As adversaries?"

"Well, aren't they? Oh, all right. Maybe that's too Darwinian. Let's just say it's always a good idea to know what one's allies are up to."

"Viktor, I am not going to play the role of agent provocateur."

He rolled his eyes and said, "Sarah, dear, I haven't asked you to do any such thing."

"I want this to work," she insisted. "We need this to work. We – and I mean all of us, not just you and me – need something to work. We have clients who are really getting tired of big invoices and slow results. I'm worried there are some who are ready to walk away from us."

"Sarah . . . do you know why our marriage ended in divorce?"

"Because you were always screwing around?"

"Aside from that – and for the record, I was faithful for the first five years. No, the central problem in our marriage was that I am an optimist and you are extreme pessimist."

"Am not!"

"I do not understand what you are so worried about. You make it sound as if Formulation and Design is going to dry up and blow away in a swirl of dust. It's not going to happen! True, there will always be little fires to be put out. Sometime in the future, there will be necessary adjustments to the course of the business. But we have a backlog that others can only envy! We are all but turning away business! I mean, seriously, we are nearly maxed out in terms of what we can handle!"

"Yes, Viktor, I agree. I am maxed out. And it's not the volume of business, it's the internal pressures."

"And so I go back to my original question: are you sure you can handle the added responsibility of . . . of something I am not sure is necessary or even valid?"

"You . . . and I . . . and everyone else here – we have built over the years an excellent research and engineering organization," she said. "We've won awards, we've made money, we've advanced the state of the art, and so on and so forth. But I feel like we're slipping. I personally don't talk to that many clients, but I do read the emails coming in and the reports going out. I know that under the surface, we are not held in all that high a regard. Therefore, I don't want us to be groveling five years from now to get some piddly little contract just to keep going."

"We won't be. Relax." Viktor glanced at his Rolex. "Now, sorry, I'm late. I have to run."

"Dinner date?"

"Um . . . actually, yes."

Sarah shook her head, even as she grinned and gritted her teeth in frustration.

"Viktor, you truly are a first-rate cad."

"Sarah, I strive for excellence in everything. See you in the morning."

As he walked out the door, Sarah said, "I won't be in early. Not for a long time. If ever."

But she was not sure if he heard her – was not even sure if she really wanted him to hear.

• • •

The evening of the day following the Rockville trip, Amy got home late. What with the regular schedule and catching up on everything that had been on hold while she was out championing for LSS, it was past eight o'clock by the time she drove into the driveway. Much earlier she had called her mom and told her to start dinner without her. So everyone else in the family had eaten by then. Amy sat in the kitchen, sipping a glass of wine while her mother warmed a plate of food for her.

"Oh!" her mother suddenly exclaimed. "Someone called for you!"

"Who?"

"A man."

"Well, that narrows it down. What, like an insurance man? A stockbroker man?"

"No. He gave me his name and I wrote it on a scrap of paper. Now, what did I do with it?"

"I'm glad Dad didn't answer the phone."

"Amy . . ." said her mother, with an annoyed edge to her voice.

"Sorry."

"Here it is. He called around six o'clock."

Tom Dawson's name and phone number were on the little slip of paper.

"That's funny," Amy said, digging through her purse for her cell phone. "He has all my work numbers. I wonder why he called me at home?"

She found her cell phone and stepped outside onto the back porch, pulling the door firmly shut behind her – and realizing even as she did that she had gone to the porch for privacy, not a better signal. In the same instant, she recognized that she was excited, and she deliberately made herself slow down, calm down as her thumb pressed the numbers on her phone.

Tom answered quickly. "Hello?"

"Hi. It's Amy. Amy Cieolara. Did you call earlier?"

"Right, I did. Hey, you left your umbrella in the plane yesterday."

Amy's memory flashed back and remembered that, yes, she had taken an umbrella because the forecast had called for late afternoon showers, which never came. And, yes, she had completely forgotten about it as she had walked away from the plane under sunny skies.

"Oh, you're right," she said. "I did. I'm sorry –"

"No, it's no problem. Anyway, I thought I might . . . you know, swing by and drop it off."

"Swing by? Here?"

"If you're not, you know, busy or something."

"Well, I just got home –"

"If it's not, you know, convenient . . ."

She realized from his hesitations and his you-knows that – to her own amazement – he was just a little nervous talking to her. This ex-Marine, this man who had faced death in combat, this pilot whose physical courage had surely been tested many times – nervous talking to her. And she felt herself being warmed and charmed by that.

"If you'd like to come by . . . that would be all right," she heard herself saying.

"Okay, great. I'll be there in ten or fifteen minutes – if that works for you."

"Sure. Do you have the address? Do you need directions?"

"Nope, I'll find you," he said. "See you in a bit."

She went back into the kitchen and told her mom.

"He's coming over."

"Who is?"

"Tom Dawson!"

"Oh, but Amy, the house is a mess," said her mother, and instantly began to neaten things.

"Mom, he's just dropping off my umbrella! Stop! Anyway, it doesn't matter! It's no big deal!"

She tossed back the rest of her wine then and flew into the living room, where indeed her father had scattered the sections of the newspaper everywhere and her children's video games and DVDs littered the floor. Ben and Michelle themselves looked like lumps in front of the television; not even couch potatoes, but worse: carpet potatoes.

She opened her mouth to say something, then stopped herself. She made herself take the advice she'd given her mother. After all, he was dropping off an umbrella. What did it matter?

It matters because I like him, said an inner voice. And what mystified her was that, until now, she had completely hidden away from herself any attraction to him. She did know that she had thought about him a number of times since they had met. Not girlish daydreams or anything like that – mainly just curiosity. She knew he was unmarried; she had asked him point blank one time when they were flying, and he had told her. But that was about all. He kidded a lot in the plane, and talked about instruments and weather and so on, but in fact said very little about himself. Meanwhile, she had blabbed all kinds of things about her own life. He always listened politely, his reactions to what she said mostly hidden behind his Ray-Ban sunglasses. Now he was coming to her house, and she felt an unexpected – and somewhat unwanted – anticipation.

Amy began picking up the sections of the newspaper and straightening pillows on the sofa, while her mother followed her with a plate and a fork saying, "Here, eat something!"

The doorbell rang. Amy answered it, and there he was, umbrella in hand. No sunglasses, a rarity. He had nice eyes, she realized. Sky blue, appropriately enough.

She opened the screen door and stepped outside, saying, "Thank you for bringing this over. I'm sorry to trouble you."

"Oh, it's no problem. So you were working tonight?"

"Right. It never ends. The workload, I mean."

Zelda appeared at her daughter's shoulder.

"Mom, this is Tom," Amy said, "Tom Dawson, the pilot."

"Oh, how do you do?" asked Zelda.

"Very nice to meet you, ma'am," said Tom.

Then, to Amy's horror, her mother asked, "Would you two like some lemonade?"

Amy shot a look that said, *Mom, I'm not twelve!* And aloud: "Or maybe Tom would like a beer, or a glass of wine or something."

"No, no," he said, "lemonade would be just fine. Thank you."

"Well, both of you have a seat," said Zelda, gesturing to the old-fashioned swing suspended from the porch roof. "I'll bring some right out."

The swing had big fluffy pillows, which were comfortable but severely reduced the available space on the seat, and after they sat down, Amy was astonished at how close he was. He, too, seemed uneasy at the closeness, and he set the umbrella on the cushion between them, almost as a dividing line.

"So . . . do you live close by?" Amy asked.

"Not far."

He described his neighborhood, and she knew where it was – a basic neighborhood of unpretentious houses a generation newer than her own. She tried to imagine what his house might look like, and into her mind popped an image of a yard and dwelling resembling a miniature Camp Lejeune. She almost laughed, but held herself to a smile.

"What are you smiling about?" he asked, as he also grinned even though he did not know the source of the humor.

"Nothing," said Amy. "It's just a nice evening. Did you have any trouble finding the street?"

He had not. At the curb was his car, a jet black Ford Mustang that looked as if it could set the pavement on fire. This must be his toy, she decided, because he always drove a clean but older pickup truck to the airport.

Zelda brought the lemonade on a tray, and Tom stood to take the two tall glasses, handing one to Amy.

"Would you like to sit down, ma'am?" he offered.

"Oh, no, I have things to do – like find where my husband wandered off to. And please call me Zelda."

They sipped their drinks and talked, and they both began to relax. He opened up just a little, told her that he had not been born in North Carolina or anywhere in the South, but in Alaska. His father had been a bush pilot, operating out of some tiny airstrip east of Fairbanks. His mother had run the local post office, and his father, among the many duties of a bush pilot, delivered the mail to places where there were no roads. Tom had first handled the controls of a plane when he was nine years old, and had repeatedly and somewhat illegally flown solo as early as his fourteenth year to help out his dad, who suffered bouts of ill health. At age seventeen he was certified as a private pilot. At nineteen, a year after his father passed away, he joined the Marine Corps.

The more he talked, the more Amy liked him – which was the opposite of the last few guys who had exhibited any romantic interest in her. Tom tended to pepper whatever he said with his wry wit, while his matter-of-fact speech never suggested that any of the many adventures in his life were the least bit special or out of the ordinary.

And yet, just as she had concealed from herself her initial attraction to Tom, so too her mind tonight had now tricked her into ignoring an unpleasant fact about their circumstances. The longer she sat next to him, the more she enjoyed listening and talking to him, the greater that fact pressed on her, though she did not at all want to acknowledge it.

Then they began talking about food, about restaurants. Tom was clearly working up to something – and clearly he was liking her more as well.

"Say, do you like soft-shell crabs?" asked Tom.

"Yes! I love soft-shell crabs."

"Well, son of a gun, I just happen to know of a great place over on the coast that does soft-shell crab like you'd never believe. And I happen to know an excellent pilot who has a spiffy red airplane and who even has a few bucks in his wallet for gas. What would you say to flying over to the coast this Saturday and have a little crab dinner? Have you home by midnight. What do you say?"

Her eyes watered. Amy opened her mouth to say, *Yes, I would love to*, but instead heard herself saying, "I can't."

"If Saturday doesn't work, what about Sunday?"

"It's not that. I can't go out with you, Tom."

"Mind if I ask why?"

She reached across the umbrella and briefly touched his hand.

"Please understand I would like to. But . . . it's business. We have a business relationship. You're a vendor, and I'm a customer – of my company, that is. There is an ethical line there that I would be afraid to cross."

He truly looked deflated – as if someone had taken ten pounds of air out of his tires.

"Do you actually think anyone would care?" he asked.

"These days, Tom, you never know. I'm the president of the company. I approve your invoices. Anymore, just the appearance of impropriety is enough to kill a career. The rumors can be more destructive than the facts. And for me, a woman . . . I have to be very, very careful."

Tom nodded solemnly, set his lemonade glass on the porch floor, and got to his feet.

"Well, it's all right," he said, "I understand . . . I guess."

Amy stood up and said, "I'm glad you stopped by. I really enjoyed talking to you."

"Please say good night for me to your mother."

He waved good-bye, stepped off the porch, went to his car. He drove slowly down the street, and she watched until the car had turned the far corner. Amy then took their glasses to the kitchen. Without a word, she wrapped her arms around her mom and rested her head on her mother's thin shoulder.

6

Wayne Reese's campaign to transform Hi-T through Lean Six Sigma began to gather momentum, and it did so swiftly. Wayne was eager to get everything moving, and Amy, with her interim status as president, was just as eager to show results before Nigel Furst became impatient. She was pushing everyone to get on board – though at times it felt like "herding cats." Despite a few protestations from Elaine, the financial manager, Amy fed Wayne a steady stream of money and other kinds of support. So it all came together at a speed that almost seemed astonishing for a mature, rather staid company.

Even as the introductory presentations had been going on, Wayne had been pulling strings inside Winner corporate management. He was able to secure a few of the corporation's most experienced LSS Black Belts to jump-start the program. These experts would lay the groundwork while Hi-T's own volunteers were being trained. Chief among the incoming Black Belts was Kurt Konani, a man in his early thirties, born in Hawaii, who was both a colleague and a friend of Wayne – as well as being Wayne's physical opposite. In contrast to Wayne's shaven scalp, Kurt sported a full head of thick, dark brown hair and a bushy mustache. Whereas Wayne was tall and lanky, Kurt was on the shorter side of average and slightly pudgy. But they worked well together, and with Kurt and the other Black Belts on board, lots of things began to happen, especially at Oakton.

The sun was a vivid orange disc on the horizon when Murphy Maguire drove up the access road to the Oakton plant. In that early morning light, something caught his eye. He saw a white SUV parked next to the Dumpsters. Leaning against one of them was a ladder. Murphy stopped his car to see what was going on – and a moment later observed that someone was *inside* the Dumpster poking around. With the thought of industrial espionage crossing his mind, Murph flipped open his cell phone and pressed a speed-dial number for plant security.

"Suggins, this is Maguire. I need you and all available guards to meet me by the Dumpsters at once. And I do mean *immediately*."

"Yes, sir."

With that, Murphy tromped on the gas of his big old Chevy Suburban and zoomed across the lot, heading straight for the white SUV. He hit the brakes and came to a stop directly behind it, pointed the lens of the cell-phone camera and began taking pictures of the vehicle and its license plate.

Then he got out of his car and called to the figure crouching in the Dumpster and apparently rooting through the plant's trash:

"Excuse me, is there something I can help you with?"

Wayne Reese stood up. Murphy blinked in surprise.

"Hey, good morning, Maguire!" Wayne said cheerily. "Hold on one second; let me just finish making a couple of notes."

He crouched down in the trash again, concealing all but his cue-ball shaven head. Just then, from around the corner of the plant came Suggins and another uniformed guard speeding toward the Dumpsters in a golf cart. Maguire flipped open his phone one more time to call off the cavalry.

"Suggins, it's Maguire again. False alarm. Go back inside, please."

The golf cart promptly made a U-turn and went back in the direction from which it had come.

"Getting back to your question," said Wayne, standing up again, "yes, you can help me by telling me what *this* is."

He tossed an object down to Murphy, who caught it and turned it over in his fingers as he examined it.

"There are hundreds, maybe thousands of those in here," said Wayne.

"Well, I cannot tell you exactly what it is, but I can tell you that it is scrap."

"Why is it scrap?"

"Wrong color. It's supposed to be green, not yellow. An operator pulled the wrong dye from the rack."

"Well, good," said Wayne. "At least we know the cause. That's another opportunity we can target."

"If you don't mind my asking, what are you doing out here? When I first saw you, I thought you might be some kind of spy."

"I am a spy," said Wayne, coming down the ladder. "I'm gathering intelligence. By analyzing what's in the trash, I get an idea of what kind of waste this plant produces – of the kind of money we are throwing away, just to have to pay someone to haul it away."

"Um, I hope you do not think this kind of thing is typical for us. I remember this incident, and I can assure you that the operator who made the mistake has been disciplined. He got a two-day suspension without pay and a formal warning that he could be terminated if an accident like this happens again."

"That's not a solution," said Wayne.

"Excuse me?"

"Unless the accident happens because of outright negligence or sabotage, you really shouldn't blame the worker. That solves nothing. Instead, I would recommend *poka-yoke*."

"Poka-what?"

"*Poka-yoke*. It's Japanese. It means to make something mistake proof. Fail-safe. The operator grabbed the wrong dye because the way the work area and the process were set up *enabled* him to make the mistake. That's something we should look into."

At first Murphy just stared at Wayne. He instantly and completely understood the essence of what Wayne had just said. On the other hand, here was this outsider – a *damnyankee* outsider, no less – digging through the trash in order, as Murphy felt, to find fault. It was rude; it was offensive somehow. Yet the man was operations manager – Murphy's superior. Wayne had the authority to go and do pretty much whatever he felt should be done. And Murphy truly hated this. Not *Wayne* per se, but the meddling. By instinct, Murph was not about to concede anything to him.

Wayne also said nothing more for the moment, but got his ladder from the side of the trash receptacle and stowed it in the back of his SUV. By the time Wayne had closed the tailgate, Murphy had concluded that for better or worse he was going to say something.

"Mr. Reese –"

"Murphy, you can just call me Wayne."

"Mr. Reese, do you know how I came to be called Murphy?"

"Because your family is Irish?"

"Actually, my family is descended from both Scots and Irish, and my great-grandmother was Cherokee. In any case, Murphy is not my given name. It was a nickname given to me years ago when I was a supervisor on the M57 Line. On my desk was a placard etched with the words of Murphy's Law."

" 'If anything can go wrong, it will,' " quoted Wayne, folding his arms across his chest.

"Yes, and I quoted those words so often that they all started calling me Murphy. So it became my name. But I'd like you to know that when I became a manager on the M57 Line, we had a reject rate of as high as forty percent. Within a few years, we had reduced rejections to four percent, and these days, on average, rejects run two percent or less. I accomplished that by pounding it into everybody's head that if something is a statistical possibility, then at some point it will occur. And little by little, year by year, we eliminated all the things that could go wrong."

"So your point would be?" asked Wayne, feeling now as if he were being lectured to.

"I may not know all the Japanese names you use, but I do know how to get things done in my own way."

Wayne shifted uncomfortably from foot to foot and looked out into the emptiness surrounding them and said, "Tell me, Maguire, do you consider a two-percent reject rate to be acceptable?"

"In all honesty, given the number and variety of challenges we currently face here in Oakton, reducing two percent rejection on M57 is not my highest priority."

"And suppose some part of that two percent gets into a Navy aircraft and fails?" asked Wayne. "Suppose we miss a defective part and it goes into somebody's car or truck, fails, and there is an accident that kills people? And then in addition to the tragedy itself, there is a lawsuit against the company. Is that acceptable?"

"We do everything possible to prevent that."

"Uh-huh. Let me tell you something, Maguire, with *me* as ops manager, settling for anything less than perfection on *any* process is *un*acceptable," said Wayne. "Only continuous striving for the sixth sigma of quality, only that is acceptable."

In silence, Murphy crossed his own arms over his chest, and the two men just stood there for a second eyeballing each other. Wayne, first to break the stance, then turned to his vehicle, and as he opened the driver's door, spoke to Murphy over his shoulder.

"I'll meet you inside the plant, Maguire. I want to get to know Oakton from one end to the other, and I'd like you to tour with me – unless you have something more urgent, of course."

Wayne's white hybrid quietly, almost noiselessly, then drove off and circled around to the main parking lot. Murphy, rather unquietly, to absolutely no one except himself, said something unrepeatable, then got into his gas-guzzling Chevy and followed, and he drove a bit faster than necessary.

Inside the plant, Murphy mooched a cup of coffee from Jayro's pot next to the Cooler. He drank it slowly as he scrutinized the worksheets for the day, and then tracked down Wayne Reese, who was at the head of the M57 Line. As Murphy approached, he saw that Wayne was having a word with his new LSS Black Belt, Kurt, and they were speaking in such hushed tones Murphy wondered if they were lip reading each other. Against his own nature, but from respect for the privacy of their conversation, Murphy slowed and was just shy of being able to hear what they were saying, when they both immediately stopped talking and turned to him.

"Don't let me interrupt," said Murphy.

"No problem," said Wayne. He then clapped Kurt on the shoulder and Kurt walked away.

"So, what can I help you with?" asked Murphy.

"Everything," said Wayne.

"Everything?" asked Murphy. "Well, that's a lot."

"It's going to be a busy day."

"Yes, we have six shipments to get out the door, fourteen new orders ready for production, and eighteen orders in between, in various stages of completion."

"If you have to break away at some point, go ahead," said Wayne, "but I intend to get to know Oakton from one end to the other, and I'd appreciate your being with me as much as possible."

"Mr. Reese, I will show you anything you want to see, and tell you anything you want to know. But I can save you a lot of time if you will just listen to me for a moment."

Wayne put his hands on his hips and said, "Go ahead."

"The main key to the throughput of this plant is a large piece of equipment that we affectionately call Godzilla."

Wayne chuckled and asked, "And why would this single piece of equipment be the key to the plant's output?"

"Excuse me, sir, but the important word here is *throughput*, not output."

"Throughput, output – what's the big deal? They're interchangeable," said Wayne.

"Sorry, but not in my vocabulary," said Murphy. "Output would refer, for instance, to the quantity of product produced. Throughput refers to the rate at which *we make money* by means of producing and selling the various products that customers buy."

"Again, what's the difference? Output translates into sales!"

"Well, I beg to differ, sir. Just because an item has been produced does not mean that money has been made."

"All right, all right," Wayne said, conceding the point. "I have to agree with you. Actually that's an important concept within Lean – that nothing should be produced until a customer wants it and will pay for it."

Murphy smiled, thinking that perhaps he and Wayne were communicating.

"So it is the performance of this one piece of equipment, Godzilla, that determines the performance of the company's entire manufacturing system," said Murphy.

"Now wait a minute," said Wayne. "Why would that be?"

"Because Godzilla is the primary constraint of the system."

"The *constraint*? So you're saying that this 'Godzilla' machine constrains the entire system, is that it? You're talking about a problem operation?"

"Ah, well, no, sir, Godzilla is not a problem at all. In fact, Godzilla performs exceptionally well – at the peak of its efficiency – because we keep it superbly staffed and maintained."

"Then why is it a constraint?"

"Here's the thing: All resources have their limits," Murphy said. "Therefore, all resources could be constraints within the system. But there is – or at least should be – one constraint within the system that acts as the primary constraint."

"What do you mean by 'should be'?" asked Wayne. "And why in the world would a manufacturing plant want a – what did you call it? A *primary* constraint?"

"To balance the flow," said Murphy.

"That is what we are going to be doing here by applying Lean," said Wayne. "We are going to balance capacity – what's the matter?"

Murphy, struggling to be polite yet assertive, was all but twitching.

"No, sir, that is the last thing that you want to do!" said Murph. "You want to balance the *flow*, not the capacity! And to do that effectively, you *want* a primary constraint!"

The expression on Wayne's face showed he was losing patience with what he perceived to be Murphy's mumbo jumbo.

"If you will bear with me, sir, for just a few moments longer," said Murphy, "let's go back to the word *throughput*."

"All right," said Wayne.

"As I said, 'throughput' is a measure of how *fast* we are making money. Ultimately, that is what we are here to do, is it not? To make money?"

"We are here, Maguire, to satisfy and delight our customers," said Wayne. "That is our ultimate purpose."

"Oh. I thought the whole point of running a business was to make money. Perhaps I have been mistaken all these years."

"Well, *of course* the business is supposed to make money!" said Wayne in exasperation. "And we make money by satisfying and delighting our customers!"

"The trouble is, Mr. Reese, I rarely see a customer in here. Certainly not on a daily basis. I have no way of knowing whether they are satisfied and no way to measure their delight. So I just keep my eye on the dollars."

"How do you know . . . ? "

"How do I know what the numbers are? I use a computer. I look them up. By the way, there are two other key measurements that are very important. There is operating expense – money spent on payroll, maintenance costs, and so on. And there is what I call inventory and investment. For the short term, inventory is the one that is important. Inventory, as a set of numbers, includes all of our raw materials and work-in-process – all the money that we intend to transform into throughput. Investment, of course, is capital – money that buys equipment and other assets that enable us to turn inventory into throughput. Are you following me, sir?"

Wayne shrugged his shoulders. "Sort of."

"It is the relationship between those measurements that tells me how well we are doing. Over time, I want to see throughput go up. That is, I want to see increases in the rate at which we are turning inventory into completed sales. I also want the amount of inventory that is needed inside my plant here to be only what is sufficient to service the primary constraint at all times. And I want our operating expenses to become lower and lower relative to the money being made in throughput. Finally, I do not want to see the level of required investment in machines and so on increase. In other words, I always want to be striving to do more with less."

Puzzlement was all over Wayne's face, and he said, "Well, if I understood you correctly, that's not at odds with Lean. Tell me, where did you come up with all this?"

"From a book. A novel, actually."

"A *novel*? What was the name of it?"

"It was called *The Goal*. Written quite a while ago by two guys . . . I forget their names."

"*The Goal*. I've heard of it; never read it," said Wayne.

"Anyway, our former president, B. Donald Williams, sent a copy to me years back when we were having a lot of inventory and expediting problems here at Oakton. After I read it, B. Don and I put our heads together and figured out that the bottleneck – the 'Herbie,' which you would understand if you read that book – was this piece of equipment we call Godzilla. And once we realized that and exploited the constraint –"

"*Exploit* the constraint?" asked Wayne, staring with incredulity at Murphy.

"Yes, sir. You see, you must exploit the constraint and make all other processes subordinate to it –"

"All right, Maguire," said Wayne. "I don't think we're getting anywhere with this conversation. Why don't you show me this problem operation, this Godzilla, whatever it is."

"It is not a problem operation! I assure you of that, sir!"

The two men strolled down the aisle together, along the M57 Line and through Lamination, past the curing racks and the staging area where batches were made up. And eventually they came to stand before one of the biggest, and one of the ugliest pieces of equipment that Wayne Reese had ever encountered in a manufacturing plant.

"This," said Murphy, "is Godzilla."

"Well, it sure is a monster. How could something that big be a constraint?"

"Because of time, Mr. Reese. Time within the overall flow. That is why we subordinate all other processes to Godzilla. Because the productivity of the 'Zilla determines the productivity of the entire production system – and so determines our throughput."

Wayne was barely listening.

"Okay, I think I kind of see what's been going on here," he said to Murphy. "Look, I don't know what you've read or what kind of coping mechanisms you've used in the past, but I promise you that Lean will be a much more elegant solution to all the issues you have raised. Trust me, Lean and Six Sigma are going to solve all your problems and revolutionize this plant. Once we apply LSS, this plant is going to be tight as a drum. Variation on all processes is going to be so minimized that for all practical purposes it won't be a factor. Now, it's not going to happen next week, or the week after, or next month or even next year. But it will happen, and when it does, Maguire, you'll be amazed."

"I do hope you are correct. But I must caution you. We do have a system that works. It might not be perfect, it might not be elegant, but it does work. If you go a-messin' around with things –"

"Now, listen, Maguire. Because I want us to work together. Improvement requires change. Improvement *means* change. I know you're accustomed to doing things in a particular way. That is not the way they will be done here in the future. Once we balance the line from one end of the plant to the other there will be no bottlenecks and whatever problems you've been having with this Godzilla thing will just be a memory. Everything will run to *takt* time, like a marching band in a parade."

"I'm sorry, but . . . *takt time*?"

Before Wayne could answer, a red light on top of Godzilla began to flash and a siren went off. Workers leaped into place and began putting on ear protection and heavy gloves. They stood ready, like a pit crew at a NASCAR track as a race car was about to come in.

"What's going on?" asked Wayne.

"It's the end of a soak," said Murphy. "They're going to offload what's been cured inside the belly of Godzilla and then reload it with the next batch."

Richy, the day-shift supervisor for Godzilla, approached with earplugs for them.

"You'll want to put these on," Murphy said, taking a set of plugs and handing another pair to Wayne. "This is going to be loud."

Richy then went to his control console, picked up a microphone to the plant public address system, and his voice went booming through the entire plant.

"Attention all personnel. Godzilla is ready to vent. I repeat: the 'Zilla is about to vent. Please synchronize. Please synchronize."

Rich then hung up the microphone, turned a handle on the control console – and Godzilla roared as the hot gases within were purged.

7

"Tack time?" asked Zelda.

"No, it's called *takt* time," said her daughter. "It comes from a German word that means 'time beat' or 'clock cycle' or something like that. It's time available to work divided by demand – the time available to make the product divided by the units needed. If customer demand called for eight units of something per eight-hour day, your takt time would be about sixty minutes per unit."

Zelda made a face and said, "I'm glad you understand these things."

It was Saturday afternoon at Amy's house, and everyone in the family – except for Harry, who was napping – was in the basement dealing with the chore of laundry. Amy was sorting the clothes, Michelle was transferring wet clothes from the washer to the dryer, Zelda was folding towels, and Ben was very reluctantly learning how to iron.

"Anyway, the point I was trying to make," said Amy, "is that Wayne Reese is practically living at the plant these days trying to figure out how to get it to run close to takt time. And when he gets it right, we will save a huge amount of money. At least, that's what he's talking about. Then I've got it made. Based on what he's whispering to me, we should easily beat the numbers that Nigel Furst wants us to make. If that happens, I think they'll probably make my position permanent rather than interim. And they'll also probably give me a nice bonus – which means I can take all of us on a cruise to someplace like, say, Hawaii next year."

This got Ben's attention. "Whoa! Mom, are you serious?"

"Yep."

"All right!" said Michelle. "Let's hear it for takt time!"

"Well, don't count your chickens before they're hatched, dear," said Zelda.

"Right, but Wayne tells me that Murphy Maguire's operation has a lot of slack in it – a lot of idle machines, a lot of people not working at a hundred percent."

"Ah, what a shame," Michelle said sarcastically.

"Well, if you're paying people to work," Amy told her, "then you expect them to stay busy – and not be standing around like a certain brother of yours."

"I think the iron is too hot!" Ben protested. "It's burning the cloth."

"Could it be that you're not moving it fast enough?" asked Amy. "Anyway, it's kind of puzzling, because my old boss, B. Don, was forever saying how good Murphy was as a plant manager, and how they nailed down something called a 'Herbie,' whatever that is, and how shipments became predictable and inventories went down. Of course, Maguire must be slipping, because we've had a lot of complaints from customers about late shipments."

"If he's not doing the job," said Zelda, "maybe you'll have to replace him."

"Wayne wants to give him a chance. But I'm not sure. I find him to be pretty annoying at times. In any case, Wayne insists there are a lot of opportunities for improvement out there at the plant. A lot of 'low-hanging fruit,' as he called it. Once Wayne balances the line and gets everyone loaded to takt as much as possible, we should start recording some quarters that'll have Peter Winn doing cartwheels across his oriental carpet."

Zelda was once again perplexed.

"Balance the line?" she asked.

"Right," said Amy. "Capacity costs money, and if you don't need it, it's wasted money. It's *muda*, according to Wayne. So you want to balance production – workers, equipment, and inventory – against customer demand. Which is where takt time comes in."

Now Zelda was doubly perplexed.

"Here, Mom, let me try to explain it. For example, take laundry –"

"Please!" said Ben.

"Thank you, Henny Youngman, and keep moving that iron. Anyway, Mom, think about laundry as a process. It has steps and each step has to be completed before the next can be started. First, we bring the dirty, smelly clothes from the hampers upstairs to the basement. Next, we sort the clothes, lights from darks, and so on. Then we set up the washer – load the clothes, add the detergent, set the cycle, and start the washing machine. Ah! But then comes Michelle's favorite part of laundry: the dryer!"

"Yes, waiting for the dryer to finish," said Michelle. "It's so exciting!"

"It is, isn't it? Then we do the last steps: ironing, folding, and distribution – taking clean clothes in neat stacks back upstairs and delivering them to the appropriate customers."

"Making sure my sister's socks don't end up my drawer," said Ben, "like they did last week."

"Good you mentioned that," said Amy, "because, yes, it all has to be done with quality and safety – reminding Michelle not to mix red shirts with white sheets, and teaching Ben not to burn his fingers on the iron or put in more wrinkles than he takes out."

"And your point would be . . . ? " asked Michelle, clearly bored.

"My point, smartie, is that this whole laundry process is a value stream – turning dirty, rumpled, stinky clothes into clean, wrinkle-free, nice-smelling clothes ready on time to start the new week. So let's say this laundry operation of ours was a business, and the basement here was our little factory. What would we want it to do?"

"Make money," said Michelle.

"Right, of course," said Amy, "but as for the factory itself, wouldn't we want it to be efficient? Wouldn't we want it to run smoothly with minimal effort and minimal waste? Wouldn't we want the whole laundry process to get done in the least amount of time?"

"You've got that right," muttered Ben.

"And," Amy continued, "we would want output to be equal to demand. In other words, we don't want to do any more laundry than necessary, but we also don't want dirty laundry piling up or a shortage of clean clothes. Therefore, we want the amount of work being done by us, the laundry workers, to be exactly equal to the weekly demand for clean clothes from us, the laundry customers. Now, takt time –"

"Finally!" said Michelle.

"Takt sets the pace of production. It's the maximum allowable time to finish each step and pass along the product to the next step. So let's say Wayne Reese was running this laundry operation," said Amy. "What Wayne would do is study the laundry process and keep good statistics on each step. Then he would balance the line to takt time so that each process would be running continuously and everyone working on the laundry line would have just enough to do to be fully productive, but still meet demand for so many baskets of laundry per hour . . . or per day or whatever."

Michelle stared at her mother with an expression of bewilderment on her face.

"What's the matter?" Amy asked her.

"You say the washer, the dryer, and the iron – they're all going at the same time?"

"Yes. What's wrong with that? Wayne would set things up so that the laundry doesn't sit in big piles. There would be a steady flow set to the pace of takt time. You know, like just as soon as Ben empties the ironing basket, the dryer stops and there are more clothes to be ironed."

"Mom, are you serious?" asked Ben. "Oh, man, that sounds like a bad dream."

"Don't worry," his mom said, "Wayne would set the pace so you're not worn to a frazzle. But everything would be synchronized. As soon as the washer was empty, there would be more clothes sorted and ready to go in. Do you see what I mean? Everything moves like *ca-chunk, ca-chunk, ca-chunk* . . . in time with everything else. And it's all pulled by demand. Like, upstairs, there would be a min-max level on each type of clothing. You get down to three pairs of underwear, the system sends a signal to the basement to wash more underwear."

"With all due respect, Mom, what planet are you on?" asked Michelle.

"What is so hard to understand about this?!" Amy said. "How have I managed to raise two kids who have no vision? No imagination?"

"But, Mom, what about the dryer?" asked Michelle.

"What about it?"

"The dryer always takes longer than the washer. Everybody knows that! Like twice as long if it's got a full load," said Michelle. "The laundry would go *ca-chunk, ca-chunk, ca*-STOP! Because the washer is finished, but the dryer still has half an hour to run."

Amy's brow compressed as she considered this.

"She's right," said Zelda. "What would Wayne do about the dryer?"

"All right, I admit the dryer would be a headache," said Amy. "But Wayne would come up with some kind of solution. Like maybe he would install a second dryer so that each one has half a load and finishes quicker, in synch with the washer."

"Two dryers?" asked Michelle. "Isn't that like twice as expensive? Twice the electricity? Isn't that *muda*? And if you only do half a load in each dryer, isn't that more *muda*?"

"Well, yes . . . but wet clothes waiting in the washer, that's *muda*. And your poor brother standing idle waiting for more clothes to iron, that would be *muda*, too. I guess Wayne would have to figure out which way is the lesser *muda* and go with that . . ."

Then a thought occurred to Amy.

"Oh, hold on! I'm sorry. Just forget the laundry example. Because the way I described it? That's what's called batch and queue. Wayne doesn't like batch and queue. That's the old industrial mind-set."

"Amy, dear, how else can you do laundry?" asked Zelda.

"Wayne would invest in new technology. Instead of doing laundry by the washerload – which is a batch – and having baskets stacked up waiting to be washed and dried, Wayne would strive for one-piece flow."

"You mean we have to do the laundry one shirt at a time?" asked Ben. "We'd never finish! I'm serious, Mom, I'm going to have nightmares!"

"Now, come on!" said his mother. "Try to envision a better way! Maybe Wayne installs some kind of high-tech laundry chute connecting the upstairs to the basement. Maybe it's automated, so that there's no hand-sorting, and the laundry goes right into the washer and a sensor identifies the fabric and gives each piece its own perfect treatment with just the right temperature and the right amount of detergent. Maybe there is no washer as we would think of it; maybe the clothes are cleaned by ultrasonic waves rather than soap and water. Maybe there is no dryer, because the clothes aren't wet!"

"Sounds great, but won't that take years and cost billions of dollars?" asked Ben.

"Yeah, is this going to be ready in my lifetime?" asked Michelle.

"All right, all right," said their mother, frustrated by now. "Let's just forget about it."

"Mom, you got us into the laundry business. You can't just walk away," said Ben, kidding with her. "You've got to manage it."

Amy gritted her teeth.

"Okay. Fine," she said. "Let's assume Wayne is stuck with a dryer that takes twice as long as the washer. In that case, the way he would balance the line is by shifting people around so that everyone stays busy all the time. Or maybe he would determine that the laundry line doesn't require four people. Maybe demand only calls for three people on the laundry line."

The instant Amy said that she regretted it, because Michelle's eyes popped.

"Mom!" Michelle said. "Can I get laid off?"

Ben's hand immediately shot up. "No! Me! Pick me! I want to get fired!"

"Sorry," said their mom, "but it is stated in the Cieolara family contract that all kids must help do laundry. If anyone is going to be laid off, it's going to be Grandma."

"Oh, I don't mind helping," said Zelda.

"And once Grandma retires from laundry, I'm next," said Amy.

But then she looked at Michelle and saw a devilish gleam in her daughter's little eyes.

"Hey, Mom, I've got an idea," said Michelle. "And I mean this one is big."

"I'm listening."

"What if we set up the laundry so that it wouldn't take four people, or three, or even two? What if we could do everything with just one person?"

Ben was immediately on her wavelength. He grinned at his mother and began slyly pointing at his sister.

Amy folded her arms on her chest and said, "No way. I know what you're trying to pull. You're just trying to get out of laundry duty."

"But Mom!"

"No. You're both doing laundry and that's final. The boss has spoken."

"Mom, listen!" said Ben. "Suppose we add up all the minutes for all the steps and it turns out that we can balance one person's time against the dryer's time – which is like at least an hour. What if it turns out that one person really can do it all. Wouldn't it make sense to give it a try?"

"And we can take turns," said Michelle. "Ben can do laundry one week and I'll do it the next!"

"Right!" said Ben. "That way we'll both be doing laundry, but only half as much!"

Amy looked at Zelda for a reaction, and Zelda simply shrugged her shoulders.

"I know you're trying to give them a work ethic," said Zelda, "but if they can really do it on their own . . . in half the time . . ."

Considering this, Amy turned to her kids and told them, "Now listen. It has to be a quality job. I'm not going to accept either of you rushing through it just to go watch television."

"Of course! We'll be careful," said Michelle.

"I have a bad feeling about this," Amy muttered. "But . . . show me how efficiently you can work, and I'll think about it."

Instantly the pace of ironing and folding picked up.

"Mom," said Ben, "I have one more question."

"Yes?"

"If we're going to treat laundry like a business, when am I going to get a raise?"

"Just as soon as I get one," said his mother.

"Well, Jayro, get out the plywood and start a-nailin' because Hurricane Wayne is about to blow."

"How come you say that?" asked Jayro, adding a nice heap of rice to his gumbo.

"The Black Belts have determined that many of our fine workers are underutilized," said Murphy Maguire.

"Under-what?"

"Underutilized. That was their exact word. And therefore, they intend to balance the line."

"Balance the line? What does that mean?"

"It means woe and trouble, or so my gut tells me. But, as Wayne Reese explained it to me, a balanced line means production in which capacity is equal to demand – exactly just enough people, equipment, materials, and time to do the job. Each and every process along the way is balanced with respect to all the others so that theoretically the flow proceeds with minimal waste. Too few resources and the process – whatever it may be – will not deliver to the next process on time, and quality may be sacrificed in the hurry to catch up. Too many resources – which is to say more capacity than necessary – drives up costs, and that means higher prices or thinner profits or both. By the way, your wife's Louisiana upbringing is shining through today. The gumbo is superb."

"Thanks. I'll tell her you said so."

"She must've kept you out of the kitchen," said Murph, "because the spicing is just right."

"As a matter of fact, she did," said Jayro as he rained Tabasco over his bowl.

They were as usual for a Monday at midday in the drab, windowless toolroom that was all but forgotten by everyone else in the plant. At the center of their table was a pot with the gumbo and another pot with the rice. Behind those was dessert: a fresh peach pie with a sugary crust, which Murphy had brought.

"So if you balance the line, what happens?" asked Jayro.

"If you balance the line, the Black Belts claim, everything is just right – materials arrive just in time, and they leave each process exactly when the next process is ready for them. Waiting times, expenses, waste – all are reduced and minimized. Everything is flattened out."

"Doesn't sound bad to me, Murph."

"Oh, it sounds just fine and dandy."

"Then why are you against it?"

"Because the world is not flat."

"Say what?"

"Go into nature, Jayro, and perfectly straight lines are difficult if not impossible to find. Look at the ocean and the horizon may seem like a straight line, but in reality that flat surface curves. There are waves. Variation. Distribution across a range of values."

"But, Murphy, we are not at the beach. We are at a modern manufacturing plant. A controlled environment. One of our major jobs here is to produce consistent results. Straight lines are not impossible."

"Even when a line looks straight, it wiggles and bends if you get close enough. There is variation, always. We do not eliminate variation here; we manage it. And then there is demand. Demand is never one constant value. There are waves in demand. And capacity must be sufficient to accommodate those waves – or losses of time and money will result. What Wayne and his Black Belts are not taking into account is the extreme difficulty of creating steady uniformity. Just to show you what they do not comprehend, they are treating Godzilla as if it was the same as any other process."

"You've explained to them that once an autoclave is loaded there is no speeding it up? That temperature and pressure must remain steady for a specific time? That the time can vary from one hour to almost an entire day depending on what's being made?"

"Yes, I've tried. I've spoken at length to Wayne Reese, but he is undaunted. He had complete faith in his Black Belts and his LSS methods. So the production line will be balanced. Our workers will be utilized to the maximum. And we are going to 'save' all kinds of money as a result."

"So what are you going to do?" asked Jayro.

"Hope that they offer me a good severance package."

"You're serious?"

"No. And yes," said Murphy. "But in the meantime, since I cain't beat 'em, I intend to join 'em. I am signed up to go to black-belt school."

"You? Isn't that like weeks, maybe months of training? Who's going to run the plant while you're away?"

"Wayne Reese himself is going to take command. He will be assisted by his trusty Black Belts and I also volunteered you."

Jayro shook his head in annoyance and reached for the peach pie.

"Gee, thanks, Murph. Trouble is on the way and you put me in the middle of it."

"You'd be in the middle of it anyway."

"Well, it's going to look great right there at the top of my résumé. 'Performed as assistant plant manager, during which time the plant saved so much money it went out of business.' Maybe I'm the one who should be going to black-belt school."

"Your day will come. They're going to train me first, then you'll go next. In the meantime, it's been suggested that you do the green-belt training, which is quicker."

"Murph, if you don't believe in this LSS stuff, why are you signing up for it? And why are you pushing me into it?"

"Worst case scenario, it'll look nice on both our résumés," Murphy said with a grin. "But really, it's not that I don't believe in all of it. Based on everything I've heard and read, LSS does have its good points. The tools you learn are excellent and worth knowing. The core ideas are very interesting and have an elegance that is not to be completely rejected. It's the reality part of it that has me worried. Anyway, by learning to talk their talk, maybe I can inject some common sense when it's needed."

Jayro nodded, but Murphy was not sure if Jayro was agreeing or he just liked the pie.

"So I'm curious," said Jayro. "What did Wayne say when you got on board?"

"He congratulated me on my profound wisdom."

"Twenty-three hours?!" exclaimed Wayne Reese.

"Twenty-three-point-five hours, to be exact," said Richy, the daylight autoclave manager, reading from the data on the screen in front of him. "You asked for the maximum, sir, and that's the maximum 'soak' time, as we call it. Then there is another spec that calls for twenty-one hours. But the twenty-three and the twenty-one-hour soaks, those are rare."

Looking over Richy's shoulder was Wayne's lead Black Belt, Kurt

Konani, who would be working on a more tactical level than Wayne to orchestrate the LSS transformation at the Oakton plant. They were gathered around the autoclave control console, and with them was Jayro Pepps, filling in for Murphy Maguire, who had departed for LSS training. They were attempting to figure out takt time.

"So that's . . . fourteen hundred and ten minutes," said Kurt, raising his thick black eyebrows. "Well, what's the minimum?"

"Um, let's see," said Richy, scrolling through the data. "The shortest is fifty-two minutes."

"That's more like it," said Wayne. "If we could get all the jobs down below an hour, we'd be in good shape."

"Yeah, this sounds like a job for Six Sigma," said Kurt. "That spread from fifty-two minutes to . . . what was it? Fourteen hundred minutes . . . man, that's what I call variation. That's just going to kill us."

"Excuse me," said Jayro, "but you do realize we're talking about a specification here?"

Kurt regarded Jayro with a blank look.

"The range from fifty-two minutes to fourteen-ten is not statistical variation," said Jayro. "The time spent in the autoclave depends upon the job. If you want the finished product to have the chemical and mechanical properties the customer wants, then you have to leave the material in there for the full fourteen hundred and ten minutes. You can't take it out quicker."

The reality of the time differences dawned on the faces of Wayne and Kurt.

"In fact," added Richy, "there is no variation to speak of within the autoclave itself. Everything is timed and run by computer, and if the spec is for fifty-two minutes, that's exactly how long the material soaks inside the unit. Each treatment starts and stops automatically."

"But, just to ask a dumb question," said Wayne, "how come one treatment takes less than an hour and the next takes almost twenty-four times longer?"

"It's whatever the good folks in Rockville specify," said Jayro. "If the chemist in Rockville specifies twenty-three-point-five hours, that's what we have to abide by. We do not have the authority here to change that."

"Now, if y'all want to go talk to Rockville and get them to make the soak times all be the same," said Richy, "that would be just fine by us. But we can't challenge what they specify."

"Right," said Wayne. "Got it."

"Well, I see what's going on, but that sure does complicate matters," said Kurt.

"Let's drill a little deeper here," said Wayne. "You said something about these long soaks being rare? How rare are they?"

Richy shrugged and said, "It depends. Sometimes it'll be three or four months until we get one. Sometimes we get five or six in a week's time. But that's very unusual. Actually, that almost never happens, that we would get a lot of them in a short period of time."

Wayne and Kurt looked a bit relieved when they heard that.

"All right," said Wayne, "and what's the norm as far as soak time?"

"The norm? Somewhere between two to four hours," said Richy. "That would account for ninety-five percent of what we do here, maybe even higher."

Kurt looked at Wayne and said, "If we calculate takt without these almost day-long soaks, we could live with four hours. And I really think we should just throw out the long soaks, because there aren't that many of them and, I mean, they're so far out in left field compared with just about all the others. We'll deal with the occasional irregularity as we go along."

Wayne scratched the back of his head and then slowly nodded.

"For now, yes, I agree," he said. "Let's work within the norm and try to get a handle on the whole thing, then we'll deal with the flukes."

"Maybe at some point in the future," Kurt suggested, "we can persuade Rockville to take on soak time reduction as an LSS project."

"Even better," said Wayne, "what could we do to get rid of this monster altogether?"

As it turned out, they could do, at least in the short term, absolutely nothing.

8

For weeks the Black Belts labored in the conference room that Wayne Reese had commandeered to serve as LSS headquarters on the fourth floor of the Hi-T Building downtown. The conference table was strewn with printed photographs taken at Oakton, process diagrams, engineering drawings, notes of interviews with plant-floor employees, as well as laptops and calculators, and various morale boosters like a bowl of lollipops and a Bose clock radio, to which an iPod had been connected. Covering an entire long-side wall of the room were sheets of brown butcher-shop paper from a big roll that Wayne had personally procured. Tacked up with pushpins and duct tape, the butcher paper was covered with hundreds of Post-it notes bearing carefully lettered descriptions, and linking the notes were lines depicting an overall flow from left to right. Wayne and Kurt Konani, with other Black Belts pitching in, had meticulously constructed this, sometimes arguing with each other, sometimes joking with boyish glee as they added detail after detail.

Amy Cieolara had generally stayed clear of LSS HQ. She didn't want to interfere – and besides that, the room had taken on a slight dormitory odor comprised of scents like Wayne's chewing gum, Kurt's aftershave, perspiration (the room was stuffy), and the stale aromas of fried chicken and Chinese food brought in from nearby restaurants offering takeout. But the day came when Amy was invited to come have a look at their completed masterpiece.

"This," Wayne said with a sweeping gesture toward the wall of butcher paper, "is our value stream map, or VSM, for short. This shows every step of every process currently used to produce composite products at the Oakton plant."

"Wow," said Amy. "It's . . ."

"Complex," Wayne said.

He pointed out, on the left, the portion of the map indicating the purchasing and stocking of raw materials; and on the right, the destinations and customer applications of the products Oakton produced. Between the two, laid out in incredible detail, was every single step that occurred between raw materials and finished products.

"What's with all the dots?" asked Amy, referring to the stick-on dots of various colors that adorned each of the hundreds of Post-it notes.

"Those show where value is added – or not added," said Wayne. "The blue dots indicate a step that adds value. The yellow dots show steps in which no value is added, but are necessary due to regulation or company policy. And the red dots point out something going on that adds no value of any significance – waste, in other words."

"There sure are lots of red dots!" said Amy.

"And just think," said Kurt, "every red dot is a potential project for LSS."

"Which means an opportunity to eliminate waste," said Wayne. "So you can see the potential."

"Yes, dozens and dozens of red dots," said Amy. "What about Rockville? How are they coming along?"

"I have a good LSS consultant working with Sarah Schwick and her people at F&D. And I think that they're putting together some excellent pilot projects – although this thing called 'the loop' that Sarah keeps complaining about is, I think, biting off more than we can chew in one year. And Viktor Kyzanski –"

"Yes, I know about Viktor. He can be evasive, passive aggressive, not to mention difficult," said Amy. "But just don't forget about F&D."

"Of course not."

"So when are you going to start making some things happen?" asked Amy.

"Soon," said Wayne. "We're now at the point that we can start selecting our first projects."

"Good. Because the clock is running, and we've been laying out quite an investment," said Amy.

"I'm aware of that," Wayne assured her. "And, believe me, it'll be worth it."

Despite Amy's impatience, a lot had been accomplished in the four months since Wayne had come to Hi-T. Key performance indicators – called KPIs – had been established and a lot of measurements were being taken in accordance with those. Formal statements of policy relating to LSS had been written. There had been the gigantic value stream maps. And there had been a lot of activity – events and meetings, and people by the dozens flying off to exotic Long Island where Winner had its corporate training center to learn Lean and Six Sigma techniques. It would cost tens of thousands of dollars per trained employee by the time it was all done.

The bills for LSS were certainly piling up, but this was not what really concerned Amy. The funding, some of it from corporate, was more or less within budget. However, there had been some disturbing "extras" that had been missed when the numbers were calculated, such as overtime for the hourly plant workers who were participating in LSS. There was also the drain on general performance caused by the numbers of people out of town on training. What was most troubling for Amy were the snide little comments Nigel Furst was making in his emails and phone calls about Hi-T's performance, which was still uninspiring and problematic.

Indeed, in late January, Amy had to go to what was informally – and only half-jokingly – referred to as the "Crystal Ball." This was when all of Nigel's presidents had to make detailed presentations, with assessments of past performance and forecasts for the year. The "crystal ball" reference was to Nigel's insistence on accurate predictions for the coming four quarters, and he absolutely insisted upon thorough, fully analyzed scenarios detailing the gains in revenue and income that were to be achieved. Furthermore, it was public in the sense that all the presidents were together in one room, and every presentation was video-recorded so that Peter Winn himself could watch his presidents perform. But there was another purpose to the video recordings: miss your projections on the numbers, and Nigel was likely to play back the video of your last presentation as a means of ridiculing you. In any case, each president – there were four of them in Nigel's group – had to endure Nigel's incisive, often critical, sometimes harsh assessments, and from what Amy had heard, he could be rather nasty about it.

As this would be Amy's first Crystal Ball, she felt she simply could not go before Nigel without being able to assert that the Lean Six Sigma "revolution" was well under way at Hi-T. Hence, the modest pressure she was putting on Wayne Reese to keep the LSS ball rolling.

• • •

So in the first weeks of January, here they were, seated at that table. There was Amy, of course, as well as Murphy Maguire, Jayro Pepps, and Kurt Konani representing Oakton. Sarah Schwick and several others involved in LSS at F&D who had come in from Rockville. But notably absent was F&D head Viktor Kyzanski, who was off on client business.

"Good morning and welcome to what I like to call the LSS Action Presentation," said Wayne Reese. "This is where we present our selections for the Lean Six Sigma projects that we feel will eliminate the most waste and explain what we want to accomplish, and then, of course, we ask for cooperation, and support, and permission to proceed. I know that all of us are anxious to get going."

"You bet," said Amy, seated in the semidarkness at the long table in the headquarters' main conference room.

"All right, well, here we go," said Wayne.

He pressed the button; the first graphic of the presentation appeared on the screen on the wall above the long table.

"What you see here," said Wayne, "is what we call a 'pick chart,' and it's simply a matrix divided into four quadrants. The two columns divide the projects into those with big payoffs and those with smaller payoffs. And the two rows further divide the projects into those that will be easy or fast to implement, and those that will be harder or more expensive or take a long time to implement.

"Now both at Oakton and at Rockville, there were many, many potential projects to choose from. If we found a process step in which there was no value being added, that was a potential project, because if it didn't add value, it was some form of *muda*. So at both locations, there were hard choices to be made.

"The decision process considered a lot of factors, the first being waste elimination," said Wayne. "But, also, every project was linked to one or more Winner corporate objectives – such as maximum utilization of resources, minimization of costs including direct labor, our commitment to safety, environmental friendliness, and our mandate from Peter Winn to achieve Six Sigma quality. Still, the chief deciding factors were the magnitude of the waste to be eliminated, the expected cost benefit, the time to accomplish the project, and the difficulty of implementing the solution. In other words, if a project can achieve a big payoff in a shorter period of time, it wins out over a project that would be hard to execute with a smaller payoff. So it's not like we just pulled these out of a hat. A lot of hard work has gone into these choices."

Wayne peered into the semidarkness to find Sarah Schwick, and said, "Let's begin with the Formulation and Design unit. Sarah Schwick is going to tell us what the LSS team in Rockville came up with."

Rockville Pick Chart	Big Payoff	Smaller Payoff
Easy/Fast	Standardize Report Formats	Duplex Printing
	Reduce Physical Steps in Sample Preparation	Toner Cartridge Refill/Recycle
		5S the Scan Lab
Hard/Slow	Passive Office Building	Reconfigure, Simplify "the Loop"

Sarah came to the podium and her five-foot-one-inch stature almost vanished behind it. To compensate she stepped to one side and bent the gooseneck of the podium lamp down to shine on her papers. She then began reading her presentation aloud in a monotone. She had written it just as she would write a lab report, just as she had been taught as a young chemical engineer. Every sentence was in passive voice: "A variety of projects was considered by the team." She utilized the word *utilized* at least once in every paragraph. And any phrasing that might have even hinted at imagery, irony, humor, or life itself had been avoided or purged. Every so often, she would look at those around the table and the clear-frame glasses she wore made her eyes seem enormous, but with tiny, dot-like pupils.

Oh, my, thought Amy. *She really is a geek.*

"A final matrix of LSS project candidates was made after thorough analysis," she read. "A standardization of report formats and a reduction in report templates was identified as having the properties of a significant reduction in resource requirements. A timely manner of implementation was determined."

Fortunately, Amy had a good idea of what Sarah was talking about from earlier discussions. She knew that Rockville, for all its rules and strict procedures, had an insane variety of different report formats, many of which were inconsistent with one another, and which could potentially lead to confusion or misinterpretation of the test results.

"Utilizing a standard report format could result in a fifteen percent decrease in the time required to generate a test report for client review, and a twenty-five to fifty percent decrease in formatting time," Sarah read.

There were other projects. They would also seek to reduce the physical distances that employees had to travel within the F&D buildings in order to prepare materials samples for the project engineers and their clients. Currently, adding together all the distances between workstations to prepare one sample required a transit of as much as 1.2 kilometers. The LSS project would seek to reduce the distance to mere meters traveled, not *kilo*meters, and cut the total time to produce the sample, from an average of four days, by 50 percent.

"Excellent," said Amy.

"The savings from such an implementation of this improvement could conservatively exceed two hundred fifty thousand dollars per year," said Sarah.

"Even more excellent!" said Amy.

Of lesser impact, but still thought to be worth doing, was a project to reorganize one of the materials labs. There, they would apply "5S," the LSS technique to raise the level of organization, neatness, housekeeping, and so on.

Then there were the "green" initiatives – reducing paper consumption, and recycling toner cartridges. Amy had already decided to give the "green light" to these, corny pun intended.

Next were the Hard/Slow projects that were longer term. In the bottom left quadrant was something termed Passive Office Building. Here, Sarah Schwick came out of her near-comatose delivery, and inexplicably began to speak off-the-cuff with some enthusiasm.

"Excuse me," said Amy. "Sorry to interrupt. But explain more about what you mean by 'passive.' "

"Right now, in northern Europe, there are houses termed as 'passive.' There are no furnaces in these houses. And the winters can be very cold. Yet the houses are warm and quite comfortable in the winter, and cool in the summer even without conventional air-conditioning. They function well because of smart design, with excellent ventilation but also excellent temperature conservation, needing only a small heat exchanger that runs on a tiny fraction of the energy consumed by conventional heating and air-conditioning. Our thought is to use the F&D buildings experimentally to create materials of the future, that Hi-T could manufacture, which might be retrofitted into existing buildings or installed in new construction to make commercial office space passive or semipassive – in any case, to use a lot less energy than currently."

Amy began playing with her pen as she listened to this. "This sounds like it was made for Hi-T, not to mention F&D. My only question is, why would this be a Lean Six Sigma project?"

"It is a little outside the Lean Six Sigma parameters," Wayne commented. "It's not improvement . . . it's like a whole new market or something. It's research and development. It's . . . enterprise thinking. I'm not sure how to categorize it."

"It's very interesting," said Amy. "Unfortunately, Sarah, you're straying from the F&D business model, which is to have a client fund the development."

"Why do we always have to follow a client's direction?" Sarah argued. "Why do we have to limit ourselves? Why can't we take the lead for once?"

"Because the clients pay us," said Amy. "And if we don't have a client to foot the bill, we're putting out a lot of money. Look, I won't rule out the project, but it's not for LSS. I think it's worthy of more fact-finding and discussion. The problem is that I think you're probably talking about millions of dollars in development costs for a payoff years away. I would have to run that by Winner Corporate to get the authorization."

"But that's why, as an LSS project . . ." Sarah faintly countered, "and with the energy savings helping offset the costs . . ."

"All right, we'll talk later," said Amy. "What else do you have?"

Sarah turned to the pick-chart graphic on the screen.

"Last . . . and least, sorry to say, is a suggestion I was pushing to reduce waste in the process called the loop. I thought, and some others as well, thought there might be a big payoff here, but I was overruled. Basically, Viktor shot us down."

"Why was that?" Amy asked. "Why was Viktor opposed?"

"He was – as he always says he is – worried about quality issues. He felt the risks were too great to be meddling with what he feels is a system that works, and the return would be small compared to the risk. We included the project here to show you that it was considered, but it's essentially dead. Maybe next year . . ."

Sarah ended on that note. After some discussion, Amy approved everything "above the line" in the Easy/Fast designation.

They then turned to the LSS initiatives at the Oakton plant, and Wayne introduced Kurt Konani to make that presentation.

Kurt used his laser pointer to refer to the huge, butcher-paper value stream map tacked to the wall.

"From our VSM," said Kurt, "we generated a very long list of potential projects. Let me assure you, we have many, many years of project opportunities ahead of us. But of course we need to select for this year only those that will have the greatest impact on waste elimination, with the largest potential gains in our journey to Leanness."

Oakton Pick Chart	Big Payoff	Smaller Payoff
Easy/Fast	Balance Line to Takt Time	Mistake-proof Resin Dye Storage
	Reconfigure M57 Line	Reorganize Cooler
	Add Kanbans	5S Shipping Dept
Hard/Slow	Balance Line to Takt Time	Re-engineer Godzilla
	Install Work Cells in T/M Shop	
	Apply Six Sigma to Solve USN Hairline Crack Problem	

The big project – and Kurt went straight to it – was balancing the production line at Oakton and producing based on takt time. This project was – oddly, to Amy's sensibilities – placed in two quadrants. Both were aligned in Big Payoff, but planted in Easy/Fast and Hard/Slow.

"Now, of course a balanced line means that we have trimmed all excess capacity from all processes, relative to demand. It's often called 'flattening' or 'leveling' because that's conceptually what we do; we level the line by moving people and adjusting job responsibilities so that everybody has just enough to do. Ideally nobody is overworked, but nobody is idle throughout the day. And the same with equipment capacities, too.

"The reason we have the balanced line in as both 'easy' and 'hard' is exactly that. In some areas of the plant it will be relatively easy to make adjustments and pull utilization above ninety-two or even ninety-five percent. In other areas, because of the diversity of the products being made, it's going to be more challenging. And so, it'll take longer. Like, you know, six or nine months instead of, say, three. Or one."

Amy was pressing the dull end of her pen into her chin as she contemplated this.

"Well, I have a question here," she said. "How can you balance the line to takt when you have such high variation in cycle times?"

"Because the only big variation in cycle time," said Wayne, jumping in, "occurs at the autoclave. We'll have to figure out how to deal with that later. In the meantime, we should be able to balance the rest of the line to takt without much trouble."

"That's right," said Kurt. "And once we accomplish that, every phase of processing will have just enough or slightly more than enough capacity to finish its task within takt time."

Amy reclined in her chair as she though about this, and let her gaze drift to Murphy Maguire, who had said nothing and showed no indication that he would. Then she said to Kurt and Wayne, "All right."

Next was the application of Six Sigma to improve quality throughout the plant, but with the special priority of solving the intermittent and vexing hairline crack problem on some but not all Navy parts orders. So far, all efforts to eliminate it had failed, and it was felt that this would be a Hard/Slow project.

"Absolutely yes. Get on it," said Amy.

And then there were the more ordinary Lean Six Sigma projects, though each one would be an involved exercise. Biggest of the "ordinary" LSS efforts, they would reconfigure the M57 Line, which was mainly where raw materials came together to form the actual composite.

Then they would mistake-proof – or apply *poka-yoke* – to the resin dye rack. They would add kanbans – a demand style of inventory replenishment – at certain places on the plant floor. They would do 5S in Shipping and make it neater, reorganize the Cooler, and so on and so on.

But what they would not do was re-engineer the Autoclave area. Much to Wayne's and Kurt's dismay, the plant's autoclave – Godzilla – had little waste to be eliminated from it, other than the excess work crew. The process was simply time-consuming and sometimes complex. With regret, Wayne had concluded that they must leave Godzilla be.

"Excuse me," Amy said, "but what is 'Godzilla'?"

"It's the autoclave, a very large piece of equipment," said Wayne. "I believe its actual, technical name is . . . what is it, Murph?"

"The AC-1240-N," said Murphy Maguire.

"And it is somewhat expensive to run, which was why I first thought it might be a good target. But it turns out that redesigning or replacing this monster would be hard and very expensive. So the only thing we can do with it in a Lean way is reduce the manpower – because between load changes, most of the crew just stands around. I think we can cut that way back. Other than that, we'll just leave it alone until there is a capital budget big enough to junk it and replace it with something that allows single-piece flow."

"Godzilla," said Amy. "All my years with Hi-T, I've never heard that name."

When Amy flew to New York City for the Crystal Ball meetings, she found the demeanor of Tom Dawson to be cool and remote – and she felt both annoyed and at the same time relieved. Since that evening on her front porch when she had turned him down, there had been a few other trips, but there had been other people along on those flights. This was the first time she was flying alone with him. He seemed to have concluded that there would be no personal relationship between them, and he was acting appropriately. Courteous. Professional. Reserved. This was not what she wanted.

The skies above Highboro were cloudy, but once in the air and climbing toward cruising altitude, the plane broke through the dense gray, and the sun was brilliantly golden in the perfect blue sky. She was seated behind him, in the passenger compartment. By now she had a sense of his pilot routines, and waited for him to trim the plane and set the autopilot.

Then, hoping to break through the frost, she asked him, "So . . . how's your business?"

"My business? It's been good," he said.

"That's nice. Aside from Hi-T, how many clients do you have now?"

"Three regulars, business clients like you. And any number of one-timers. Depends on the month. They tend to come in waves for some reason."

He began turning a knob on one of the instruments. As if to tune her out, she thought. Presuming the conversation – if it could be called that – was over, Amy opened her laptop to review her presentation one more time.

But then Tom turned to her and said, "I'm thinking about leasing another plane. Something bigger, more comfortable."

"That would be nice. I like this airplane, but it is a little . . ."

"Small," said Tom. "That's true, and I know I do lose some business because I can't seat larger groups. On the other hand, a bigger plane means more money, higher costs. And if I go to a two-plane operation, I'd have to bring on a second pilot, at least on a part-time basis."

That meant, of course, that he would not be the pilot every time, she reasoned. As she thought about this, they fell quiet again.

"What about you?" Tom asked, filling the silence. "How is business at Hi-T?"

"We've started a big continuous-improvement program. I have high hopes for it. In fact, it had better deliver, because the reason I'm flying to New York today is to make a presentation declaring the gains we're going to make in the coming year. Most of those gains are going to have to come from the improvements this program is supposed to deliver."

"That's Lean Six Sigma? The program?"

"Right."

"I remember talking to . . . that guy, what's his name?"

"Wayne. Wayne Reese."

"Right. Nice guy and all. Very bright. He's all gung ho. On a trip to Maryland, just the two of us, he filled my ear with all the great things about Lean. Didn't have the heart to tell him, I already knew most of what he was telling me."

"Really?"

"We used it in the military. To improve logistics – surely one of the biggest, if not *the* biggest, supply chain systems in the world."

"How did it work out? The LSS, I mean?"

"The toolsets are very good. Very powerful if they're applied the right way."

"But what kind of results did you get?" she asked, pressing.

Tom shrugged his shoulders. "That was some years ago. I retired."

He was becoming reserved again, and Amy decided not to push.

"Good luck with it," Tom said, turning away.

There was something in his tone Amy didn't like, something that implied she might need the luck, but she let it go.

The Crystal Ball presentations were held in an elegant but windowless room inside the Winner corporate headquarters in Manhattan. The walls and ceiling of the room were adorned with antique oak paneling taken from the mansion of an English estate. A long table, also of oak, with lion's-claw feet, dominated the room. Nigel Furst sat in the center of one of the longer sides, in the position where, beneath the edge of the table, there were a number of buttons and switches to turn microphones in the ceiling on and off, control the video cameras, summon refreshments, etc. At the press of one of the buttons, the paneling opened to reveal a huge flat-screen monitor for displaying graphics.

Including Amy, there were four business-unit presidents. Excluding her, all were men. This was the first time a female of equal rank had been in this type of meeting, and the others treated her a bit like delicate glass.

"Why don't we abide by tradition," said Nigel, "and declare that ladies should go first."

Amy in fact was glad of this, happy to get it over with. She stood next to her chair, introduced herself and began. Half an hour later, she sat down again, feeling confident that she had done well. Yet as Nigel pressed the rocker switch to bring up the lights, she was struck by the hard glints in the eyes of her peers, and on the face of at least one, the trace of an icy smirk.

"Amy, are you truly satisfied with what you have forecast?" asked Nigel.

"Yes. Absolutely," she said.

"You're banking very heavily on the Lean Six Sigma stuff to come through, aren't you?"

"Yes, and according to Wayne Reese, it will."

"All right," said Nigel. "Who would like to be next?"

One by one, the others delivered their presentations, and as they did, Amy felt the cold sting of inadequacy. Each of the other presidents in his forecast was much more aggressive than she had been. Whereas Amy had promised year-over-year net income growth of 7 percent – a rather conservative number that she felt Hi-T was all but certain to meet – the others had predicted growth in the double digits, from 11 percent to as high as 22 percent. A game of one-upsmanship was being played here. By the end of the presentations, she felt like hiding under the table.

"Very well then," said Nigel. "I think it's time for the awards."

He pressed a switch under the table, and into the room came an assistant bearing what appeared to be a small treasure chest. This was set before Nigel, and the assistant withdrew. Nigel then stood and looked at Amy.

"Miss Cieolara, come here, please. I have something for you."

The other presidents were either stone-faced or smirking, seeming to know what was coming. Amy nervously approached, and Nigel took from the treasure chest a box the width of a salad plate. The box, as Amy saw, was covered in purple velvet of a garish shade, with fake gold embroidery that was unraveling, and the lid bore a dark stain. Opening it, Nigel produced a green, outsize lapel button, large enough to be read from the far side of the room, and on the face of the button was the cartoon character Bart Simpson taking aim with his slingshot.

"Let me read for you, Amy, what the button says," said Nigel. "It says, World's Greatest UNDERACHIEVER! Now, let me pin this on you."

"Oh, please . . ." she murmured.

"No, no, you've earned it," said Nigel, smiling as he plunged the sharp pin into the fabric of her jacket's lapel and fastened the clasp. "There. Go and take your seat."

Her cheeks burning, she did so – even as Nigel was working himself into a rant against her.

"*Seven* percent?! That's the best you can do, Amy? Well, that's not going to satisfy *Peter Winn*! Or our *investors*! And it certainly won't satisfy *me*! Our corporate objective is for year-over-year, bottom line earnings growth of *double digits*. Ten percent . . . um, let me do the math . . . yes, that would be the *minimum* acceptable gain for a projection such as you have given. I take it you were not aware of that?"

"I based my projections on what I think is realistic," she told him.

"Realistic? Or *easy*?"

"I didn't want to overpromise!" she insisted.

"Good. Because I don't want you to overpromise either," said Nigel. "I want you *to deliver*! Your *predecessor* delivered *eleven* percent his very first year! What ever made you think you could deliver less?"

"We have a lot going on. A lot of changes. It's going to take time."

"Time for *what*? I do not want excuses; I want results. The only time this corporation relaxes the double-digit, ten percent growth threshold is in times of recession – and even then we expect year-over-year improvement. Is the economy currently in a recession? I think not. In every market your business serves, the economic climate ranges from average to excellent. So don't tell me *seven percent* is the best you can do."

She decided it was better to keep quiet.

"I am going to give you a choice. Either tender your resignation right here and now and let me find a manager who *can* meet our corporate objectives. *Or* go back to Carolina, and find another three percent. And if I were you, Amy, if you don't want to keep wearing that lovely pin the rest of your tenure here at Winner, I would be looking for something on the order of an extra five to six percent, if not higher."

He paused, awaiting her answer.

Amy, sitting in fury, inhaled a calming breath. *He will not break me,* she said in her mind.

"Well, what's it going to be?"

"I have to talk to my staff," she said.

"Fine. I'll give you two weeks to re-evaluate and resubmit your plan," said Nigel.

Then he pivoted away from her. Looking at the other presidents, his cold, livid face abruptly changed, and Nigel lit up with big smile.

"Well! Now that we have that unpleasantness out of the way, let's see what's in the chest for the rest of you!"

He made a show of rooting through the little treasure chest, and produced three small jewelry boxes, which he tossed one by one to the other presidents.

"Wow," said one, as he opened his box. "Are these . . . ? "

"Yes! Diamond-stud platinum cuff links!" said Nigel. "Just a small token of Peter Winn's esteem. The full measure of Winner's appreciation, of course, will soon be reflected in your bonuses."

When the expressions of gratitude and the little quips between the men had receded, Nigel again turned to Amy.

"And now, Miss Cieolara, I believe you have a plane to catch," said Nigel. "The rest of us shall adjourn to my club for a few games of racquetball, an elegant dinner, followed by brandy, single malts, and cigars."

Red-faced, humiliated, Amy removed her Underachiever pin, closed her laptop, and began gathering her things as the others stared at her. She could not bring herself to look at any of them.

"Oh, and one more thing, speaking of planes to catch," Nigel then said to her. "The WING reports have brought it to my attention that you and your staff are using a private aircraft on a regular basis for your travels. That is *over*. From now on, until you have earned the privilege, you will fly commercial."

"But we have an arrangement with the pilot —"

"Fire him," said Nigel.

She wanted nothing more than to flee from New York, but Tom Dawson did not answer his cell phone. The original plan had been that she would stay at a hotel in Manhattan overnight, following an evening's revelries with Nigel and the other presidents, and that Tom would meet her at Teterboro Airport in the morning. What he did in the meantime had not even been discussed. All that Amy wanted was to go home, find a hole, and crawl in.

A cursory check of flights using her BlackBerry showed every flight headed south was booked solid, and only standby was available. Even if she was lucky enough to get a seat, the closest she could get to Highboro that night was Charlotte, which meant renting a car and driving the rest of the way. She debated checking into the hotel where Winner had reserved a room for her, but the last thing she wanted was to bump into one or more of the other presidents, who would be staying there as well. So she was standing outside the Winner headquarters building, grinding her teeth in frustration, utterly unsure of where to go or what to do – when Tom returned her call.

"Where are you?" she asked.

"I'm in New Jersey at a motel near the airport. I figured it was cheaper and less wear and tear on me and the plane just to stay over. Sorry I missed your call; I was in the hot tub."

"Tom, could you possibly take me back to North Carolina tonight?"

"Well, this motel has great in-room TV. But, for you . . . all right, sure, no problem. How soon do you think you'll be here?"

Given traffic, just getting across the Hudson and into New Jersey took the better part of an hour. Tom Dawson by then was waiting for her, looking all scrubbed and crisp despite the hour. But his face clouded over when he read the dejection on her face.

"Are you all right?" he asked, opening the door for her.

"Please," she said, "just get this thing in the air."

But it was rush hour in the sky as well as on the ground, and the wait to get clearance for takeoff seemed interminable. In her mind, Amy kept hearing Nigel berating her, over and over, as they waited. The sun was setting by the time they lifted into the air.

Tom finally turned to her to make small talk, but one glance told him to maintain the silence.

"I'm sorry," Amy called out to him. "It's been a really rough day. Maybe the worst day of my career."

"Anything I can do?" he asked.

"No," she said. "Thanks."

Amy put her face in her hands for a moment, then ran her fingers through her hair.

"Tom . . ."

"Yes, ma'am?"

She figured that she might as well tell him now; no point in waiting.

"I have some bad news. The group president I report to has told me that Hi-T is not allowed to use your services anymore. I'm really sorry."

Tom turned in his seat and stared blankly at her.

"Everybody in the company has to fly commercial from now on," she explained.

"Does your boss know that there are no commercial flights out of Highboro?"

"I don't think that matters to him right now."

"Well . . . shoot," Tom said. "I guess that answers my question of whether or not to lease that second plane."

They flew on and the sky deepened in color as twilight came. After ten or fifteen minutes, Tom turned to her again.

"Are you hungry?" he asked.

"A little. But I don't have much of an appetite. Why?"

"Because I'd like to take you to dinner," he said.

"Tom, I thought I made it clear –"

"If you're no longer going to use the services of Dawson Aviation, ma'am, then there is no longer a business relationship between us, and with no business relationship, there can be no conflict of interest in me asking you to dinner, or in you accepting."

She hesitated.

"Unless you have something against retired Marine aviators who know how to make lemonade when handed lemons," he said.

Half an hour later, they were landing in Maryland beside Chesapeake Bay. Next to the airstrip within walking distance was a little restaurant that Tom claimed served the best crab cakes on the Eastern Shore.

"What a prick," said Amy.

She was of course referring to Nigel Furst. In her curled fingers was a glass of Chardonnay – her second. With the help of the wine, she had told Tom about her day, talking freely, maybe too freely, but she did not care.

Tom, still having to fly, was drinking iced tea but was eyeing her wineglass – though not from envy; he was wondering if her grip would snap the stem.

"Yeah, well, the world sure has a lot of 'em," he said. "Pricks, I mean."

"I gave him my honest, best plan," said Amy. "And it wasn't good enough. All right, I was conservative. Maybe too conservative. But it makes me wonder what I've gotten myself into. I never liked Nigel, and now I don't even respect him. Why am I even working for him?"

"I don't know. To pay your mortgage?" Tom suggested. "To support your kids, give them a good life, and get them through college? To give yourself some financial security? Amy, you probably don't want to hear this right now, but prick or not, this guy *is* your boss. You've got to do everything, as long as it's legal and ethical, to accomplish whatever mission is given to you, no matter what the pressure. That's your job."

"Spoken like a true Marine."

"Always," he said. "It'll always be part of me."

Amy sat back and regarded him. Behind the good-natured humor and the overall competence his demeanor suggested, there was a resolute forcefulness. A sense that, whatever he had to do, whatever it took, he would get it done. She found herself admiring that quality, yet she also found it just a little frightening. She wondered what he would be like to be around on a daily basis.

"Well, I am not a Marine," said Amy. "And I *am* doing my job. Trying to. And I don't like the way I was treated today. On the other hand . . . I'm not going to let that prick beat me."

Tom nodded at her and smiled. It was as if she had just passed some secret test of his.

Their crab cakes arrived at the table. They had long thick flakes of crab, were golden brown on the outside with the whiteness of the crab showing through, slightly crispy but moist on the inside, with just enough breading to hold them together. If they were not the best on the Eastern Shore, they were worthy contenders.

Back in the air, they flew through a cloudless sky. Amy sat "up front" in the copilot's seat, looking out into the blackness. Below them on the dark earth were constellations of light made by cities and towns and the webs of streets and highways. Between the big pools were tiny pinpricks of the light from rural homes and the slow-moving headlights of those traveling lonely roads. Tom touched Amy's arm and pointed out the blue dot of planet Venus, visible in the western sky.

A few minutes later he touched her arm again and pointed to a small, vague disc of light visible through the windshield on the horizon far ahead.

"That's Highboro," he told her.

With that, whatever spell had been cast by the beauty of the night was broken for Amy. For out there, down there, was so much that she would have to deal with.

"Tom . . . can I ask you a question?"

"You can *ask* . . ."

"This morning, you said you knew Lean Six Sigma, that you'd used it in the Marines. But you never told me how well everything worked out with LSS. Did it work?"

He rolled his eyes and then smirked at her. "On a gorgeous evening like this, you have to ask me *that*?"

"Well, sorry, but it's important to me! I'm taking my company down the LSS road and there is a lot riding on it – not only for me, but for a lot of other people."

"When you ask, 'did it work,' what do you really want to know?"

"I want to know if you achieved what you set out to achieve."

"We accomplished a lot of good things using LSS," he said. "Why are you asking? Do you have doubts?"

"No, I believe in LSS . . . based on everything I've been told. But, well, I've never done anything like this, and I was just wondering what your experience has been."

"Most of my experience with LSS was positive. Lean and Six Sigma are excellent. The trouble is that these are programs, and all programs have a tendency to take on a life of their own. They become the end, rather than the means to the end. People can get wrapped up in making the program perfect, and lose sight of the mission the program is supposed to accomplish."

She thought about this, and then said, "We've been pushing hard with LSS, and I'm just wondering if I push even harder, will I get the results that Nigel wants?"

"I can't tell you," said Tom. "One of the things a new pilot has to learn is to read the instruments and trust what they're telling you. Because your perceptions might be telling you that the plane is flying straight and level and on course, and the *reality* may be on that you're on the wrong heading, or losing altitude, or flying too slow. My only advice is that believing in LSS is far less important than knowing what the hell's really going on."

Not quite getting the reassurances she so wanted, Amy stared toward the blur of lights, larger and closer now, that was Highboro. Even as she stared, the wine and the rich dinner, the stress of the day, and the lulling drone of the engines overcame her.

"Hey, look," said Tom a few minutes later, pointing out the window on his side of the plane. "The moon is rising."

Indeed, a full moon had risen and was shining huge in the eastern sky, but Amy was not awake to see it.

In her office some ten hours later, Amy held a closed-door meeting alone with Wayne Reese. She confided to him the gist of what had happened in New York the day before – not the details; those were too embarrassing. She presented to Wayne "the challenge," as she put it, that Nigel had laid down to her of finding another 3 to 6 percent of bottom line improvement in addition to the 7 percent that she originally thought that Hi-T could achieve.

"First of all," she said to Wayne, "before we even probe ways to increase what we're promising to Nigel, I want to be clear on this: are you totally sure that Lean Six Sigma can deliver real bottom-line gains?"

"Well, sure, absolutely. I mean, I certainly believe it can."

"I know you *believe* that it's possible. But are you really going to get it done?"

"What? The program? Will we implement it?"

"No! Not the program! I *know* you will implement the LSS program," said Amy. "My question is, will Lean Six Sigma actually deliver the millions of dollars in savings that will boost the profitability of this company?"

"I don't know why you're even asking me this," said Wayne. "Of course it will . . . over time."

"*This* year, Wayne. Not a decade from now. What is Lean Six Sigma going to contribute to this company's earnings *this* year?"

"Amy, I'm sorry, but it's difficult to say. I mean, we're really just getting started with the actual projects."

She glared at him. "Wayne, can I count on you or not?"

"Yes," he said finally. "Yes, I'm going to go out on a limb, and I'm going to say that LSS will deliver five to seven percent in additional profitability this year."

"Good," said Amy. "Now . . . how can we make the savings larger?"

Within ten days, Amy had ferreted out, pasted together, or otherwise browbeat from everyone who reported to her another 5 percent in projected gains on top of the 7 percent originally forecast. Most of the 5 percent came by increasing the revenue targets for the sales force, and extrapolations thereof. But the bedrock foundation would come from Lean Six Sigma and the operational improvements it would deliver – which in any case would be necessary in order to make good on actually filling the orders of the increased sales.

Nigel Furst accepted the revised plan that Amy submitted, saying to her, "This is much, much better."

A day later, a small package for Amy arrived from New York. It was from Nigel. Inside the padded envelope was a jewelry box, and inside the box, a pair of diamond-stud platinum cuff links, the same as the other presidents had received. And there was a handwritten note:

> Dear Amy,
>   I am sorry I had to be hard on you, but so often that is the only way to bring out the best. Give us a great year!
>
>   Cordially,
>   Nigel

The diamonds were flawless and sparkled in their platinum settings. But Amy closed the lid of the jewelry box and put them away, far back in the center drawer of her desk, next to the tacky Bart Simpson Underachiever button. Before she closed the drawer, she wondered which of the two would be the more appropriate for her in one year's time.

9

The first time Amy went out with Tom Dawson, they played golf on a Saturday afternoon and had an early dinner together. The second time, he flew them to Charleston and they took a taxi to a restaurant on the waterfront. She bought dinner; he provided the transportation. The third time, he invited her to dinner at "Chez Tom" – his place.

As she parked in his driveway, everything she had imagined about what his house would be like was confirmed. It sort of looked like it might have been picked up from Camp Lejeune and dropped here from the sky. A small brick house with freshly painted white trim. A well-tended lawn surrounded by a perimeter of perfectly trimmed hedges. And not one, but *two* flagpoles: one pole flying the stars and stripes, the other the scarlet, gold, and gray Marine Corps flag, both fluttering lightly in the evening breeze. And the concrete walk to the front door had a border of white-painted round rocks. Amy fought a fleeting urge to back up the car and drive away.

"This is never going to work," she thought, sitting there in her BMW, holding a gift bag with an expensive bottle of wine with frilly colored ribbons she had carefully tied to the neck of the bottle.

Then Tom appeared, waving hello and wearing shorts. She had never before seen him in shorts. He had mentioned that he jogged in the morning, rain or shine, and it showed.

"Nice rocks," she said, handing the gift bag to him.

"You like 'em? I painted each one myself."

Inside, the decor was less Marine. True, there was the wall in the dining room filled with photographs from his days in the Corps – the centerpiece being a picture of Tom seated in the cockpit of his F/A-18 Hornet grinning and giving the camera a thumbs-up. But there were knickknacks from all over the world, and some watercolor paintings that Amy really admired. Then she discovered, slightly to her surprise, that he was a reader. There was a large bookcase in the hall filled mostly with history texts, but also mystery and spy novels, a lot of Pat Conroy – *The Great Santini* caught her eye – and Larry McMurtry.

He cooked dinner: grilled shrimp marinated in a teriyaki sauce, served with grilled asparagus, white rice, and a basic lettuce salad. Everything was tasty and good, although Amy suspected that this was about the limit of his culinary repertoire. Dessert was Buster Bars from Dairy Queen.

They ate on the back porch, then sipped the wine she had brought until well past sunset, talking easily about everything and nothing in particular. He told three or four stories from his Marine days that had her doubled over with laughter.

Afterward, in his living room, they watched a movie. But they never made it to the ending – or in any case, were paying no attention to it as the credits rolled by.

Driving home some time past midnight with a big, lazy smile on her face, she said herself, "Well . . . it *might* work."

"Amy!"

Seated at her desk, but with her back turned to the door, Amy Cieolara startled at the cry of her name. She turned to find Elaine Eisenway, who was Hi-T's vice president of finance, and who had barged into Amy's office without so much as a knock.

"What's the matter?" she calmly asked Elaine.

"It's the inventories again! Here, see for yourself!" said Elaine tossing down a printout of the latest financial reports onto Amy's desk blotter. "Both finished goods and work in process, they're high and getting higher!"

From long experience, Amy knew that Elaine was an alarmist. Elaine had her virtues as a financial manager; she understood the business, she was ethically rigorous yet inventive at problem solving, and she did answer to reason. Yet she was also a drama queen. At even a modest downturn, she was given to running willy-nilly and proclaiming that the sky was falling.

Amy reached for Elaine's printout and slowly went through the pages, which bore a multitude of Elaine's notations, including exclamation points, big circled question marks, and various remarks in the margins.

"Okay, you're right," Amy said to her. "The inventories seem a little high."

"More than a 'little'! Look at the comparisons with last year!"

"All right, all right, I agree; inventories are high."

"I thought Wayne Reese was supposed to get this under control. Didn't we talk about this last month?"

"They've been having some problems at Oakton. To be honest, I don't fully understand why. But Wayne says he's dealing with it."

"Amy, it's not just a matter of inventories. Look at the payroll. Look at the overtime, and especially look at the temporary workers they've added."

"Yes, I know about the overtime and the temps. I authorized them. Wayne assures me that it's all just, you know, *temporary*."

"Well, all of this is starting to affect our cash flow! Our cash reserves are down and our receivables are slowing. Our accounts payables are through the roof!"

"Through the roof?"

"As in rising! It's not a good trend, believe me! And then on top of everything else, we've got all the costs for Wayne's program – the training costs, the travel costs, and so on."

"Now, Elaine," Amy said, deliberately lowering her voice and slipping into her soothing tone, "we've been through all this. And as I have explained, we are in the midst of a turnaround."

"Turnaround? I would hardly characterize what I am seeing as that. A turnaround implies that there has been a turn in performance. Yet there has been no turn in all these months. We are still headed downhill and the pace is accelerating."

"What I mean," said Amy, "is that we are making some big changes at Oakton and also at Rockville – changes for the better. Did we not agree months ago that Lean Six Sigma would in the short run raise costs slightly as we made improvements for long-term gains?"

"We are no longer talking 'slight,' " said Elaine. "I don't think you realize this, but if this trend continues, I am soon going to have to tap our reserve credit lines in order to meet payroll and pay our vendors."

Amy blinked.

"That's not good," said Elaine.

"You're right. That's not good. I didn't know it had gone so far."

"I was awake half the night thinking about it!" Elaine claimed.

"That's not good either," said Amy.

"And as for Rockville," Elaine said as they concluded, "that business is in somewhat better shape, but you also cannot say that F&D has improved to any measurable degree."

Amy grimaced. Then she said, "Elaine, I will get on top of this. Thank you. I appreciate the early warning."

She stood and escorted Elaine toward the door, then went back to her desk and reviewed the pages of numbers one more time. She next brought up the WING reports on her computer.

What was especially odd, she thought, was that WING was showing marked improvements in the metrics. At Oakton, resource utilization was the highest it had ever been. Nearly all workstations throughout the plant were reporting higher productivity. Most were running at over 90 percent of capacity, and many were producing at close to 100 percent. Yet the productivity was not translating into *profitability*. How could that be?

"Linda!"

"Yes?" said her assistant.

"Would you please check Wayne Reese's schedule. I need a meeting with him today!"

"Wayne has canceled all his meetings. He's out of the office again."

"Well, where is he?"

"Where he usually is these days. He's at Oakton."

Amy thought about this, then about her own schedule for the day.

"Linda, cancel my eleven o'clock, and send a text message to Wayne telling him I plan to stop by at Oakton around eleven thirty. I think maybe I should see what's going on out there."

Wayne Reese received his boss's text message announcing her midday visit as he was on his way down the main aisle of the Oakton plant in search of Kurt Konani to talk about yet another "issue," as Kurt described it.

"Oh, *pissa!*" Wayne muttered, reverting to the slang of his youth. "Just what we need!"

He thumbed a quick acknowledgment in reply and continued, finally locating Kurt in Laminating. Kurt was pacing next to a machine that was joining and fusing together three sheets of material at what seemed like a agonizingly slow rate of speed.

"*Now* what's wrong?" Wayne asked him.

"They're short on sheets," said Kurt.

"Short?"

"As in not enough. We're seventy-seven sheets short."

Just then a finished sheet of material exited the rear of the fuser machine and into the gloved hands of a worker, who spread it carefully on the shelf of a curing rack.

"Now we're seventy-*six* sheets short," said Kurt.

"Why is this a problem? And what are you doing out here? Can't you just let *them* – the plant workers – deal with it?"

"I came out to see for myself, because there have been so many complaints," said Kurt. "Look, Wayne, I hate to say this, but I think we may have to rebalance the line."

Wayne put his hands on his hips and in a demanding tone asked, "Why?"

"Because we keep getting these . . . I don't know what the word is. These *glitches*, and they never seem to pop up in the same place. Last week, it was the M57 Line. The week before it was in Coatings. This week it's in Laminating. You know what it's like? It's like that arcade game, Whac-A-Mole. You know the one? The mole pops up out of a hole on the panel and you whack it with a hammer and it disappears, but then a second later it pops up from a *different* hole. So you keep whackin' and whackin' but the moles keep popping up."

Wayne rolled his eyes and said, "*Whac-A-Mole?* Kurt . . . I don't think Whac-A-Mole is in the Lean lexicon."

"I'm just using an analogy!"

"Let's stick with logic," Wayne insisted. "Let's stick with data."

"The data tell us that we do not have smooth flow through the plant."

"And why is that? I'll tell you: variation. That is the core issue. Fluctuation, deviation beyond tolerances, excess change – however you want to say it, that's the root of the problem. *Not* Whac-A-Mole."

"All right, forget I mentioned it! But that's what it seems like."

"The solution is to keep applying Six Sigma to eliminate the variation," said Wayne.

"But that's going to take years," said Kurt, "and meanwhile, we've got all these moles popping up."

Just then, Murphy Maguire came from around a corner and headed directly for them. There was heat in his eyes.

"Excuse me, gentlemen, but are you aware that Godzilla has been idle for the past forty-five minutes?"

Kurt turned to the worker and asked, "How many more?"

"Sixty-two."

"You heard her," said Kurt. "They're waiting on these last sheets."

"*Why* are we waiting?" asked Wayne.

"They're waiting because there are not enough pieces to fill the customer's order," said Kurt. "And this order requires one of those low pressure, special atmosphere soaks in the autoclave. So the whole batch has to go in at the same time. Once the door on Godzilla is closed and locked down, it can't be opened again to put a few more in."

The frustration showed in Wayne's face, and he said, "We are supposed to be guided by Lean principles now! We are supposed to be moving toward one-piece flow! Why are we still talking about *batches?*"

"Because the nature of the autoclave process requires a batch," said Murphy. "As Kurt was saying, once the door on Godzilla is shut, it has to stay shut until the process is completed – times ranging from three-quarters of one hour to twenty-three-point-five hours, depending upon the specification. With the current technology, that is the reality."

"There has to be a better way," said Wayne.

"Sir, while we are standing here discussing that better way, the fact remains that Godzilla is *waiting* to be loaded," said Murphy. "And because you have reduced the work staff dedicated to Autoclave, every load and unload takes *longer.*"

"Maguire, we have balanced all work staff throughout the plant to takt time," said Wayne. "You had people standing around doing nothing, and that was waste that we have eliminated."

"To what gain, sir?" asked Murphy.

"How can you not understand this?" asked Wayne. "People waiting for something productive to do is *waste*. And waste is the enemy!"

"Murph, you approved the staff changes," said Kurt, attempting to intercede. "Don't you remember?"

"As I recall, I said I agreed to give it a try; I did not necessarily agree that the changes would work," said Murphy. "What I would emphasize is that I would much rather have a few workers waiting than to have Godzilla waiting."

Wayne was now about to blow a fuse.

"I would very much appreciate it, Maguire, if you would give up this obsession with the so-called Godzilla," said Wayne. "It is *one* piece of equipment. One process out of many processes. Start thinking about the performance of the entire *system*."

"I *do* think about the performance of the entire system!" Murphy insisted.

"This plant is going to run to takt time, with every resource balanced to customer demand," Wayne insisted. "That is our objective, and we will reach it!"

Not wanting to provoke Wayne Reese further, Murphy – who was quite angry himself by now – held up his hands in surrender and walked away.

As soon as Murphy was out of earshot, Wayne turned to Kurt and quietly said, "He is the problem."

"Why?" asked Kurt. "You think he's sabotaging the program?"

"No, I wouldn't go that far," Wayne admitted. "He's just set in his ways. Lean Six Sigma is a new way, and he is never going to accept it."

"I don't know," said Kurt. "He's been running the plant a long time. You've got to give him his due."

"You just hit the nail on the head. He's been here a long time. I think it's been *too* long," said Wayne.

Just then the fusing machine shut down, and the soft whine it had been making went silent.

"What's wrong?" Kurt asked in alarm. "It didn't break, did it?"

"No," said the woman tending the fuser. "We're done here. Y'all got your full batch now."

She began to walk away, leaving the curing rack where it was.

"Wait! Aren't you going to move it?" asked Wayne.

"I'm not allowed," she said.

"She's right," Kurt said to Wayne. "A class-two materials handler has to move it. It's a safety rule."

"So where *is* the materials handler?" Wayne asked in exasperation. "Hey, excuse me, can you get us this class-two mat handler?"

The woman stood on her tiptoes and looked around, then cupped her hands around her mouth and yelled:

"Hey, Jeeter! Git your ass over here and move this rack!"

"I'm busy!" Jeeter yelled back.

"I sa-yid, git over here!" the woman responded. "The 'Zilla is waiting!"

And Jeeter, as if magic words had been spoken, stopped what he was doing and came right over to move the rack.

When Amy arrived at Oakton around 11:30 a.m., she swapped her stylish Italian heels for black safety shoes, took her safety glasses, and headed for the plant. The guard at the receiving desk was on the lookout for her, and he called Wayne Reese. But rather than wait for him, Amy simply thanked the guard, said she would meet Wayne

inside, and walked onto the plant floor – and the guard, of course,
knowing who she was, had no authority to stop her.

From the customer tours over the years, she had a general knowledge of the layout, and she strolled down the main aisle at first with a sense of familiarity. But then she noticed that a lot of things were different from what she remembered. The organization now seemed less segmented, less "departmental." It was clear, as she looked around, that different areas were performing different functions, but the dividers between them were less exact.

On the actual floor, there were the dark outlines, like dirty shadows, of where some of the machines had been before they were moved, and the holes where the bolts fastening them to the concrete had been. Now a number of the machines were arranged in groups – "work cells," she remembered Wayne calling these – so that one or more workers could perform a series of tasks in one place, rather than physically move product material from one department to another. This was a move toward the Lean ideal of one-piece flow, in which – ideally – there would be virtually continuous movement and processing of material, with comparatively little time spent sitting or waiting. And the rate of processing and movement would be set to takt time and – again, ideally – the rates of consumption by each customer along the value stream from raw material to the ultimate buyer.

But Amy, as she walked along, also began to notice what Elaine had been warning about. There were racks and multishelved carts and bins on wheels – all filled with unfinished materials, what was known as work-in-process inventory, or WIP. The many and various holding devices laden with WIP were lining the walls and between the groups of work cells. They were arranged in neat, orderly rows, but clearly there was a lot.

Amy wondered what was going on. Huge quantities of work-in-process inventories were exactly what Lean was supposed to eliminate. Yet here was the physical evidence to the contrary right before her.

On the outskirts of Highboro was a warehouse and distribution center that housed finished goods that Hi-T kept in stock – standard items and replacement parts. Remembering the numbers that Elaine had pointed out, Amy could only imagine what that must look like. She envisioned opening the warehouse door and being buried under a deluge of quality, Hi-T parts.

From down the aisle came Wayne, striding along at a crisp pace.

"Good morning!" he called as he closed the distance. "You caught us on a busy day."

"I can see that," said Amy, pivoting in a full circle t... urvey all the activity. "Sure seems like everyone is hard at work."

"That *is* the beauty of takt time. Everybody works a... able, even pace so as to be busy all day, and yet not be comfort- or strained to keep up. Most people really like it; they say essed goes faster when they're busy. So, what brings you to ...e today?"

"A couple of reasons," said Amy. "I haven't been able to stop lately, and I just wanted to see how things were going. But, um, this i... not just a casual visit. I had a meeting with Elaine earlier this morning, and she was very alarmed about the growth of inventories over the past six months. And now that I'm here – I can see why. Wayne, what's with all this inventory?"

Wayne in fact began to turn slightly red.

"Well . . . ! The best I can say is that we're working on it. I can assure you that's not intentional and that it is temporary. In a couple of months at the most we should have the whole thing sorted out."

"But what is the cause? I thought Lean was supposed to *reduce* work-in-process inventory."

"It *is* supposed to reduce the WIP, but . . . there are some things we haven't quite sorted out yet."

"Such as . . . ? "

"This is kind of a delicate topic," said Wayne, "but one of the causes seems to be the WING system that we're mandated to use by Corporate. Based on what my lead Black Belt, Kurt, has been able to learn talking to some of the production people, whenever WING detects that a machine is idle and waiting for something to produce, it triggers a build order, usually for a stock item that can go to the warehouse."

"WING just does this automatically?"

"Yes."

"You mean, it's like the Sorcerer's Apprentice? You turn it on and you can't get it to stop?"

"Pretty much."

"There's no manual override? No off button?" she asked.

"Yes, there are work-arounds, but it's like the software has a mind of its own. It is very determined to keep every resource working one hundred percent of the time."

"Well, wait a minute, I thought Lean Six Sigma was supposed to
do that too – you know, what you just said a few minutes ago. Every-
ne is busy all day, working to takt time."

'The trouble is that WING triggers the build order with only a
loose correlation to customer demand. The assumptions in the
are are based on the old 'push' model."

, I'm familiar with push – the assumption that 'if we build it, it
' " said Amy.

n sure I've explained to you, Lean is based on the opposite.
on a 'pull' model. Nothing is built until and unless a cus-
ts it. Or, on a practical level, only so much is built to fill the
a timely basis. So WING3.2 is actually at odds with Lean
's a constant battle."

just pull the plug?" asked Amy.

ut what we're going to do is implement a newer version
d WING4-L, which incorporates a number of Lean
meantime, we're doing a lot of manual entry, which
and incomplete entries, and all kinds of problems.
ically a little sensitive. WING is enthusiastically
Winn, who just loves the ability to drill down
d find out what's going on."

ery Winner employee is working at a hundred
o what's the solution?"

lled some Lean software plug-ins that should
ush effects of WING3.2," said Wayne. "But
is overriding the *overrides*. The program-
st be some very powerful subroutines bur-
that what Hi-T is using is not a standard
en modified."

my's face.

ikes again," she said.

lecessor. He was forever fiddling with
ld make sense. Because his goal was
etrics. That's probably how he got
in – and, come to think of it, why
iscounting on stock inventory the

e. "Can you ask him where he
e?"

"No, I can't call him. But maybe I can ask one of the Microbursts – his IT staff. A few of them are still around."

"That could be very helpful," said Wayne.

"I'll let you know whatever I can find out," said Amy, then added in conclusion, "Well, I'm glad we figured out where all this inventory is probably coming from. But I should get back downtown. I've got a two o'clock with my new head of sales and marketing."

"I'm glad you stopped by," said Wayne, "but, hey, before you run off, how about a quick tour of some the LSS improvements we've made?"

"Sure, I have time for that, as long as I'm not keeping you from something urgent," said Amy. "And, actually, I *would* like to run by you these numbers that Elaine showed me this morning – just so you know. Is there someplace nearby where we can talk in private?"

"Sure. After I give you the quick tour, there's a little toolroom I'v discovered that nobody uses. Yet another small example of the was in this plant!"

The two of them continued through the plant, with Wayne point out some of the changes that Lean Six Sigma had brought about was in the process of trying to bring about. At one point Amy sto and pointed to an enormous, ugly, cylindrical piece of equipme

"Wait a minute," she said. "Is that Godzilla?"

Wayne frowned.

"Um, yes. *That* is Godzilla."

"I remember it now. I've seen it lots of times. I just didn't l had a nickname."

"Murphy Maguire's favorite obsession," muttered Wayne.

"Why do you say that?"

"Sorry, never mind. This autoclave process is a real hea love to get rid of Godzilla if I could. But . . . we're stuck wit

He led the way through the plant, and they soon arri little toolroom at the end of the corridor that Wayne had

As they approached the toolroom, Amy noticed that in all the chemical and industrial smells throughout the pla detected a smoky, spicy scent, an aroma that was both p enticing. But from the far side of the toolroom door ca and loud voice.

"One full hour! An hour, Jayro! They got Godzilla doin' nothing! That is lost throughput, Jayro. And wh why: they've taken out all the slack! And they think they can handle it with five percent buffers! Five percent? No way is that enough! It's all a bunch o' damnyankee nonsense! Balanced line? Balanced my butt!"

A lower, calmer, but unintelligible voice spoke from behind the door as Amy and Wayne hesitated outside.

"I've tried tellin' him!" the angry voice resumed. "He won't listen!"

Before Amy could stop him, Wayne had set his jaw and was pounding his knuckles on the door.

"What?!" shouted the angry voice.

Wayne turned the knob, as the door swung open, there was Murphy Maguire red-faced and glowering. With him of course was Jayro Pepps, who went slack jawed at the sight of the intruders. And between them was a table laden with a small feast – a black kettle of pulled pork, fluffy white buns, a plate of fried chicken, homemade coleslaw, fresh strawberry pie, and a Thermos jug of cold tea – all nearly untouched as yet given the distress of the moment.

"What the hell is going on in here?" Wayne demanded.

"Lunch!" shouted Murphy. "What's it look like?!"

A brief silence of outrage and fuming ensued. And to fill the silence, an embarrassed Jayro Pepps, whose expression was not unlike a deer caught in the headlights, said to Amy:

"Would you care for a pulled-pork sandwich, Miz Cieolara?"

"Um, no, but thank you. Everything looks and smells very good!"

"I think you have some explaining to do!" Wayne shot at Murphy.

Amy promptly inserted herself between the two, put a hand on Wayne's chest, and pushed him gently back toward the door.

"Excuse us," she said. "We didn't mean to intrude. We'll talk later."

And she steered Wayne Reese out of the toolroom and closed the door behind her.

"You see what I'm up against?" Wayne asked rhetorically as they walked back through the plant.

"Wayne, what is going on between the two of you?" asked Amy.

"The simple answer? I think it's called a turf war – on his part, not mine."

Amy considered this, but then said, "Wayne, he was really angry. What he said sounded to me like more than just a clash of egos."

"To tell you the truth, Amy, I don't know what it is with him, but I'm glad it's out in the open. I've had my doubts about Murphy Maguire for a long time."

"What do you mean by that?"

"I hate to tell you this, but in my opinion, he's part of the problem. He's pretended to go along with LSS. He's done some of the training – and I do give him credit for that. But he just doesn't get it. He's too old school. He's locked in the past. Frankly, I don't think he's ever really going to make the transition to the new culture we need to create."

Amy nodded slowly, but since it was clearly turning into a personnel issue, she made no comment.

"But, Wayne, what about the substance of what he was saying? What was it, something about Godzilla being idle for a full hour today?"

"That was earlier. For some reason, there was a shortage of material, of a specific part, and we had to fill the shortage before proceeding. So, yes, the processing in this big autoclave – Godzilla, a name that I hate – was delayed until we had a full count. I mean, I'm not happy about it. Kurt and I are already making adjustments. But Murphy . . . he's obsessed with this one piece of equipment – as if Godzilla controls the whole plant or something! The whole business, for that matter!"

They had reached the entrance. Amy signed herself out on the guard's clipboard. Then something occurred to her.

"Wayne, we have very high levels of inventory. How could there be a *shortage*?"

"I don't know. It bothers me, too. We just didn't have enough of a certain part for a certain order at a certain time."

Wayne opened the steel door to the outside, and they stepped into the hot midday sun. The heat rolled over them.

"Before I go," said Amy, "let me just ask you, what do you think should be done about Murphy?"

Wayne hesitated, knowing what was at stake and what the consequences might be. Then he spoke his mind.

"I think that Maguire should go. I think he should be moved out – for his sake, as well as the good of the company. He's becoming an obstacle."

"Has he been insubordinate?"

"No – although he came close just now, I thought."

"I want to talk to him," said Amy. "But not today. Let him calm down. I'll call him tomorrow morning."

On the drive back to Highboro, Amy had plenty of time to think about Oakton. The construction zone was more torn up and a bigger delay than it had ever been. But the only conclusion she came to as her BMW sat in traffic gathering a fine powder of dust was that she could make no absolute conclusions.

10

After marrying his third wife, Garth Quincy decided it was time to settle down. He had been a salesman for almost twenty years by then, and he felt as though the vast majority of those years had been spent sleeping at night in places where he did not live – hotels and motels in cities all across North America, South America, Asia, and Europe. The travel demands of his work were certainly a factor in the ruination of his two previous marriages, so when Garth married Fanny, he resolved that this union would be different. So he sought out and won the position of Hi-T's sales manager for the western United States. He made less money as a manager than he had as a salesman, but he slept in his own bed most nights, and beautiful Fanny proceeded to demonstrate her happiness and appreciation by delivering three kids in four years.

Then came the opportunity to fill Amy Cieolara's former position of vice president of marketing and sales. Here, Garth faced a dilemma. On the one hand, he relished the title, the higher salary and benefits, and the job itself. On the other, it had become clear to him and to everyone else selling Hi-T's products and services that since the acquisition by Winner not all was going swimmingly. Something was amiss. The customers were getting grumpy and telling the Hi-T salespeople this, and Garth was hearing the complaints both indirectly and directly. As was Amy. So the question, for Garth, was whether to take the VP position and perhaps help steer the Hi-T ship toward a better course, or whether to jump over the side and swim away before the ship ran aground or sank. He kept these considerations to himself, and during the interviews and discussions, never revealed anything other than complete loyalty.

In the end, after the job was offered, Garth still was not sure what to do. He could not make up his mind. He liked Amy and had worked with her for years. But he knew that she was untried. He was not sure how well she would measure up as Hi-T's president. Yet that factor was small compared to Hi-T's fluttering and flagging reputation in the marketplace.

Ultimately, it was Fanny who swayed him to accept. Most of her family lived in Roanoke, Virginia, which was relatively a stone's throw from Highboro compared to the transcontinental trek from and back to Los Angeles – and with three young kids, two still in diapers. When Garth expressed his doubts to her one evening about a future with Hi-T, Fanny made it abundantly clear to him that this concern was minor. So Garth, wishing to avoid a quest for a fourth wife, called Amy the next morning and accepted the position.

Garth had in fact been born in Roanoke, which was how he and Fanny had first struck up a conversation in an airport terminal waiting for a plane to L.A. But he had spent most of his life on the West Coast and had become completely Californian. He looked it as well. Golden tan. Sandy brown hair with highlights. The body of a surfer, though a few pounds heavier due to age and fine living. A craggy, yet handsome face. Perfect white teeth. Many of the younger women in the Highboro offices were abuzz when Garth arrived. Amy, though she would not deny that he was an attractive man, had far more appreciation for his track record of delivering respectable gains in sales revenue over the years.

His approach to selling focused on simplicity. It relied upon a rather small number of essential tenets, and Garth was fond of rattling these off whenever he needed to sound philosophical.

"Customers always want just a few basic things," as he said to Amy when they met in her office at two o'clock that afternoon. "Customers always want a lower price. They always want perfection not just in the product itself, but in all the details – delivery, packaging, and so on. They want the salesperson to manage all those details and guarantee they'll be handled for them. They want to know the salesperson, and know that this person is dependable, but they don't want to know you too well. And they want the buying experience to be efficient, but they also want it to be a little bit entertaining – you know, they want dealing with you to be enjoyable, fun. It's really not that complicated. And it is the job of the salesperson to facilitate those few, basic things."

Amy was nodding as he went on. She certainly did not disagree with what he was saying.

"Unfortunately," he continued, "this company is making it harder, not easier for our salespeople to do their jobs."

Amy frowned. "Why do you say that?"

"I need to level with you, Amy."

"Sure. Go ahead."

"Ever since Winner took us over, some things have not gotten any better, and some things have gotten worse."

"Such as?"

He used his fingers as if to enumerate and emphasize his points, and his nails were immaculate.

"First, our prices," Garth said. "They've always been a bit high, and that hasn't changed. Second, our lead times have never been very good, and if anything they seem to be getting longer, not shorter. And third, whatever is going on at Oakton is losing us business. I know of two accounts that have completely gone away because Oakton has been screwing up – and I would say there are at least half a dozen others just on the West Coast that are starting to look around."

"I just came from Oakton," said Amy. "They're doing a major implementation of Lean Six Sigma out there, and I firmly believe that LSS is going to resolve all your execution issues."

"How soon?"

"A few more months and you should start to see a noticeable improvement – and it's going to be *continuous* improvement. Quality and everything else will just keep getting better and better. In fact, I think that the sales force should be talking to customers about LSS. Maybe you could have a laptop presentation on Lean Six Sigma put together for the salespeople."

Garth was shaking his head.

"Why not?" asked Amy.

"Because customers don't care about that stuff. They don't care about Lean or Six Sigma or any of the rest of it. They care about the things I just mentioned: Price. Perfection in all aspects of what they're buying. Shorter lead times and more flexibility. Things like that. But they don't care how it happens. In my opinion, LSS belongs at the bottom of page three of the brochure. That's all the mention it deserves."

Amy was becoming somewhat annoyed with him.

"I know a certain admiral in the United States Navy who would disagree with you on that," she said.

"All right, you have me on that one," Garth conceded. "But the average customer? I really don't think they care. The *results*. The *execution*. Working with a salesperson they know and trust who can also put a smile on their faces. That's what they care about. Sorry, but I have to be honest."

"Yes. And please, always be that," she said.

She was quiet for a moment, considering what he had said.

Then she asked him, "Do you really think Oakton is becoming a severe negative for us?"

"Look," said Garth, "as we all know, Hi-T is the world leader in precision, high-performance composite materials. What we can do with, well, what is essentially a piece of plastic is unmatched technically. There are some customers who almost have to deal with us, because we can do things no one else can. But those customers are few in number. The vast majority have other alternatives for suppliers, and those suppliers have excellent facilities in Asia and in Europe, as well as the United States. If Oakton keeps screwing up, and driving away accounts that we've worked years building up . . . well, it doesn't get much more negative than that."

Late in the afternoon, and almost dreading it, Amy called Murphy Maguire.

"Murph, I need to have a meeting with you. How does tomorrow morning around eight o'clock sound?"

Murphy paused and then said, "I think I know what this is about. And let me just say that I do apologize for my outburst earlier today. It will not happen again."

"I appreciate the apology, but I'm afraid there's more to talk about than just that. My office, eight o'clock tomorrow?"

"Yes, I'll be there," he said quietly.

Such was his bitterness and anger over what was happening that Jayro called Murphy that evening on his private number to make sure he was all right.

"No, I am not all right," said Murphy. "Jayro, I cannot abide this. The most foolish thing I have done in recent months has been to pretend to myself that I could just go along. I have too much of my life tied up in that place to stand by while someone ruins it."

"How do you know it's going to be ruined?"

"I don't. But I've got twenty-five years of experience at that plant, plus a gut as big as the great outdoors that tells me we should be nervous, not confident."

"These folks seem to know their stuff, Murph. They got spreadsheets and data and formulas. Wayne and Kurt, and everyone else, they sure look like they know what to do. And there are a lot of people who are on board. They – and I am one of them – really would like for this to succeed."

"That stings me, Jayro. I'd have thought that you, of all people, would have more common sense."

"Well, no offense, Murph, but Lean Six Sigma appears to be the wave of the future."

"Then you go ahead and ride that wave, Jayro. Because I cannot."

The next morning at seven thirty, when Amy Cieolara arrived at the offices downtown, Murphy Maguire was waiting for her. Dismayed to see him there, Amy stopped in her tracks.

"You're early," she said.

"Well, I hardly slept at all last night," he said. "And if it's convenient for you, I'd prefer to get this over with as soon as possible."

"I'm not going to fire you," she said, "if that's what you're worried about."

She took a key ring from her purse and unlocked her office.

"Come in," she said.

Murphy took a seat in front of her desk. She noted that his blue eyes were indeed tinged with red, as if he'd had a bad night. She settled herself behind her desk.

"Now, what I want to know most of all is what is going on between you and Wayne Reese?" Amy asked. "Why are you two so angry with each other?"

"I would say that we have a professional difference of opinion," said Murphy. "Wayne is absolutely committed to Lean Six Sigma. And I abide by what is known as the Theory of Constraints or TOC."

"Theory of Constraints?"

"Yes, ma'am."

"What's that?"

"To give you the briefest possible explanation, the Theory of Constraints holds that every system – in our case, a business system, or at Oakton, a manufacturing system – is made up of resources that each have varying limits. Performance of the total system is constrained by whatever resource is the most limited. We sometimes refer to that resource, the one with the tightest constraints, as the bottleneck of the system. Therefore, the most efficient way to manage the entire system is to optimize the flow by maximizing processing at the bottleneck and making all other resources subservient to the needs of the bottleneck in terms of their own processing. Do you follow me?"

"No," said Amy. "I haven't the foggiest notion of what you just said."

Murphy sighed. "Well . . ."

"Just tell me this," said Amy. "Why are you, with this constraint theory, and Wayne with Lean Six Sigma, why are you at odds with each other?"

"First of all, there is much that we agree upon. Small transfer batches, for instance. And quick changeovers in equipment setups to enable greater flexibility. And, of course, quality and continuous improvement – though I do have to admit that at Oakton, we have become a little complacent about ongoing improvement in recent years," said Murphy.

"But the differences?"

"Yes, there are several, and they are very important. Wayne believes in a balanced production line. I subscribe to an unbalanced line. Wayne's objective is to reduce capacity to exactly whatever is customer demand, and then exploit that capacity to one hundred percent. I accept that extra capacity is very necessary for maximum throughput, and that using more than a few resources at a hundred percent is extremely inefficient. Wayne strives endlessly for perfection. I cope with the reality of endless *im*perfection. Wayne believes that through continuous effort and investment, all meaningful variation can be eliminated. I say, horsefeathers; there will always be some variation, and even if you do succeed in eliminating all variation, by then decades will have passed and you will have exceeded the design life of the technology. But most important, I believe – indeed, I know for a fact – that there must be a primary constraint regulating the entire system. For us, that constraint is Godzilla, the autoclave. And Wayne refuses to acknowledge the supreme importance of keeping Godzilla operating at peak efficiency."

"Okay, wait! Hold on! Time out!" said Amy. She leaned her elbows on her desk blotter and rubbed her temples. "Wow, this is like the Democrats and the Republicans."

"Please, ma'am, I don't think we're *that* bad."

"But clearly you have different philosophies about managing Oakton, as well as the business in general."

"We each subscribe to a philosophy that has much in common purpose with the other, but a few differences that are irreconcilable."

"Seriously? You really think these cannot be reconciled?"

"Not without Mr. Reese accepting some realities at Oakton that I came to terms with years ago. There are actually many things I admire about Wayne, but he is a very stubborn man."

Yeah, well, take a look in the mirror, she thought.

"Let me cut to the chase," said Murphy. "Amy, I have given the matter a great deal of thought. Please understand that I am at heart a team player. But after a lot of soul-searching, I have come to the conclusion that I cannot remain at Oakton. There is a saying, 'Lead, follow, or get out of the way.' No one will let me lead, and I cannot follow, so I have to choose the third alternative."

Amy blinked as she realized that he was in earnest.

"Murph, are you sure? Is this what you want?"

"No, it is not what I want. I am just a few years away from retirement, and I always thought I would retire from Hi-T."

"Do you intend to leave the company?"

"I would prefer not to. If there is anything else, any other position where I could be useful . . ."

Amy pressed her lips together and thought for a moment.

"Why don't you take some time off," Amy then said to him. "Take a few days, whatever. Let me talk this over with Human Resources. Right now, I don't know what, if anything, we can offer. If there is a position or if we could create one for you, it might involve a move down and less money. But *if* we can come up with something, would you be interested?"

"I certainly will give it fair consideration," said Murphy, brightening a bit, clearly relieved that some other position might be an option. "And I do thank you. I'll appreciate anything you can do."

"Well, I appreciate your being forthright," said Amy. "By the way, is there anyone you would recommend as your replacement at Oakton?"

"Jayro Pepps," said Murphy without hesitation. "He is a believer in LSS, and as far as plant operations, he knows as much as I do – almost. And if he ever invites you over for barbeque, be there."

Reactions to Murphy Maguire's decision to leave Oakton were varied and not all were what Amy had expected. When Amy spoke to Wayne Reese later that morning, he at first expressed surprise.

"I didn't think he would just up and quit," said Wayne.

"We're trying to work it out so that he doesn't have to leave the company," said Amy. "But I'm not sure if we can find him anything that's mutually acceptable."

"Well, it's too bad in a way . . . but I think it's really for the best," said Wayne. "You know, we're trying to make big changes, and if he can't wholeheartedly embrace what we're trying to accomplish, then it's a good thing for everyone that he's stepping aside. And I respect him for that. Maguire is actually a very smart guy – just stubborn and set in his ways. I hope he lands on his feet."

"You're sure you don't want to talk to him and get him to reconsider?" asked Amy.

Wayne hesitated.

"No, I'm sure he made the right call," Wayne said.

But when Amy mentioned the matter to Garth Quincy, Garth's reaction was quite different.

"Murph is quitting? Oh, man. That sucks big time."

"Why? Were you friends?" asked Amy.

"No, I hardly know the guy. It's just that Murph was, I've always thought, one of the best people in this company."

"Now, wait a minute!" said Amy. "Just yesterday you were saying that if Oakton doesn't get its act together, it could bring the whole company down. Now Murphy quits and you're upset. Why the change of heart?"

"I never said Murph was the problem! What I *said* was that since Winner took over, Oakton hasn't been the same! I didn't mean that it was Murphy's fault. Over the years, in my opinion, he's been dependable. It's just that in the last few, especially this past year, things have been slipping. If that's because of him, then I'm glad he's out. If not . . . well, I hope you get somebody good in there."

"Mom, I need my baseball uniform."

"Ben, you've got two of them. Where are they?"

"They're in the laundry."

"Both of them?"

"Yeah, and it's Michelle's week."

Amy sighed. It was Saturday and she was at the kitchen table working on her laptop, reading the latest figures on shipments, which were showing no improvement.

"Did you ask your sister nicely to wash at least one of them right away?"

"Yeah, and she told me, too bad, she's washing delicates."

Amy got to her feet and started for the basement stairs.

"You know," she said to Ben over her shoulder, "I bought you the second uniform so we wouldn't have this problem."

The idea met with enthusiasm.

"Okay, great," said Amy. "I'll call in the pizza order, but while we're waiting for delivery, I want us all to play this little game together."

"What kind of game?" asked Michelle.

"I learned it in the Marines," said Tom. "It's a dice game."

"Marines. Dice. I might have known," said Amy.

"Well, it's not craps, if that's what you're thinking," said Tom. "Anyway, I need a few things."

Amy scrounged up everything that Tom asked for – a dozen dice from various board games, a big jar of pennies, and a tablet of paper and a pen for keeping score.

The six of them sat around the dining room table. Tom was at one head of the table. To his right were Ben and Michelle. Amy sat at the far end of the table. Then to her right sat Harry and Zelda. Tom explained the rules.

"The idea of the game is to move pennies from one person to the next, starting from my end all around the table. We're going to play the game two ways. The first way, each of us will have one die to roll, and we all roll together. Whatever number turns up – from one to six – determines how many pennies you can move from your position to the person on your right. Any questions?"

"Yes," said Harry, raising his hand. "Where are we? Have I been here before?"

Zelda and Amy made the explanations, then Tom resumed.

"All of you start with four pennies. I am the bank, with the jar of pennies. Whatever I roll, I move that many pennies to Ben. And whatever Ben rolls allows him to move that number of pennies to Michelle – and so on around the table to Grandma Zelda."

"So in manufacturing terms," said Amy, "you would be raw materials inventory, the one who gates materials into the system."

"Right," said Tom. "Now if you want to think of this as a game, we're all on the same team. Either all of us win or none of us win. There are no points for individual achievement. In order to win, we as a team have to get the expected number of pennies around the table and past Grandma Zelda, at which point they are through the system."

"Finished goods," said Amy.

"So how many pennies do you think the system – the six of us – can process in one turn?" asked Tom.

"An average amount," said Ben.

Tom smiled, and said, "That's right! An average number. And what would that number be?"

"Three," said Zelda.

"Well, not quite," said Tom, "because if you add the numbers one, two, three, four, five and six, the total is twenty-one. Divide by six to get the average, and –"

"Three-point-five. That's the average," said Ben.

"Right! But you can't have half a penny, can you?"

"No," said Amy, "but over time, you'd expect the system to deliver three to four pennies per turn."

"That's what you would expect?" asked Tom. "You'd bet your career on that?"

"I think you're setting me up," said Amy. "But sure. Why not?"

"Each round has twenty turns, to simulate a month with a five-day work week. So the *expectation* would be a total of how many pennies per month?" he asked.

"Seventy," said Amy.

"Yes, three-point-five times twenty equals seventy," said Tom. "But, hey, let's cut ourselves some slack. Let's say our target is sixty-five."

"No, I think if we all try hard, we can do seventy," Amy joked. "We just need to blow on the dice once in a while for luck."

"Okay! She's the boss! Seventy is the target," said Tom. "Now remember, what we're simulating here is a balanced system – a balanced processing line. We each have one die, even me. So we each have exactly the same capacity. It's a level playing field, just like Lean says you should have."

"Okay," said Amy. "Let's go."

"One last thing. Everybody, except me, starts with four pennies each on the table. I am the penny vendor, so I have lots of pennies. We all roll dice at the same time, and you can only move the number of pennies that your die rolls – *if you have them*. So if Ben rolls a three, that allows him to move three pennies to Michelle *if* he has them in front of him to move. Let's say that during the game he only has two pennies and he rolls a four, then he can only move two, because that's all he's got. And it's the same for everyone else. Are we ready? Everybody roll . . ."

The dice chattered on the tabletop.

Tom rolled a four, Ben rolled a two, Michelle a three, Amy two, Harry four, and Zelda two. That meant Tom took four pennies from the jar and moved them to Ben; Ben moved two and was left with six pennies (four from Tom, and two left over from his original queue). And so on around the table.

On the first turn, they moved two pennies across the finish line – Zelda, having rolled a two, was only able to move two pennies of her four-penny inventory. But on the second turn, Zelda rolled a six. And she had six to move, because – with Amy helping her dad – she had received four from Harry on the previous turn.

"Come on! Roll those sixes!" Amy squawked.

They joked back and forth with each other. Ones were booed; sixes were cheered – and there were groans when the high rolls were for naught because the pennies in queue were less than the number rolled.

"All right! A six!" called Amy on the first turn of Week Three.

"Boxcar!" said her dad.

"Ah, nuts. I only have two," Amy said, moving her two cents over.

Tom kept a tally on the pad of paper. In the first week, they "finished" fifteen pennies. The second week, sixteen. But the third week, only twelve. And in the fourth week of the month, also only twelve pennies. The grand total for the month: fifty-five cents.

"Not exactly the seventy cents you were targeting for the month," said Tom. "It's not even the easier target of sixty-five."

"If we played it again, couldn't the average improve?" asked Amy.

"In the Marines, we played this multiple rounds," said Tom, "and let me tell you, fifty-five for the balanced system model is pretty good. Most rounds, we ended in the forties. I think one time my team did hit sixty, but we never once made the target. And did you notice what happened with the inventory?"

"The work-in-process? The pennies in process? The number grew," said Amy.

Indeed, at one point in the third week, Ben had eighteen pennies in front of him. And it was not uncommon toward the end of the game month for there to be a dozen or more pennies waiting in queue in front of one or more of them around the table.

"We started with twenty pennies on the table," said Tom, "and we ended the month with more than double that number – forty-six."

"True, but this is not really a Lean model with pull-through inventory," said Amy.

"No, it's not. On the other hand it *is* a balanced system, and you can see the tendency of a balanced line when you have variability in combination with dependency."

"Dependency? What does that mean?" asked Zelda.

"One thing depends on another having happened," said Amy. "For one event to occur, a prior event has to have occurred. In order for the kids to be allowed to watch TV, they first have to have finished their homework."

"And then there is interdependency," said, of all people, Harry, chiming in. "Two or more conditions dependent on each other."

"Right, Dad!" said Amy.

"Where are we again?"

His daughter patted him on the shoulder, saying, "You know, Dad, parts of your mind are still sharp."

"And other parts," Harry muttered, "not so good . . ."

"That's the way the disease is," said Zelda.

"Let's do one more round," said Tom. "But this time we're going to run an *un*balanced system, rather than a balanced one. We will unbalance the line by adding a constraint."

"This sounds weird," said Michelle. "Why would you do that?"

"Just because it's Saturday night and we want to be wild and crazy," said Tom. "Now, the way we're going to unbalance the process line is everyone will now have two dice, but your mom will only have one die. So she will be the constraint. She will have half the processing capacity of each of the rest of you."

Amy stuck out her lower lip and pouted.

"That means the least she can process will be one penny, and at the most six pennies. But the rest of us, including me as penny vendor, can move anywhere from one to twelve pennies. What do you think is going to happen? Will we move more pennies or fewer pennies than before? Will we do better than sixty-five? Seventy?"

"Less," said Zelda. "Because Amy will be holding everything up."

"I think it'll be about the same as the first round," said Ben.

"All right, let's see," said Tom as he finished passing out pennies and dice. "Now, all of you start with the same four pennies as before. Are you ready?"

The dice again chattered on the dining room table. The pennies were slid from person to person. And in the first game week, they moved a total of twenty pennies across the finish line. In the second week, they moved a mere thirteen, due mostly to Amy's lower-than-average rolls as the constraint. All five turns, she never rolled higher than a three with her one die. But in the third week, the unbalanced line processed nineteen pennies. In the fourth week: a fabulous twenty-one cents. These made for a grand total of eighty-three pennies – handily beating the lean, level balanced line.

As expected, the pennies in process had soon backed up in front of Amy. By the end of the fourth week, there were forty-two pennies in queue in front of her. But once through the constraint, the pennies had flowed quickly to and across the finish line.

"Wow. That's very different from what I expected," said Amy. "I really thought the best that we would be able to do would be to equal the balanced line. Because the most I could roll was the same as before."

"That's true," said Tom, "but you always had plenty to process. The inventory came to you quickly and was moved to the finish line quickly."

"Right, although of course it took twice the capacity, which in the real world costs a lot more than dice," said Amy, "and look at the work-in-process!"

"Yes, the WIP at the end of the month was . . . sixty-three pennies," said Tom, checking the tally. "With the balanced line, WIP was in forties, or double the starting WIP. The constrained line tripled the WIP by the end of the month. *But* your throughput more than met the target."

"So assuming all the pennies went to market and were sold," said Amy, "we probably made a good profit."

"We made a pretty penny then!" said Zelda.

The kids groaned.

"If you're up for playing a third round," said Tom, "I can show you how you can keep the system constraint, get good throughput, *and* have low work-in-process inventory. What we need is a signal –"

At that moment, the doorbell rang.

"For pizza!" shouted Ben, leaping out of his seat.

"I'm getting it!" yelled Michelle, running after him.

"I'm buying," said Zelda, motioning her daughter to stay seated as she got up to get her purse.

Tom looked down the table at Amy and said, "Well, I guess the game is over. We lost half our workforce."

"But thanks," Amy said to him. "That was enlightening."

"So have you punched out from work?" he asked. "Are we going to have some fun tonight?"

"I hope so."

The pizzas – Amy had ordered two – were devoured. Harry raved that he couldn't remember ever having pizza so good, and he alone consumed four pieces and would have had more if Zelda had not pushed the pizza box out of reach. Twenty minutes later, Harry was in the bathroom, sick.

"I'd better get him home," said Zelda. "I'm sorry."

With Tom in his Mustang as a chase car, Amy drove the big Ford to her parents' house and helped her mother settle Harry in for the night. She rode back with Tom. But that blew their plans for the evening, because now there was no one to stay with Amy's kids.

"Aren't they old enough to stay home by themselves?" asked Tom.

"I just don't feel comfortable with that," Amy told him. "How about watching a movie in the living room?"

"Fine," he said without much enthusiasm.

She let him pick it, thinking that would pacify him. But halfway through, in the middle of the car chase with orange explosions on the screen lighting the room, Tom looked at her face and observed that Amy had drifted off – not to sleep, which had often been the case before, but to somewhere else, away from him. He pressed the pause button on the remote.

"What?" she asked, snapping back.

"Are you at work again?" he asked with disgust.

"Well . . . I just thinking about the dice game. I'm going to question Wayne about the constraint idea on Monday, and I was just thinking about the best way to do that."

Tom got to his feet.

"Where are you going?" she asked.

"Home," he said calmly. "No, on second thought, I'm going to a little place I know, maybe bump into some old friends who like to have fun and will actually be in the same room with me when I talk to them. Good night."

And Amy sat there stunned as he walked out the door.

"Tom!" she called.

By the time she got to the front porch, he was in the car. He made a somewhat noisy departure down the street, and was gone.

It had been their first real fight. It would not be their last.

On Monday, Amy did her best. She showed Wayne Reese the tally sheets from the two rounds of the dice game on Saturday night, one round with the balanced line and the other round with the constraint installed. She tried to explain what the results seemed to prove. But Wayne was unmoved.

"First of all – dice?" he asked. "A one-to-six variation? That's *high* variability, Amy. What we're striving for is *no* variability. Zero. Or a very small amount – not anything like what a roll of the dice would suggest. We want dice that always roll the same number."

"Yes, but is that achievable?" asked Amy.

"We're working on it."

"Is it achievable this year?"

Wayne looked at her as if she had asked for the moon.

"No, of course not! But look at what we have been able to do," he said. "Look at the M57 Line! Simply by reconfiguring the M57 Line we have been able to achieve a twelve percent reduction in cost and a *twenty* percent increase in throughput! And you can take that to the bank!"

"Can I?"

"Well, I didn't mean literally," he said.

"You say there's a twenty percent increase in throughput? Why am I not seeing a twenty percent increase on the bottom line?"

"Because we have more work to do!" Wayne protested. "Our next target is going to be Final Prep, then probably Coatings, then Packaging and Shipping. I mean, we can't do everything at once!"

"All right," Amy said. "But you think we will have a significant improvement – with clear financial gains – later this year?"

"Yes, absolutely, I believe we will. I mean, it's not entirely up to me or Oakton, but if the sales are there to support it, I think we're going to have a blow-out fourth quarter. We'll be capable of it anyway."

"Really?" asked Amy. "Well, just the same, maybe I should throw out a few words of caution to Nigel."

Wayne shook his head.

"Of course, it's your call," he told her, "but if I know Nigel, he's not going to take kindly to your backing off. If he gets impatient and demands rigid cost controls, it might even jeopardize some of the progress we're making on keeping the line balanced."

Amy sighed and pressed her lips together as she felt the stress weigh on her.

"I'll think about it," she said. "But one more thing. Since we currently don't have dice that always roll the same numbers, and there is variability, and there is interdependency and all of that – what about the need for a system constraint?"

"A *system* constraint?"

"Yes, like my, um, friend, Tom, says has to be there?"

For a second, Wayne was working to cover his amusement. *Her, um, friend. Tom. The flyboy.* Like he would know anything about manufacturing high-tech composite materials. Then Wayne sat back.

"Amy, you can relax. We've already thought of that. We've got it covered."

"You do?"

"Yes, we're going to be establishing a pacemaker on the M57 Line."

"A pacemaker? What's that?"

"It's the same thing as a system constraint. That is, it accomplishes the same purpose. A pacemaker process does what it sounds like – it sets the pace for the entire value stream. It's a single scheduling point for the entire system. Every piece of inventory above the pacemaker is pulled to it. Everything below in the value stream flows in a nice, smooth, level manner."

Amy began to nod in agreement as she visualized what Wayne was talking about. Then a question came to mind.

"Why the M57 Line? Why should that determine scheduling? And anyway, I thought you were done with the M57," she said.

"Kurt and I have had a lot of discussion on this. There is some question on where to locate the pacemaker. For made-to-stock products, typically you would want it more downstream, like in Final, where everything comes together. But for a portion of what we produce, there is no assembly; it's one piece. That stuff comes out of the autoclave and goes to Coatings or even straight to Packaging."

"Right, I'm with you," said Amy.

"So Final didn't make sense. And anyway, most of our profit and even the majority of our volume comes from made-to-order, custom-designed products. In that case, you want the pacemaker upstream where the final specification is set. Therefore, to me, the M57 makes the most sense. That way we won't overwhelm the system – and unbalance the line – with the efficiency gains we've achieved on the M57."

"You mentioned the autoclave," said Amy. "If I recall correctly, Murphy Maguire was telling me that Godzilla was the system constraint. Like, you know, a *real* bottleneck?"

This clearly touched a raw nerve inside Wayne.

"Look, Amy, we are designing Oakton for the future, not for the past. The autoclave – and I prefer to call it by its correct name, the AC-1240 – is so problematic in terms of Lean production that at some point it's going to have to be replaced. Why should I let a batch-oriented piece of junk that's going to be replaced dictate our takt time? We cannot allow our entire product flow to be set by yesterday's technology and yesterday's thinking!"

As she listened to this, Amy in fact did begin to relax. Clearly Wayne Reese knew what he was doing, she thought to herself. She decided she should continue to give him a free hand.

"All right," she said. "I'm going to let you handle it."

"Amy, I think we have accomplished an awful lot at Oakton in a relatively short period of time," Wayne said in conclusion.

"Yes, you've worked hard, and I don't in any way mean to question your sincerity or your integrity," said Amy. "It's just that there is a lot riding on this – for me professionally, and for everyone in the company. You *have* to come through, Wayne."

"Understood. Look, I meant what I said earlier. I truly believe that by the fourth quarter, Oakton will be capable of delivering whatever Garth Quincy and the salespeople can bring in. We just have to let the Lean techniques run, keep Six Sigma in there reducing variability, and stay the course. Something this good has to pay off."

That same Monday, Amy sat down briefly with Garth Quincy in his office.

"Wayne just told me a little while ago," said Amy, "that he firmly believes that Oakton will have most of its issues resolved toward the end of the year. He thinks we'll be capable of delivering what he called 'a blow-out' fourth quarter."

"No kidding?" asked Garth.

"That's what he said. So my question to you is, will the sales be there to make it happen?"

Garth interlaced the fingers of his salon-tanned hands and put them behind his golden head as he thought.

"Well, the fourth quarter, as you know, is historically our best time of the year, for various reasons," he said. "So . . . yeah, it's possible. If Reese and Oakton are sure they can deliver, I can throw together some incentives, and we can do a beat-the-bushes campaign to rev things up. What about Rockville? Is F&D on board? Because, you know, they have to review the designs of anything non-stock."

"I have a call scheduled for tomorrow morning with Viktor Kyzanski," said Amy. "I'll be sure that he's alerted."

"All rightie then," said Garth. "I'll get my team on it. But Reese had better come through for us."

As soon as Amy returned to her own office, Linda brought in a long white box tied with ribbon and a crisp red bow.

"They just arrived!" Linda chirped. "Looks like somebody likes you!"

Amy's fingers pulled off the ribbon, and she opened the box to find a dozen long-stemmed roses inside. Roses, in fact, were not her favorite – she loved gladiolas, and was charmed by the simplicity of daisies – but he didn't know that yet. These roses were fresh and beautiful, and most certainly expensive.

Linda cooed over them and then went to get a vase. Amy opened the little envelope with the card. The message was almost blunt:

> Sorry,
>   T. D.

Well, she thought, it does at least mean that he cares. She picked up the phone and called him.

"Dawson here."

"I'm sorry too," she said.

There was a long pause.

"All right," he said, "we're both sorry. Do you want to try again?"

"Do you?"

"Well, I wouldn't have sent you the roses if I didn't."

She smiled. *Spoken like a true man*, she thought.

"This time," she said, "I will not talk to you about business when we're together."

"Hey, I don't mind if it's once in a while. Some of it is interesting," he said. "It's just that there's a time and a place for everything."

"I agree," said Amy. "I absolutely agree. Sometimes it's hard to find the right balance."

On Tuesday morning Viktor Kyzanski called from Rockville.

"Amy, it's Viktor. Listen, before we get into everything else, I want my factory back."

"Your . . . factory?"

"Right. The little factory that Random Tornado, in his infinite wisdom, did away with. You know what I'm talking about, don't you? That factory we owned over in Virginia, near Dulles. We used it for all kinds of things, small-lot classified work, single-piece projects – and more important, we used it to build prototypes and to test manufacturability. It was very handy, and if a problem came up, we could scoot right over there and have a look. I mean, it was like our own, private Skunkworks."

Amy dredged her memory. "Excuse me, but *Skunkworks*?"

"It was a sort of factory-within-a-factory that Lockheed set up to build advanced aircraft."

"Oh," she said. "Yes, go on."

"Well, *now*, post Tornado, having found that we just can't get any cooperation out of Highboro or Oakton, my people have resorted to using outside suppliers for prototypes and testing. And it is damned expensive, plus there are often proprietary and security concerns, not to mention delays and the inefficiencies of dealing with vendors who are hundreds or sometimes thousands of miles away. Seriously, Amy, I'm having to put my analysts and engineers on airplanes, causing them to lose days, whereas if we had a place nearby, they could resolve everything in a few hours. So I want my factory back."

"Viktor, I don't disagree with you on this, but who's going to pay for it? There is no money in this year's budget for building a new factory – even a small one."

"Can't we go to Winner for funding?"

"We can, but I know they won't give it to us."

"Why not?"

"Because their own manager – Randal – was the one who closed the Dulles shop! Nigel Furst is not going to take kindly to investing in a new mini-plant to replace the one that was shut down just a couple of years ago. No way."

"Well, something has to be done, because we are getting serious push-back from clients about the costs, and the lost time, and all their other concerns, which are legitimate," Viktor insisted.

"I understand what you're telling me. But the facility that you're talking about is out of the question. We're going to have to come up with some other solution."

Viktor was barely listening. He rambled on with his complaints.

"Don't you find it ironic that you have this Lean Six Sigma program going on that is supposed to eliminate waste – and we have a real problem that is extremely wasteful in any number of ways! Why can't we solve this?"

That was when the idea popped into Amy's mind.

"Maybe we can. I just thought of something," she said. "Let me do some checking and call you back."

Two weeks later everything had been worked out. With the approval of Human Resources, Murphy Maguire took a new position called Manufacturing Liaison. He would be assigned to Formulation & Design in Rockville, and would be on their payroll – at a 20 percent cut in pay – but would split his time between there and North Carolina. His responsibilities were to coordinate anything F&D and its clients needed with respect to manufacturing at Oakton, and also to serve as a kind of internal consultant on all things manufacturing related. In particular, one of his major objectives was to reduce the professional time and expense associated with building prototypes. Longer term, he was to come up with a feasibility plan to determine whether a new mini-plant, like the one that had existed near Dulles, was a cost-efficient option – or if not, then to come up with alternatives.

At first, Viktor Kyzanski vociferously resisted this arrangement – Viktor wanted *his* factory. Amy finally convinced him that he was not going to get it, and Viktor relented.

To replace Murphy at Oakton, Kurt Konani was named production manager. Jayro Pepps was closely considered for the position, but Wayne argued that at this crucial time he needed someone fully imbued in Lean and Six Sigma. Jayro was only an LSS Green Belt. Amy agreed to give Wayne what he wanted, on condition that once Kurt had moved on – as presumably he would once the Lean cultural change was in place – Jayro would be first in line to replace him.

Jayro, for his part, was fine with this. He quietly let it be known that he was not sure he really wanted to run Oakton. Not now at least.

"Some little feelin' I got," Jayro said under his breath.

Amy was pleased with herself in arranging the whole thing. From her point of view, moving Murphy to Rockville was win-win all around. Murphy's experience was bound to be of value to F&D. The move would let Murphy stay within Hi-T probably until retirement without losing much, and he would keep all his benefits. Moreover, the new position was a means of moving Murph out of Wayne's way, but still keep him a phone call away – just in case.

She asked Murphy to sit down with her for what was in effect an exit interview, although the move was a transfer, not a termination. When Murphy's stocky frame filled her doorway on the appointed day, she sat him down and looked at his broad face and his receding silver-gray hair, and then decided his face had more color and his blue eyes were much cheerier than they had been. When she commented tactfully on this, he said that he had been sleeping better of late.

They talked about things, and then Amy said to Murphy, "I just have one more question. Not to open old wounds, but the system constraint at Oakton. You say it's the autoclave, Godzilla."

"Yes, ma'am, it is."

"Wayne says that he is setting the M57 Line to be the system constraint."

"No way," said Murphy. "It won't work."

"But he's establishing the M57 Line as being what he called 'the pacemaker process.' "

"I do not understand Lean as completely as Wayne Reese. Heck, I don't even advocate Lean necessarily. But a system constraint and a pacemaker process are not the same."

"They're not?"

"No, though I believe they are often confused with each other. A system constraint, managed properly, functions very well given ample reserve capacity both upstream and down. A pacemaker attempts a similar function, but does so with everything quote-unquote 'leveled' – the balanced line. When real-world variability enters the equation, you've got problems."

"Like what kind of problems?" asked Amy.

"The pacemaker process is still ticking along, trying to act like a clock, like everything else will also behave like a clock. But if any of the little clocks get out of synch with the big clock – the central clock, the pacemaker – they do not have the *juice* to run faster."

"Why not?"

"Because Wayne *leaned* them. He trimmed the mainspring on every clock. They can only tick so fast. He's balanced the line, but that means everything has to run perfectly at close to one hundred percent. So he's tightened the capacity of every resource. He did it in the name of eliminating waste. But you know what happens when you do that, don't you?"

"I don't know, Murph. Tell me."

"You end up with the potential for any resource to become a bottleneck."

"How so? I'm trying to understand here, but . . ."

"With a system constraint, you have *one* bottleneck – a primary constraint – and you know where it is. With a balanced line, even with a pacemaker, due to trimmed capacity and too little reserve, you potentially can have a lot of bottlenecks. So they will seem to pop up here and pop up there, all over the place."

Amy stared at Murphy, unsure whether to believe him.

"Well," she said, "I appreciate your comments, Murph. But I feel I have to give Wayne his opportunity. Let him run with it."

"I understand completely," said Murphy. "Hey, it's his plant now. And his problem, however he wants to handle it."

"Good luck, Murphy."

"Good luck to you, too, ma'am."

11

The email from Sarah Schwick was brief:

Due to the demands of my primary responsibilities as chief chemist within the Formulation & Design unit, I am resigning effective immediately from my Lean Six Sigma project team. I have spoken with Dr. Kyzanski about this matter and he agrees with and has approved my decision to do so.

Thank you,

Sarah Schwick
Chief Chemist
F&D – Rockville

It was addressed to Wayne Reese, but there were a dozen or so people in Hi-T who were copied. One of them was Amy Cieolara. As soon as she had read it, Amy shot back a terse reply:

Sarah, please call me ASAP. I'd like to talk about this.
Thx – Amy

About ten minutes later, Amy's desk phone rang; Sarah was on the line.

"Hi," said Amy. "Hey, listen, your email about quitting LSS really took me by surprise. What's going on?"

"Nothing," said Sarah. "I just have too many other things on my plate to stay involved."

"Did your workload increase?"

"No, not really. It's the same ten thousand th[...] every day. It's just that . . . well, I want to apply i[...] most effective, and something had to go."

"But why Lean Six Sigma? Why are you walking awa[...] asked. "When we started down this path however many m[...] you seemed very enthusiastic about it, and said you'd make ti[...] and now you're dropping it. What changed?"

Sarah hesitated.

"Is it something to do with Viktor?" Amy asked.

"No, it's not Viktor," Sarah said quickly. "I mean, he didn't pressure me to quit or anything like that. It's just that . . . if you want to know the truth, I've kind of lost confidence that Lean Six Sigma will be effective here. Maybe it'll work at Oakton, I don't know. But the way we've set it up here in Rockville, I just don't see LSS as making much of a difference to the business overall."

On the other end of the line, Amy was stunned.

"And why is that?"

"Well, because look at the projects that were approved. Like we've reduced the actual distance required to make a material sample for our clients. It used to be the technicians making up the samples had to walk all over the building to do what they needed to do, and if you added up all the steps, the distance was more than twelve hundred meters. Now they've got it down to less than a hundred meters, and they think they can eventually get it to less than sixty-five meters."

"Well, they've eliminated wasted effort. What's wrong with that?" asked Amy.

"Nothing!" said Sarah. "On the other hand, what does it matter? So *what* if the people making the samples walk fewer steps? Actually, I think they're all gaining weight because they're getting less exercise."

"So you're saying the end result has been negative?"

"No! I don't mean to imply that at all. We've made this one process more efficient. That's fine. Great. But how does that improve what's really driving the business? How does it help with all the things that are driving *me* crazy? Let me assure you, I don't lie awake at night worrying about whether some technician has to walk eight hundred meters or eighty meters or sits on his butt all day."

"What *does* keep you awake at night?" Amy asked her.

"Worrying about the analysts. Worrying about getting results from the loop *to* the analysts – and *through* the analysts. I worry about where things are inside the loop, and whether they'll be ready on time. And I worry about how much we're –"

Sarah abruptly shut up, almost as if she'd bitten her tongue. It was not lost on Amy.

"How much you're what?" Amy prompted.

"How much we're billing our clients," Sarah said quietly.

"And why is that a concern?"

"Because we've got some pretty grumpy clients out there. I'm hearing from the project managers that we've got major accounts that are really upset over the invoices they're receiving. Meanwhile, Viktor isn't really doing much about it. He just –"

Sarah cut herself off again. For a second, Amy thought the call had been dropped. Then:

"Amy, I shouldn't be talking like this."

"Yes, you should," Amy insisted. "Now, *please*, talk to me."

"Viktor just keeps patching things over. He doesn't want to fix what I – and a lot of others – see as the problems. He doesn't want the loop to be efficient."

"I'm sorry, say that again."

"He doesn't want the testing loop to be more efficient or more productive. He wants the loop to turn out accurate data. He wants dependable, verifiable results. He wants the loop to be fully utilized. But he wants the loop to be only as efficient as it needs to be."

"Why is that?" Amy asked her.

"Because Viktor thinks that if the loop is more efficient, we'll make less money."

"Huh?"

"Amy, you have to protect me on this."

"And I will. Keep talking."

"The vast majority of our projects are billed on an hourly basis," said Sarah.

"Right. Like lawyers."

"So every working minute is logged against a project and a client account. Viktor thinks that if the loop is more efficient, there will be fewer billable minutes, therefore monthly billings will go down, and we'll be less profitable. So anytime that anyone talks about improving the loop, Viktor starts to sing his standard opera about quality, and dependability, and why all the tests we do are so vital, why the exhaustive testing and retesting inside the loop is essential to predictable results, and priceless experience of the analysts, and the ingenuity of the chemists, and on and on."

As Amy was absorbing this, the thought crept coldly across her mind that indeed Viktor might have a valid point. And if Viktor was right about lower billings, in a year when she was on the line to deliver higher earnings to Nigel Furst and Winner . . .

"The only reason Viktor allowed LSS to reduce the number of steps in sample prep," Sarah was saying, "is because the time of those technicians is not billable to the client; they're overhead. The same with clerical staff, which is why he allowed report formats to be standardized."

"But wait, Sarah, those are real savings, aren't they? And don't those savings trickle to the bottom line?" asked Amy.

"*What* savings? We still have the same headcount, the same number of staff!" said Sarah. "Expenses have not gone down, and we're not bringing in more accounts or more business. By the way, that mini-factory that Viktor wanted? When we send professional staff to other locations, their travel time – if it's billable at all – is charged at half the normal rate. Viktor wants to keep the analysts and chemists in Rockville as much as possible, so that they stay fully billable."

Listening to this, Amy was struck by how much it made sense. She knew that she would not be able to disagree with either point of view – with Sarah for wanting to resolve the issues that caused her insomnia, or with Viktor for supporting a system that was no doubt wasteful and highly inefficient, yet time-tested, functional, and profitable.

"So you should not expect Victor to be a Lean champion," Sarah said. "He may support Six Sigma and quality improvement, as long as it doesn't interfere with billings. But not Lean. And that is why he has allowed, and even encouraged, the Lean Greenies to take over."

Amy snapped back from her own thoughts. "The who?"

"The Lean Greenies. That's what they call themselves. They've kind of hijacked LSS here in a political sense, with Viktor's tacit approval, and they will only consider improvement projects that have a strong environmental tie-in. Like reducing paper consumption and recycling toner cartridges. If you suggest something to improve one of the lab processes, the first thing they ask is, 'What does that have to do with saving the environment?' For next year, they're talking about replacing all the windows in the building to conserve energy. Viktor thinks it's great, thinks it'll make for good public relations. A nice fluffy story in a magazine. I say, screw the PR, I want *real* improvement in the things that worry me."

"You are worried, aren't you," said Amy.

"Yes. The project managers tell me we are getting some serious push-back from clients. Yet just last month Viktor raised the billing rates again. That's what he does almost every few years to boost profits; he bumps the hourly rates by ten bucks or so. And if clients complain, which they do, he just patches things over. So that's why I'm dropping LSS; I want to focus on the things that really matter."

Amy then thanked her for explaining and hung up.

"Wow," she murmured after a few minutes of sitting there feeling overwhelmed and slightly numb.

Amy decided she would talk to Wayne Reese to get his reading on what was going on in Rockville. She did not mention the conundrum of the hourly billing conflict with efficiency, because she was still mulling that over. But she did mention the Lean Greenies and Sarah's withdrawal from the program.

"Look," said Wayne, "I know they're a little bit off track up there. But for right now, I feel it's better to let them take the ball and run with it. Did they pick the best targets to shoot for? No, probably not. Then again, hey, what's wrong with cutting energy costs or boosting recycling? If that's what brings them into the Lean culture, that's fine. If we try to force them into some narrow little channel, they're not going to be as engaged as they would be working on something that turns them on, something they really want to work on."

"Okay, I can see that," said Amy. "What's it doing to improve the business?"

"It's giving them experience in LSS tools and methods! It's indoctrinating them into the Lean culture! So why not let them have some fun! And once they have enough certified Green Belts and Black Belts up there in Rockville, then we can steer them into some of the customer satisfaction issues, and so on. Besides, if the Rockville program achieves what they've set out to accomplish, they're going to be saving something on the order of a quarter of a million dollars a year – which is not to be sneezed at, given that it's a relatively small operation."

"All right," said Amy, not relishing a confrontation with him. "We can let it ride for now. Oakton in my opinion is more important. How is everything coming along out there?"

"Fine! It's going great," said Wayne. "We've almost rebalanced the production line, and this time I think we'll start to see some real improvements in the metrics. I just know we will."

• • •

For the first week or so that Murphy Maguire worked at Formulation & Design in Rockville, he kept to himself, feeling as he did like a new dog in a world of cats. Just figuring out what the heck he was supposed to be doing was enough of a challenge.

Even so, Murphy could not help but notice that there was a quiet tension hiding in the placid ambience of the F&D offices. And sometimes not so quiet: all of a sudden, a door would slam; there were outbursts of temper, exchanges of angry words in the hallways. Frowning faces would pass by Murphy's cubicle and give him just the briefest of cold glances. The iPod was both allowed here and widely used, as if to screen out everyone else and stay isolated in a private auditory sphere.

One afternoon, from out of the general silence came shouting:

"Where is it? I need it now!"

"I'll find it for you! But get off my back!"

Then silence again. Murphy stood up in his cubicle and searched over the tops of the dividers, just to see who was yelling. Though he never did detect the source, he made eye contact with a woman in a neighboring cubicle.

"Happens all the time," the woman said to him. "My advice? Get an iPod."

At first Murphy attributed the tension to the relative rudeness of northern, urban culture. But soon that explanation began to seem inadequate. He started taking more notice of things he overheard.

"Nothing ever gets finished around here until it becomes a crisis," said someone in a small throng by the elevator.

"I know," said another. "It's all crisis management."

Later, from somewhere near Murphy's cubicle:

"I am *not* working this weekend. I swear I'm not. I don't care what anybody says. I have not had a weekend off in a month. And you know what? It never gets any better. We never get caught up! I feel like we're just spinning our wheels all the time."

And:

"Why are you working on *that*?"

"Because Bob told me to!"

"Forget what Bob told you! Get going on the tensile strength report! Joe Tassoni needs it by the end of today!"

Then there were the emails – hundreds daily flying back and forth. What Murphy noticed as he read so many of them was the same underlying tension. People often went to considerable lengths in their writing – and no doubt invested considerable time – to defend even petty positions.

Every night Murphy called his wife, Coreen, from his hotel. More and more as time went on, he began to voice his own frustration.

"I'm telling you, honey, it's a zoo up here," Murphy told her. "For such a bunch of smart people, I sometimes wonder if they could manage to organize a two-car parade."

Early in his tenure as manufacturing liaison at Rockville, Murphy Maguire was called upon by Sarah Schwick to attend a meeting to talk about something code-named Cobblestone. In addition to Sarah and Murphy, there were two others in the meeting, the project manager and the lead chemical engineer. They assembled around a table in a conference room done in neutral colors that made Murphy long for the vivid, if sometimes ugly sights of his old Oakton plant. The diminutive and pale Sarah, who usually dressed in bland pastels, was wearing something that was a washed-out greenish gray, and she almost disappeared against the walls when she entered the room and sat down at the table.

"Where is Joe Tassoni?" asked the project manager.

"I asked him to be here, and I reminded him this morning," said Sarah.

"That doesn't mean he'll show up," said the engineer.

"Why don't you text him," said Sarah, looking at the project manager, "just to be sure."

"Excuse me," said Murphy. "This Joe Tassoni. I've heard that name. Who is he?"

"He's a senior analyst," said Sarah.

"And for my benefit, being the new kid on the block," said Murphy, "an analyst is . . . ? "

"Analysts are kind of central to everything we do here at Formulation and Design," said Sarah. "They do a lot of things. They specify which procedures and tests are to be run. They approve the research schedule. They evaluate the test results. Based on those results, they then recommend whatever further actions need to be taken. They either write up the conclusions themselves or they approve what others have written up."

"If F&D was a hospital," the project manager said to Murphy, "then the analysts would be the doctors. The rest of us would be the medical staff – the nurses, the therapists, the pharmacists, the lab techs, the administrators, and so on."

"In fact, all of the analysts here have their doctorates," said Sarah. "They all have PhDs in whatever their specialty is. They're so valu-

able that it's in their contracts that they take flu shots every fall –
because if one of them gets sick, it backs up everything."

"I see," said Murphy.

"Joe is a brilliant guy," said the engineer. "Kind of eccentric, I
guess you'd say, but nobody knows carbon fiber like Joe Tassoni."

"And he's a gourmet cook," added the project manager. "He
can spend a whole Sunday just making veal stock. His *osso buco* is
unbelievable – if you like that kind of thing."

"Can't say as I've ever had it before," said Murphy, intrigued.

"All right, we have to move forward," said Sarah. "Any word
from Joe?"

"He just texted back saying start without him," said the project
manager.

"Great. Well, while we're waiting for Joe," Sarah said, "let me bring
Murphy up to speed on Cobblestone. This is a project that's been going on for well over two years. We're working with Caterpillar, which
is funding the development of a new class of carbon-fiber materials
that are three times as strong as the strongest commercially available
steel, yet only a quarter of the weight for an equivalent strength."

"And for better or worse," said the project manager, "what is currently working the best is a fiber matrix in combination with some
rather exotic and volatile resins. In an uncured state, the resins become unstable within minutes of reaching room temperature. So
they have to be worked with in a refrigerated environment prior to
the curing stage."

"Sounds like a production nightmare already," said Murphy.

"Which is why you're here," said Sarah.

"Now, ordinarily," said the project manager, "we would go out to
a consultant at just about this point to come up with manufacturing
recommendations. But since you're on the payroll, we'd like you to
take a crack at it."

"Be glad to," said Murphy.

"Good," said Sarah. "So first of all, let's go over the report we're
going to present to the client next week."

In front of each of them at the table were comb-bound copies of a
report with the single word "Cobblestone" on the cover.

"Let's all turn to page two," said Sarah, "and have a look at the lab
test summary . . . wait a minute. Where the heck is page two?"

"Mine starts with page five," said the engineer.

"I'm sorry," said the project manager, "I forgot to tell you. Sanjay
hasn't written it yet."

"Why not?" asked Sarah.

"Because Sanjay hasn't gotten everything he needs from Joe. That's what he told me yesterday."

Sarah jutted her jaw forward and blew through her mouth, causing her bangs to rise from her forehead.

"All right," she said, "let's move on. Let's look at the cross-section analysis. Is it in here? Oh, good! It is!"

They made it through the cross-section analysis, only to find that two of the mechanical tests that were supposed to be included were not. They were missing.

"Crap!" said Sarah. "How come they're not in here?"

"I have no idea," said the project manager.

"You know, we're supposed to present this to the client *next week*!" said Sarah.

"Well, there's still time," said the engineer.

"Not much! And I'm wondering, what else is missing?" asked Sarah, flipping through the pages. "Where's the environmental section?"

"It's in here," said the project manager, "I just saw it."

"I saw it too, but I hate to tell you," said the engineer, "it's outdated. There is newer environmental data, and what's in here is from six months ago. But I don't think Joe has signed off on it yet."

"Who put this report together?" asked Sarah.

"I don't know," said the engineer. "But Joe Tassoni was supposed to approve it."

"Where *is* Joe Tassoni?" asked Sarah.

"Um . . . I just got a text message," said the project manager, checking his cell phone. "Joe's not coming. He's in a meeting with Viktor. He says it could go on for a while. He says to go on without him."

Sarah flung her small body back into her chair, then sighed and said, "We can't! We cannot go on without him."

That evening, Murphy had to stay late at work to participate in a conference call involving people on different continents. The call was scheduled for 7:00 p.m Eastern time, but at 6:55 it was postponed until 8:00 p.m. Murphy had put off dinner in order to prepare for the call, but by now he was seriously hungry. So he went to the vending machines on the third floor, which were just down the hall from the thermodynamics lab.

Murphy stood in front of the vending machines, looking at an array of bad choices. As he deliberated, another man walked up, and put money into one of the machines to buy a bottle of water. Murphy was just about to purchase a packaged sandwich, which he suspected might have been in the machine for days, when the other man said:

"You don't want to do that."

Murphy turned. The man was in his late forties, portly and rather large in all dimensions, had a broad face, a curved nose, dark brown hair that had receded from his temples, and a well-trimmed thick dark mustache.

"You're right, I really don't, but I've got to eat something," said Murphy.

"You like-a pizza?" asked the man.

He had a slight accent.

"Excuse me?" asked Murph.

"Pizza. You like pizza?"

"I sure do."

The man nodded toward a door nearby.

"You come with me."

He led Murphy into the thermodynamics lab, past various warning signs saying things like Danger: High Temperatures.

"How'd you get a pizza delivered here?" asked Murphy.

The man turned as if insulted and said, "Delivered? No! I make it myself. From scratch."

He went over to a piece of lab equipment that in actuality was a very precise, high-tech oven. To one side was a wooden cutting board dusted with flour where the pizza had been rolled out. Over his office clothes, the man was wearing a lab coat, and Murphy noticed red smears – tomato sauce – where he had wiped his fingers.

"*Un minuto*," said the man, pointing to a timer on the oven that was counting down. "One minute more."

He noticed on the digital display of the oven that the temperature was 481 degrees Celsius.

"Wow, that is . . . what? Nine hundred degrees Fahrenheit?"

"For great pizza, you want the oven be hot, hot, hot."

"No one objects to you making pizza in a lab oven?"

"Oh, it's a new product," said the man, "We're coming out with it next year. Hi-T Pizza."

Murphy bent in laughter and almost slapped a knee.

"But . . . you're sure this is safe? I mean, to eat?"

"*I* am going to eat it! You don't have to. But yes, I make sure there is no residual toxicity, everything is neutralized, sanitary. Not to worry, I know what I am doing. My title? I am senior chemical analyst and carbon fiber specialist. Let me tell you, I know every carbon molecule in this pizza."

The mention of the job title rang a bell. Murphy peered at the other's F&D security badge.

"So you are . . . *Guisep*?"

"Giuseppe," said the other, extending his hand. "Giuseppe Tassoni. But they call me Joe. Joe Tassoni."

"I've heard of you. Pleased to meet you. They call me Murphy. Murphy Maguire. If you don't mind my asking, you are . . . Eye-talian?"

"I was born in Italy, in Siena, so yes, that makes me Italian – but United States citizen for fifteen years now," said Joe. "And you are . . . Southern?"

"Why, yes, I am," said Murphy. "North Carolina to be precise."

"Oh, yes. I have heard of you as well," said Joe. "You are the new manufacturing guru."

"Well, I would hardly call myself that, but, yes, I do have manufacturing experience in abundance. The title they gave me is 'liaison,' which is pretentious enough for an old cracker like me."

Joe chuckled as he put on heavy mitts. Just as the timer clicked down to zero, he opened the oven door – whereupon a blast of heat rolled out, and with it a wonderful scent of fresh-baked crust, melted cheese, onions and garlic, and a mingling of other aromas.

"Come," said Joe, "we dine in my office. And the time we take to get there, it lets the pizza cool, and the cheeses, they set up perfect."

Joe Tassoni's office was itself an experience – the walls filled with photographs of Florence, and little towns in the Italian countryside, and the Mediterranean coast, all taken by Joe himself. There were along the windows potted flowers and herbs – rosemary, basil, parsley, thyme, and who knows what others – all lush and green, and the scent of these was heady. Braided garlic hung from the ceiling.

But, if anything, just as remarkable was the fact that the office had no horizontal surface that went unoccupied by profuse clutter. There were stacks and stacks of binders and reports and envelopes and magazines and everything else. Big diagrams of molecules. Huge engineering drawings unfurled hither and yon. Stacks of hand-labeled discs. And somewhere amidst all of this chaos, a desk and a computer and a whiteboard with chemical formulas scrawled top to bottom – and all the other things one might expect in an office.

In one corner was a round table, and the stacks and clutter had been pushed back just enough to allow for a single place setting with a plate, an elegant coffee cup, real silverware, and a cloth napkin – and the cutting board bearing the pizza. Joe set the pizza down, moved a few piles from the table and set them on the floor, then went to the large safe next to his desk. He opened the safe and produced a second place setting and cup for Murphy. Then he cut the pizza.

"In Italy," he said as he sliced, "pizza is no big deal. We have many other dishes that are . . . *ottimo*. Excellent. Extraordinary. But I come to America to do my graduate work, and everybody is eating pizza, so I try it, and I like it a lot. But is too much salt. So over the years I make my own, and I try to make it so all the natural flavors come through. Here you are . . . *buon appetito*."

If it was not the *best* pizza that Murphy had ever tasted, then it was in the top three – and he was extremely complimentary.

"Thank you. *Grazie*, as we Eye-talians say," Joe said, poking fun. "It is good to have someone join me for dinner. I feel I all but live in this office, so I try to make it a little bit like home."

"What's keeping you late tonight?"

"Yesterday, Viktor – you know Viktor, of course – comes to me and he tells me that in a certain project we have over sixteen hundred hours billed, for which we cannot be paid until I finish the analysis and write the conclusions. So Viktor is whining and crying and pleading, and here I am."

"That wouldn't happen to be the Cobblestone project, would it?" asked Murphy.

"Cobblestone? No, not at all. Cobblestone is another one. I cannot get to that until next week."

"How many overdue projects are there here?"

"A few. Listen, I do my best. All the analysts do. Well, I should say most of them do. One or two are . . . *cosi-cosi*. They are so-so in their work ethic. But listen. This project keeping me here tonight, I have been trying for six weeks to wrap it up and get it out of here."

"How come you can't?" asked Murphy.

"It's always one thing and then another," said Joe. "I get data back from testing and some of it isn't clear. So I need other tests. Or I get the data and it looks accurate, but I need it in a different format. So that's another couple of days until someone reformats it. Or I get this and that and the other thing, *but* one other piece is missing, so I have to put everything away until the missing piece arrives, who knows when. By then I can't remember all of the details, so I have to read it all again to refresh my memory. But the worst thing is when there are two or three or four analysts involved in a project – and I am waiting for this one, then the other one is waiting for me, and it goes on for-ever. By the way . . ."

He reached beneath the table and brought up a stainless steel ca-rafe, unscrewed the top, and poured into his coffee cup.

"Would you like some?" Joe offered.

"Is it decaf?"

"Decaf? It's *Chianti*," he said. "*Chianti classico*. From my uncle's vineyards."

"I'd better not," said Murphy.

"You can't have a decent dinner without a little wine!" Joe pro-tested. "Hey, it's after hours anyway."

"I'd still better not," said Murphy.

"If Viktor is going to keep me a prisoner, working late, then I re-fuse not to live like a human being," said Joe.

"Well, just a wee little bit," said Murphy, showing no more than an inch with his fingers.

It was then, as Joe poured, that Murphy just happened to notice right in front of him a tall stack of papers and reports, and they were sitting in an in-box on the table, and the box was labeled with a name: Oakton.

"Excuse me," said Murphy, "but this big pile here, sitting in the Oakton box . . . why is it labeled like that?"

"Those? Those are the background materials for all the run-of-the-mill production orders that I have to clear."

"*You* have to clear?"

"Yes. A number of years ago, maybe you recall, Hi-T was sued for hundreds of millions of dollars – and lost – because of a material we made that was used in infants' car seats. Some infants were able to chew on this material, ingested it, were poisoned, and a few of them died. So ever since, for liability reasons, all production orders going to Oakton have to be reviewed by an analyst – for safety, quality, and other things. That's my share in that box. I get to them whenever I can. They're low priority."

"Low priority? Says who?" asked Murphy.

"Says Viktor, my boss. He sets the priorities. The billable work for F&D clients, that work comes first. The Oakton clearances, mostly the review is just a formality, so it is less important," said Joe, raising his cup of Chianti.

"*Salute.*"

"Cheers," said Murphy, with a lack of enthusiasm.

• • •

The following morning Murphy telephoned Jayro Pepps at Oakton.

"How is everything?" asked Murphy.

"Oh . . . all right. The kanbans are mostly in place now, and Final has gone to this, what they call, one-piece flow. And I have to say it is pretty slick. Once we got enough out of Godzilla to make it worth the while."

"Uh-huh. That's the way it's always been, Jayro. Anyway, I have some interesting news."

"What's that?"

"Jayro, you know how production approvals from Rockville usually come in fits and starts? You know we'll get five or ten in one day? And then we might not get anything from Rockville for three or four days, maybe even a week or more?"

"Yeah."

"You remember how the salesfolks always wonder why it takes so long for some of their orders to get into the production queue?"

"I don't have to *remember*, Murph. It goes on all the time."

"Well, I now know why."

"Is that a fact."

"Yes, and next time some sales guy yells at us because some hot order isn't in production when it's supposed to be, if it involves carbon fiber, I know exactly which pile to look in to find it."

"Pile of what?" asked Jayro.

"Yes, exactly," said Murphy. "I will explain next time I'm back in Carolina."

Murphy Maguire understood that in order to have influence, one must have rapport. And to have rapport required an extension of goodwill.

Therefore, Murphy ventured out, driving his Chevy Suburban into the vastness of the metropolitan Washington, D.C., retail experience. Ultimately he found and purchased the equipment for his tactical olive branch, his pacific Trojan horse: a WSM smoker. This was not his preferred sort of barbeque smoker, but it was a cute little black barrel thing that would do the job and would fit on the microscopic porch of the company-rented town house where he resided while in Rockville. And so on Monday, there were ribs.

Murphy came into a 3:00 p.m. meeting with Sarah Schwick, Joe Tassoni, and a few others, holding a platter covered with heavy-duty aluminum foil. It caused a stir. As he unveiled the ribs – which he had kept in a cooler until a few hours before, when he had gone to the parking lot and placed the foiled slab on the dashboard of his Suburban, parked with the windshield at southern exposure, so as to heat them to perfection in the bright hot sun – there were gasps.

Joe Tassoni uttered most of his compliments in Italian, a testament of his appreciation. The others, between bites of the succulent meat – crispy at the edges yet moist inside – also raved. But Sarah would not partake.

"Sarah, have a few," Murphy offered, holding the patter toward her.

"No, thanks."

"Are you sure? Joe likes 'em! And I do believe Joe knows his food!"

"Um, Murphy, I'm Jewish," Sarah said.

"Oh?"

"And I don't eat pork."

"Oh."

"And I'm also vegetarian," Sarah said.

She might just as well have said she was from a different galaxy. Murphy attempted to smile politely as he withdrew the platter.

"But I do eat cheese," Sarah said, as if in consolation.

"Yes, so do I," said Murphy. "I like cheese."

"And I like spicy," she added, "especially hot Thai food."

"I don't believe I've ever had any," said Murphy.

The following week Murphy appeared with two platters, both with small, round, tempting morsels.

"What are these?" asked Sarah.

"ABTs," said Murphy. "They're kind of an appetizer in the barbeque world. And I made two kinds, regular and vegetarian."

Joe Tassoni immediately reached for one of the "regulars," which consisted of a jalapeño pepper stuffed with cream cheese and a small amount of sausage, then wrapped with bacon secured with a toothpick.

"*Splendido!*" said Joe, delivering his blessing and having another.

With some trepidation, Sarah reached for the veggie variety, which substituted seasoned bulgur wheat for the sausage and a brined, hand-roasted sweet red pepper for the bacon. Into her mouth went the ABT, and a second later her small brown eyes became enormous behind the outsize lenses of her glasses.

"*Fantastico,*" she raved. "What do you call these again?"

"ABTs," said Murphy. "Atomic buffalo turds."

At which, Sarah nearly choked.

From that point on, they got on quite well, worked harmoniously together, and in a suitable way became friends.

• • •

One evening a few weeks later, Sarah Schwick coaxed Murphy to an Indian restaurant, thinking he would enjoy some of the hot curry dishes, which she loved and which were extremely spicy. As she did not own a car, Murphy drove. And as he had no idea even how to pronounce much of what was on the menu, she ordered for them – a meatless *rajma masala* for herself, and a *rogan josh* with lamb for him, knowing his carnivorous propensities, as well as some curried side dishes for them to share.

"So how do you like life in the big city?" she asked. "Or I guess I should say, the big suburb?"

Murphy smiled in a wry way, which said everything necessary.

"Well, I sometimes feel the same way," said Sarah, "but, on the other hand, I like my work – even if it does drive me crazy."

"Yes, I know what you mean," said Murphy. "It can be a little . . . what's the word?"

"Chaotic? Dysfunctional? Insane?" Sarah supplied. "Depending on the day, any or all of those might fit. By the way, what do you think of Joe Tassoni?"

Murphy chuckled and said, "A very odd, but very likable and interesting man. And I'm not sure the degree you're aware of this, but Joe *is* the bottleneck of your operation."

"What do you mean, 'bottleneck'?"

"Excuse me, let me try to state that more precisely – and I mean no disrespect to Joe or you or anyone at F&D. Things are the way they are. Having watched him and everyone else, Joe Tassoni is a bottleneck, and the analysts in general are the F&D system constraint."

"I don't understand," she said. "Constraint? Bottleneck? First of all, what's the difference?"

"Well, a constraint is something that limits flow – like a one-lane bridge on a two-lane road. When traffic increases beyond what the one-lane bridge can comfortably handle, the bridge becomes a bottleneck. You see, in general manufacturing lingo, a bottleneck is a constrained resource that is incapable of filling the demand set for it. For example, a pipeline must deliver one hundred gallons per minute, but a sticky valve limits the flow to seventy-five."

"So a bottleneck is bad," said Sarah.

"That is the world's view on bottlenecks, but my own view is different. Now, I sometimes use 'bottleneck' and 'constraint' interchangeably, though I probably shouldn't. To me, a bottleneck is a key feature in the functioning of the bottle. It is there by *design*. It's purpose is to help regulate the flow."

Murphy had a bottle of beer at hand on the table, and he raised it and poured into his glass to demonstrate.

"If a bottle had no neck, what would happen? Why, the beer or whatever would run all over the place! You'd have a mess!"

"Unless you were extremely careful." said Sarah, "and your pouring angle was precisely controlled."

"But why not just keep the neck in the bottle and be done with it? Well, it's the same in a factory, or in an office, or a lab, or any organization with a systematic output of something through a series of steps. A constraint is desirable, or even necessary, to regulate the flow."

"What about Joe? Why is he a bottleneck?"

"Nothing against the man, you understand," said Murphy. "Joe is clearly brilliant, but he is messier than my wife, which is saying a lot, although I love her dearly. I've been watching Joe for a while now, and he meanders through his duties, working on what he feels like at the moment. In order to compensate for his inefficiencies, he works extremely long hours, but still, everything that has anything to do with Joe is always late. And the policies at F&D, the work rules, often serve to make him even less productive than he otherwise would be."

"What about the other analysts?" asked Sarah.

"The other analysts are more capable in terms of output, but so much is demanded of them that they can barely keep up. So if there is any disruption, they *cannot* keep up. Projects become overdue. Mistakes are made and have to be corrected. Everything is late."

"And clients become upset, and we all go insane," Sarah added. "So what is the answer? Hire more analysts? That's what Viktor says — not that we can."

"If you hire more analysts and put them into a chaotic system, what will that yield?" asked Murphy.

"Probably more chaos. While spending a lot more money."

"Yes. Exactly."

"What would you do?" Sarah asked.

While forming his answer, Murphy sampled one of the side dishes, which had an intensely hot Madras curry. and was further delayed in his response until he could drain his beer and mop his forehead with his napkin.

"Whew!" he said. "Jayro Pepps would like that one!"

He ordered another beer and a pitcher of water from the waiter, and then recomposed himself.

"What would I do?" he continued. "The first thing would be to recognize that the analysts are the system constraint for F&D. Second, would be to decide what is the best application of their time – and remove anything extraneous to that decision. Third, would be to align, synchronize, and otherwise subordinate everything else going on at F&D to the analyst process – which should bring order to the chaos. And then once the chaos has been removed, the fourth step would be to improve the system by increasing the flow through the analysts – which is maybe when you would hire another analyst or two if the market supported it. Finally, you just keep doing those improvements until you're doing the best that your markets will allow. What you do not do is allow, say, a shortage of lab techs to become the constraint."

Sarah was considering all of this as she ate – and loving the heat the curries were making.

"What I would really like for you to do, Murph, is explain what you just told me to Viktor," she said.

"Surely I can try," Murphy said.

"Well, good. I'll set up a meeting for you and I to talk to Viktor. I don't know what his reaction will be, but he should at least hear how you view things."

But the meeting with Viktor was a disaster. Sarah, who had planned to sit in, was called away to deal with some client crisis. Viktor was borderline rude, pretending to listen to Murphy even as he went about cleaning up his desk. In fairness, the meeting was poorly timed; Viktor had to leave for the airport within the hour to travel to California in order try to save a troubled account – and with so much on Viktor's mind, the introduction of any new idea was practically impossible.

Murphy became acutely aware that Viktor was dissing him. He became tongue-tied – a rarity for him – as Viktor began throwing out challenges, as if to show he was paying attention. And when Murphy would attempt to explain his logic, Viktor would interrupt. Finally, and perhaps mercifully, Viktor took an important phone call.

"We'll talk again some time," said Viktor as Murphy exited.

"Not if I can help it," Murphy muttered to himself as he retreated down the hall.

From that day on, Murphy Maguire resolved that he would come to work, do whatever he was paid to do, and that was all. Except for Sarah, no one was really interested in what he had to say, so what was the point? That very evening he drove to the mall and bought an iPod. It was a lonely time for him.

12

As the end of the year drew near, Wayne Reese and Kurt Konani began to trumpet the victories of Lean Six Sigma. By then Wayne had been on the job about fifteen months, and from the way he saw things, a lot had been accomplished – which was true.

The application of Six Sigma had determined the cause of the hairline cracks that had intermittently plagued production of certain advanced composites for the United States Navy. The cause was a laminating process that drifted out of control in a way that was impossible to detect by casual observation. The solution was relatively simple, and the cracking problem would never again occur so long as vigilance was paid to the control charts.

Then there was the reconfiguration of the M57 Line, the project of which Wayne and Kurt were the most proud. In a single weekend, the line operators and some maintenance staff, under Kurt's direction, had completely rearranged the placement of the equipment. By Monday morning, the line was up and running again, and there were high fives all around. The new configuration yielded a 12 percent increase in process speed, plus faster setup and fewer quality issues. Four line workers were transferred to other areas of the plant, resulting in a reduction in direct labor but no additional stress or strain to the remaining operators, as takt time paced their work such that no one became unduly fatigued.

There had been other improvements through the year as well. The 5S discipline had been applied to several areas in both Oakton and Rockville. By doing 5S, tools were within easy reach, everything was better organized, and the entire area was easier to keep clean and maintain. Not that any place inside Oakton had been a pig sty, but the improvements were clearly appreciated by the plant workers in the 5S-ed areas.

Then there were the racks brought about by Kurt's push for POUS, or Point of Use Storage, filled with materials and parts – but placed close to where this inventory would be used in production, mainly at the front end of the plant. A prime example was the insertion of POUS into the M57 Line. Similar but different in Lean terminology were the "supermarkets" – racks holding work-in-process inventory until the next operation in the stream could accommodate it. There were a number of these supermarkets, notably in Coatings and in Lamination. Jayro Pepps had participated in these changes, and for a while at least, he had been a staunch advocate. In any case, the POUS racks and the supermarkets made certain areas look different, and often in a plant anything different seems like an improvement.

The new WING4-L software that supported the Lean balanced line had been installed. Wayne and Kurt both acknowledged that there needed to be some "fine-tuning" done to the algorithms and values, but at least they were no longer saddled with the old Winner "push" style of production, jamming inventory into the system and obliging everyone to work at 110 percent or be buried in the avalanche of parts coming at them. WING4-L supported "pull" inventory methods – with kanbans triggering reordering once a minimum level was detected – as well as the general philosophy that nothing be produced until a customer downstream had asked for it. Also supported in 4-L were takt time and tools for balancing the line. Unfortunately, WING4-L presumed that the world really behaved exactly as its programmers were told that it behaved – hence the need for "fine-tuning."

In mid-December, as Winner's fourth quarter neared a close and the year-end holidays put most people in a merry mood, Wayne found money in the budget for the first annual Oakton Lean Six Sigma Awards Dinner. There were little plaques and speeches and lots of applause. Spouses had been included in the invitations, the restaurant did a nice job, and in general a good time was had.

What was puzzling, or should have been, was that everyone knew or at least suspected that Oakton was still having real problems – and the problems were not getting better. Yet according to all proclamations, the implementation of Lean Six Sigma that past year had been a glorious triumph. Kurt Konani, who believed his own cheerleading, was highly optimistic for the coming year. Wayne Reese stubbornly insisted everything they were doing was on the right track, though in private he was known to mumble otherwise.

None of this was lost on Elaine Eisenway. During the year, Elaine had been promoted from finance manager to vice president, finance and administration, with human relations now reporting to her, in addition to all of the accounting functions. But her new status as veep did nothing to tone down her alarmist ways. Even as Wayne and Kurt were trumpeting their claims of success, Elaine was trumpeting all her worries and warnings directly into Amy Cieolara's ear.

Amy herself spent the final days of the year in bed fighting some "weird virus," as she described the malady, with symptoms of sweating, headaches, and the inability to sleep without medication. In a few weeks this would pass, but later she would wonder about the degree to which those miserable nights had been brought on by stress.

That New Year's Eve was Amy's personal worst. Not only was she sick, she was, romantically at least, alone.

Late in October, Tom Dawson came to Amy's house one evening, just dropped by unexpectedly. She could tell that he was antsy, restless – as he had been the past few times they had been together. He suggested they go for a walk, and once they were outside, he wasted no time.

"I'm going to be leaving soon," he told her.

That stopped Amy in her tracks.

"And going where?"

"Africa."

"May I ask, why?"

"A good buddy of mine is over there, a guy I knew in the Marines. He's working for some outfit in sub-Sahara Africa. They need a pilot, and he thought of me."

"How long are you going to be gone?" she asked.

"I don't know. At least three months. That's the minimum. Maybe longer. Depends on how things work out. If they like me, I like them, that kind of thing. I will be back eventually. I just don't know when."

"Oh, well that's cool," she said – coolly.

"Really? That's great, Amy, because I didn't know how you'd take it."

"*No, Tom, it's not cool!*" she said.

He folded his muscular arms across his chest and said, "Well, I'm going. I already signed the contract and faxed it back to them."

"Tom, why would you think I'd just go along with something you decided completely on your own and that I didn't even know about until now?"

He blinked his eyes a few times, as if the question made no sense whatsoever.

"You've never been a military wife, have you," he said. "They put up with this shit all the time."

"Well, they have my sympathy. Point of fact, I'm not a wife at all –"

"That's right! And why shouldn't I decide something that's about *my* life?"

"There's 'decide' and then there's 'discuss.' And we could have at least discussed it!"

"We are discussing it! Right now!"

Amy shook her head, then decided to take a softer tack.

"Tom, why are you doing this?"

"It just seems like a good opportunity. Something different."

"What about your flying business?"

"My business sucks, Amy. I really don't make that much money doing charter flights or flying lessons. And with cost of fuel going up the way it has, everything's been off. Heck, your company was the best client I had – and look what happened."

"You're bored, aren't you," she said, saying it like an accusation.

"All right, yes, I am bored. I just need a change."

"From me," she said, angry now.

"No, now come on, Amy! This has nothing to do with you."

"Yes, I've picked that up," she said. "This is all about you, and not about me, and definitely not about *us*. Well, you go right ahead, Tom. You go to Africa and have a nice life. Then maybe you want to try Australia. Hell, you can go to Antarctica and stay there for all I care!"

"I told you, I'll be back!"

"Not with me, you won't."

She then turned on her heel and began walking rapidly back to her house. He jogged alongside her.

"You know, I didn't think you'd be *this* pissed off," he said.

"You were wrong! 'Bye!"

And she sprinted to her front door, went inside, and locked the door. The lingering image for her seen through the front window was of him standing next to the curb, those strong arms of his held out in exasperation, then dropping limply in hopelessness.

That had been it. No mournful good-byes, no letters, and no

calls – not until Christmas Eve. He had called, but her cell phone had been turned off, and she had missed it. There was no voice mail; just his number in the missed-call log. She debated calling him back, and then decided not to. There had been nothing since.

On the day the fourth quarter financial report for Hi-T was finished, on a sleety Tuesday in January, Elaine Eisenway did her customary and thorough final review, then logged off and wrote down the password on a slip of paper. She folded the paper in half, and hand-carried it across the floor, through the maze of cubicles to Amy Cieolara's office, where she placed it in Amy's outstretched hand.

"Happy New Year," Elaine said, the tiniest smirk crossing her face.

"Happy? Really? Are there good surprises in there?" asked Amy.

"No. I was being sarcastic."

"All right, are there *bad* surprises?"

Elaine shrugged her shoulders. "I would have to say that there are *no* surprises, at least as far as I'm concerned. Since the second quarter, I've been waving so many flags my arms got tired."

"Yes, you like to wave your flags," muttered Amy, and instantly regretted saying it.

"No, excuse me, but I do not *like* to wave flags. As vice president of finance for this company, I feel it is a key part of my responsibilities to provide the proper alerts to management."

"Yes," said Amy, "absolutely, I agree. By all means, keep waving those flags whenever you think there is something I should be aware of."

"I only crunch the numbers; the rest of you are the ones who create them," said Elaine.

And as if she had scored some sort of moral triumph, Elaine pivoted and left.

Amy turned to her computer, unfolded the slip of paper, and keyed in the password to bring up the report. She paged through it all quickly so as to get an overall impression. At first glance, to her own surprise, the numbers did not look horrible. Hi-T had recorded a profit for the quarter and for the year. Sales had increased from third quarter to fourth, though only by 3 percent. Somehow, with all of Elaine's hand-wringing in recent weeks and months – her flag-waving – Amy had been bracing herself for something really ugly. But it wasn't a disaster.

Then Amy drew in a breath, as she thought, *yes, that's the point.* It was not horrible, but it also was not great. The quarter and the year were so *lackluster*. She had been expecting . . . more. She had been expecting, she realized, something *impressive*. Or at least the beginnings of what might become outstanding performance.

She began to drill down into the details. And to her disappointment, this was where she began to notice some disturbing trends. Indeed, sales were up, but the backlog of orders was up as well – and it had risen in greater proportion than the sales increase. Shipments were down; they had fallen by 4 percent from the third quarter. Inventories – no surprise – were up; greater backlog, lower shipments would equal higher inventory. Even given marginally higher sales, the finished products were not being delivered fast enough to reduce the backlog. Then she noticed something that she found very upsetting: sales were up, but so were order *cancellations*. Yet the backlog was high. Which customers were canceling their orders? The report did not provide that information.

But the real jaw-dropper came when she got to the breakout of numbers for Formulation & Design. During the fourth quarter, the Rockville operation had received a gigantic payment for completion of a multiyear project, and this along with some other one-time accounting credits had masked the weaknesses in the core business. Here, the backlog was large, and yet relatively stagnant. It was for the most part being shifted from quarter to quarter, and not being converted into income. At the same time, over the course of the entire past year, there had been a decline in the bookings of new projects. F&D seemed to be working and working on the existing projects, and not much was getting finished.

"This is not good," Amy whispered to herself. "Not good . . . not at all good."

She closed her eyes, refusing to look at the report anymore. She leaned back in her chair. She felt slightly sick. Clearly, she was going to have to have a talk with Viktor Kyzanski about what was going on. And she knew that charming Viktor would try to oil his way past all of her concerns. He would sidestep her every attempt to corner him or pin him down. He would juggle his words. He would instantaneously come up with irrefutable technical reasons why things could not be done any differently than they were being done at present. He would make her feel unsophisticated, out of her element, even stupid. She dreaded talking to him. Yet it would have to be done.

Then there was Wayne Reese. She was going to have to speak

with him as well. She squeezed her eyelids shut, and she pinched the bridge of her nose at the prospect. He, too, would try to put his own spin on the situation. Wayne, she expected, would be more forthright and more outwardly concerned than Viktor. But Wayne was so optimistic about his Lean Six Sigma methods – his belief so total – that he would also try to convince her to stay the course. Inertia, though he would never call it that, was what was best. In the end, it would all just work out. The savings from waste elimination would trickle to the bottom line, and all would be well.

When Amy finally opened her eyes, she saw that outside her windows the winter's evening sky was now dark.

"Before we get started on the details, let me just say that I do think we're holding our own."

Those were the first words from Wayne Reese after he sat down to meet with Amy Cieolara. This was three days after Amy had read the fourth quarter report. The following morning she had signed off and authorized Elaine to send the report on to New York in order to meet the Winner corporate deadline. She had shortly afterward sent a copy to Wayne and given him time to review it. Now, they were seated across from each other at the table in Amy's office. Wayne was fidgety, perhaps sensing what might be coming, but making every effort to project confidence. Amy's face was dour.

"I mean, seriously, we're headed in some good directions," he continued. "Last week I was talking to Kurt out at the plant and according to his projections we ought to have the perfect black-belt to green-belt ratio sometime within the coming year. That's just one more indication of the momentum we're building, and as that momentum continues, we're really going to see some great things happen in the years and even decades to come."

"Decades," Amy repeated.

"Sure. Absolutely. Once the culture is in place, the improvements will just keep going and going."

"Great. When do the improvements start?"

"When do they start? The improvements have already started! Amy, look at what we've been able to achieve so far: we almost have a perfectly balanced line! Employee utilization is just about as high as we can hope for! In one year we have saved one-point-two million dollars' worth of wasted resources!"

"Then where is it?"

"Where is what?"

"The one-point-two million in savings," said Amy. She lifted her printout of the financial report she had sent to corporate, and shook it so the pages riffled, as if dollar bills might fall out, all the while asking, "Is it in here? Because if it is, I don't see it."

Wayne frowned, then attempted to mount a defense.

"Amy, as I said at the very beginning when I first came here, Lean Six Sigma is a long-term proposition."

"Yes, but we started down this road over a year ago. I really thought that by now we would be seeing some kind of real improvement –"

"But we are!"

"No, Wayne, I am not talking about the black-belt to green-belt ratios. I am not talking about employee utilization. And I am not talking about a balanced line; I am talking about the *bottom* line."

He stared back at her with a rather hurt, glum expression on his face.

"Look. Hi-T is basically not making any more money now than we were a year ago," said Amy. "That much is terribly clear from the financial report I just turned in. And despite a good economy, we made slightly less than we did before we started LSS – and far less than we did during that one year when Randal was president. Furthermore, we are also actually earning less now than we were before Winner acquired us. So we have not been able to beat any of the numbers going back four or five years. My question is *why*?"

Wayne cleared his throat, but then sat there in silence for a few seconds, and finally blurted out, "I – I'm afraid I don't have a good answer for you. After all the progress we've made, you would think that the financial performance would show it – that *some* of it would have trickled to the bottom line."

"What disturbs me almost as much as the lack of improvement to the bottom line," said Amy, "is my sense that Oakton as a whole is not running smoothly. Look at the rise in WIP inventory – the very thing that Lean is supposed to prevent. Look at the overtime we're paying. Look at the delayed shipments. *What* is going on?"

"I share your frustration," Wayne muttered.

"And then we've got Rockville. That operation is as problematic as ever."

"Now, hold on, please. Formulation and Design is not under my wing," said Wayne.

"This is not just about you!" said Amy. "Unlike you and everyone else around here, *I* have to look at the whole picture!"

She rubbed her temples with her fingers for a moment, trying to massage away the stress.

"Do you know what I'm hearing from Garth Quincy?" she asked him. "He's telling me that the sales force is becoming disillusioned. A lot of the salespeople are just going through the motions. Why? Because we're losing credibility with customers. This is *bad*, Wayne. This is *serious*."

"I'm sorry! What do you want me to do?"

"I want you to fix whatever is wrong! I want improvements that show up in a financial report! And I want it to happen soon, not five years from now!" she told him. "All along, you've been telling me to just be patient, just a few more months and we'll have turned the corner. You've been telling me, and I've been telling Nigel Furst. I'm on the hook for twelve percent growth, and it hasn't happened! What am I going to tell him now?"

As if on cue, her phone rang. Amy let Linda pick up, but a moment later Linda peered around the edge of the office door.

"It's Nigel on the line," said Linda.

"I'll take it," said Amy.

Wayne slunk out of her office.

Amy prepared herself for a moment, then lifted her phone and said, "Yes, Nigel."

The only good thing about Nigel Furst's call was that it was relatively brief. For the first part of it, Amy sat tight and silent while Nigel delivered a blistering diatribe expressing his displeasure – his "*extreme* displeasure" – with yet another "flop" of a quarterly performance.

"One year ago, approximately, you gave me a plan promising twelve percent earnings growth," said Nigel. "By the end of the second quarter, you told me that there had been some learning curve issues, transition issues, whatever, but you thought you could at least do nine to ten percent growth given a strong fourth quarter. Well! Here it is, the fourth quarter has come and gone, and you have delivered *nothing*! You have delivered one percent year-over-year *negative* growth!"

He paused. Then:

"Well? Have you nothing to say for yourself?"

"Mr. Furst, when you made me company president –"

"Interim company president," he interrupted.

"Yes, when you made me *interim* company president, you gave me

Wayne Reese and a directive to implement Lean Six Sigma as quickly as possible."

"Oh, come on! Don't think that you are going to blame your way out of this, walking on the back of Wayne Reese!"

"My only point is that I did what I was told to do!" she said. "You told me Wayne was strong in operations, that I needed him, that I should listen to him – and I did! You told me that Lean Six Sigma was endorsed by Winner and that it would solve our problems!"

"I don't believe I said any such thing."

Amy forced herself to calm down.

"Well, sir, I believe it was implied. In any case, I took it on faith that LSS was the answer, and believe me, we gave it a sincere try. And the evidence suggests, we really have made improvements. We're just not seeing the results on the bottom line."

"My dear Amy," Nigel said in his imperious tone, "let me offer a piece of advice: save your faith for religious services."

She gritted her teeth.

"Would you like to know a little secret?" Nigel continued. "Actually, it's not much of a secret at all. The truth is that I do not care about Lean or Six Sigma or any other management flavor of the month being touted. All I care about – essentially – is growth. Earnings growth in particular, with revenue growth and growth in free cash flow and so on playing secondary roles. But *growth*! You know, as in earnings going up and up and up! Compounding endlessly! To the sky! Like a stairway to heaven! Up, up, up, forever! At least until I retire or move on."

"But sometimes growth in every quarter or every year just isn't possible," argued Amy.

"Well, of course we sometimes tolerate an occasional step or two downwards, as long as it's brief, as long as the upward slope is resumed within a quarter or two," said Nigel. "But Amy, I must say you fail to inspire my confidence."

Amy took a breath and said with determination, "My pledge to you, Mr. Furst, is that I *will* get Hi-T Composites growing again."

"Right. Well, listen, I'm leaving for Europe in a few hours. And after Europe comes India, and then China. Anyway, I'll be gone for three weeks. The week after I return is Management Council – the Crystal Ball, as many quaintly refer to it. I've been debating whether I should even include you. However, I will give you until then – almost a full month – to come up with a turnaround plan. Why I am so lenient with you, I do not know. That said, your plan had better be logical, fact based, and show conclusively that you will return Hi-T to profitability and . . . ? "

"Growth," Amy parroted.

"Exactly. And, Amy, if you show up as you did last year with some pathetic rag of a thing that underwhelms . . . well, *don't*. This is really your last opportunity. You had best get it right."

Wayne wandered around his office – which was not huge – too agitated to sit down and too distracted by any number of feelings to deal with any of the slew of tasks that demanded his attention. He felt stung by what Amy had said to him. He was angry at her, and angry with himself at the same time. Yet he knew, too, that down the hall at that moment she was getting beaten up, and that on some level he was responsible for it.

He had known, or at least had suspected, that this day would come – while hoping all along that it would not, that somehow things would just fall into place and everything would start to work. And yet, despite his own zeal for what he was doing, he had been having his own doubts about this wonderful thing that he and many others were attempting to bring about.

When in charge of LSS at the corporate level, he had constantly fought a growing disillusionment about Lean from a number of Winner managers. Granted, some of them never really grasped the premise. At least a few were so jaded that everything coming out of their mouths was lip service of one form or another. Just the same, he could not deny that many of the LSS efforts within Winner were lackluster in terms of impact. Wayne himself had always believed it was a matter of implementation, that, for instance, political agendas – and Winner was highly political – and lukewarm commitment must have mitigated the results.

But now here he was facing the same thing, a kind of "so what?" result from all the hard work, even though he and everyone associated with LSS had enjoyed the complete support of Amy Cieolara. In all honesty, he could not fault her for expecting more. Still, it was very puzzling to him. How could a set of concepts seemingly so powerful – and just plain right – yield so little in terms of overall performance?

In his office now, Wayne brought up his schedule on his computer. There were two meetings that day, one of some importance, but neither of them as important as sorting out what the heck was going on – not so much what had gone wrong, as what had not happened?

He sent emails to everyone saying that he would not be attending, and then quickly left the building, got into his white SUV hybrid, and drove toward Oakton.

Going to Oakton was hardly necessary. By now Wayne could close his eyes and see in his mind everything in the place. But the drive was at least uninterrupted time alone, and he wanted very much to walk through the plant and try to assess firsthand what the impact of LSS had been so far. He called Kurt Konani to say that he was on his way.

"Good," said Kurt, "because I'm kind of in a jam, and I need a decision on something."

Just as Wayne came onto the plant floor, Kurt sent him a text message asking Wayne to come to the Autoclave area "ASAP." When Wayne arrived, the situation could not have been more discouraging. Kurt was there arguing with Richy, the day-shift manager, with the ugly, sinister Godzilla hissing in the background.

"You're going to have to stop this soak right now," Kurt was telling Richy.

"If we interrupt this soak," Richy countered, "everything that is now inside of Godzilla has to be scrapped!"

"We have no choice!" said Kurt. "If we do not get this order for the Navy into autoclave processing *now*, we will not be able to ship it by tomorrow! And if we cannot ship the order on time, the Navy will assess penalties, which under contract they are allowed to do! We may even lose the contract, which would be a disaster! Can't you understand that?"

"What's going on?" asked Wayne. "Kurt, are you . . . ? Are you *expediting*?"

"Yes," Kurt admitted. "I – we – are expediting. As I just said, we have no choice. We *have* to get this shipment out the door by tomorrow, and the only way it's going to happen is if we start the autoclave processing *now*."

"Oh, for crying out loud!" cried Wayne. "How could we be so up against the deadline?"

"Because we just got the material – the pre-preg – from the supplier," said Kurt. "And the only way we got it this morning was by making *them* expedite. It's a specialty pre-preg and only two vendors offer it."

"Well, let's try the other one next time!"

"I'm told that the other one is even less reliable – and thirty percent more expensive than the one we use now."

"Shoot!" muttered Wayne. "Why haven't we implemented a kanban procedure with every vendor we work with?"

"Well, we're working on it. But some – like this vendor – don't want to cooperate. So we're using the normal min-max reorder procedure, and for whatever reason, there are times when the resupply does not show up when we need it."

"Excuse me," said Richy, looking toward Wayne, "but what do you want me to do? There's thousands of dollars of product inside Godzilla, and it's all going to be ruined if I stop the process now."

"But there are *millions* at stake with the Navy contract!" argued Kurt.

Wayne raised his hand and curled his fingers as if to strangle some invisible phantom. Richy just patiently stared at him.

"Just do what Kurt tells you," Wayne said with resignation.

"Mr. Reese, that also means we lose thirty to forty minutes of setup time –"

"Just do it!" said Wayne.

Richy grimly turned to Godzilla's controls.

"Kurt, this is exactly the kind of waste I've worked most of my career to eliminate," said Wayne, "and here it is right in front of me, on my watch, in our plant."

"I know, I know!" said Kurt. "But I don't know what else to do!"

As Wayne walked away, he heard the *boom-whoosh* as Richy went through the venting procedure to purge the hot gasses from the belly of the monster machine.

Wayne desperately needed solitude, a place to be alone to sort out his thoughts. Even without a conscious decision to do so, Wayne headed in the direction of the drab little toolroom tucked away at the end of a seldom-trafficked corridor of the plant. When he reached it and opened the toolroom door, he was relieved to find the room in its usual state: empty.

He sat down at the table, and opened the laptop he had brought along. Through the plant's wireless network, he was able to log onto WING, and he began calling up pages of data and various reports looking for clues as to what might resolve the multifaceted dilemma he faced.

Soon after he began, Wayne was interrupted. The toolroom door opened, and there stood Jerome Pepps with a brown paper sack in one hand.

"Oh! Excuse me," said Jayro in surprise. "Sorry. I was just looking for a quiet place to have lunch."

"Come on in," Wayne invited. But Jayro hesitated. "Seriously, come in. Have a seat. I've been wanting to talk to you."

Jayro took a seat at the table and slowly removed various items of lunch from the paper sack.

"What did you want to talk about?" Jayro asked.

"Well, this morning, I got reamed out by Amy Cieolara, who is herself taking a lot of heat from her boss in New York."

"Over what?"

"Lean Six Sigma and why all the efforts we've made toward improvement haven't really accomplished much in terms of things like net income and so on."

"The financial end of things, I wouldn't know hardly anything about that," said Jayro.

"All right, but financial performance stems from operational performance, and that you do know something about – especially because you are a veteran here at Oakton. And at this point, you also know a lot about LSS. So I want to ask you, what is your take on everything that's happened at Oakton in the past year?"

Rather than responding immediately, Jayro flattened out the brown paper sack on the table, took a pen from his shirt pocket, and began to sketch a diagram. In the middle he drew a circle, and to left and right of the circle he drew some boxes. He then wrote some numbers above each of the elements and drew arrows depicting the flow.

"Here's the problem," said Jayro. "The circle is Godzilla. Upstream from the 'Zilla you've got a number of processes going on, and likewise downstream . . . more than I've shown, but hey, there's only so much room on a paper sack."

"Yes, I get the idea," said Wayne.

"So we have done LSS and made these improvements on both sides of the 'Zilla. Downstream, for instance, LSS reconfigured the equipment layout of Final Prep. A typical flow time through Final used to be eight minutes, but now, because of LSS, the flow time averages four minutes. That's a fifty percent improvement."

"Right. It was one of our big accomplishments," said Wayne. "I'm very proud of that."

"Well, sir, I don't mean to rain on your parade, but what does that fifty percent improvement really mean?"

"I have a feeling you're going to tell me."

"Maybe a better question is what does the fifty percent improvement *not* mean," said Jayro. "For instance, it does not mean that Final is actually processing fifty percent more. It does not mean that the company is really saving any money, because the cost of running the equipment is about the same as it was before – it's just been reconfigured."

"Now wait a minute. We moved two employees out of Final Prep. *That* was a savings."

"But I saw those two folks just this morning. One works now in Shipping and the other works in Maintenance. They're just working in different parts of Oakton. So the company is still paying their wages."

"Right. I can't dispute you on that one," said Wayne. "But you know, those two both cooperated in making the project a success. We can't just turn around and terminate them after helping us out. In order to get continuous improvement, people have to have some level of security – or they won't cooperate and they may even sabotage whatever improvement you're trying to make."

"Oh, I'm not saying that keeping those two on was a bad thing," said Jayro, "but the plain fact is that the company didn't really *save* any money."

"Yes, it did! Final now processes more with less! That is a savings!"

"I'm sorry, I don't mean any disrespect," said Jayro.

"That's all right," said Wayne. "Please, speak openly."

"I'm afraid that what the fifty percent improvement really means is that Final is *capable* of doing assembly in four minutes rather than eight minutes. It doesn't mean that Final is actually working at that rate – or that Oakton is actually shipping more product than it used to or doing it any faster than it used to."

"Hold on here. Why not? And how do you know?"

"I've walked through Final any number of times in the past couple of months, and they are not going flat out, I can tell you. Sometimes on second shift, they don't have anything to work on."

"How can that be? We've *balanced the line*! They are always supposed to have enough material to keep busy!"

"Well, sir, look upstream from Final, and what do you see? I'll tell you what you see: Godzilla. Now the 'Zilla does its pressure-cooker thing with an average time of a hundred twenty minutes. But that's an *average*."

"Yes, I know. The so-called soak time can range from fifty-two minutes to twenty-three hours, or whatever. The scheduling software in WING4-L is supposed to deal with those complexities."

"Yes?" she asked.

"May I come in?"

"I'll tell you right now, I am not in the mood."

"Tonight, I'm the one with the headache."

She walked away from the door, leaving it ope[n] behind him as he came inside.

He was still dressed in his office clothes, b[ut] his shirt collar was unbuttoned. And somet'[ ] ter she turned on some lights and plopp[ed] room: he was ashen-faced. He looked tr[ ]

"What's the matter? Were you in a[ ]

Viktor grimaced, shook his head[ ]

"Why? What's wrong?"

"We're about to lose the Ma[ ]

Sarah's mouth opened. "[ ] with them."

"I thought I had, too." [ ] on the phone with the[ ] will come tomorro[w] drop. . . . Listen, [ ] you for some li[ ]

"You know[ ]

He head[ed] glass. Vi[ktor] hand.

"You said[ ]

He nodded, [ ]

"I had dinner wi[th] very happy with us. T[ ] I'm afraid." He raised his g[ ]

Sarah had shut her eyes.

"Viktor, why . . . ? "

"Because we're expensive and we're [ ] Then, more softly: "In essence, that's wh[ ] yes, you warned me; you were right. Good for [ ] thing else; something I wouldn't have expected[ ] about the reliability of our findings. They are skeptic[al] of our work. To me, that's the devastating part of it."

Sarah was grimly silent, then ventured to say, "We spin ou[r] a lot, Viktor. There is a lot of waste in the way we operate."

"Oh, please, Sarah! Are you serious? Do you really think that but sh[e]

"Sarah, I'd really like to stay."

"Yes, I know you would, and I told you when you came in _ "

"I just don't want to go home to an empty house. Not tonight."

He took one of her hands in his and gave her the most beseeching, pathetic look.

"You can sleep on the sofa if you want."

"Well . . . better than a cold empty place, I suppose."

She got a pillow and blanket for him, then quickly exited up the stairs and into her bedroom. She started to press the privacy lock on her door, but hesitated, then set it, and got in bed.

Not long after, she heard him. He was outside her door. He tu[ ] the knob, and the locked knob clicked back and forth. He t[ ] softly on the door. She did not answer or make any sound.

"Sarah? Please . . . ?"

She sat up and yelled: "Either sleep on the sofa, or go h[ ] Nothing more from him. She pulled the covers ove[ ] few minutes later, outside, the Porsche's engine fire[ ] off, redlining in first gear, or nearly so, using th[ ] express his displeasure.

Sarah waited, half expecting him to come [ ] downstairs. She made sure the front door wa[ ] there in her robe in the darkness for some [ ] lay down where he had been, kissed the [ ] been, and finally drifted off.

That evening after dinner, just past[ ] in the single glass of wine she all[ ] when she actually had time to [ ] off. She muttered something[ ] mother, and checked the in[ ] number was Tom Dawso[n] She let it go on ring[ ] wanted to do, and the[ ] said:

"Suzie here."

"Oh," said T[ ] Amy? A[ ] this [ ]

"I know lots of things."

Another pause, and then Tom asked, "So what else do you know?"

"I know I am at home in my own house," she said. "Where are you?"

"I am in some shithole of a town in the middle of Africa with a name that sounds like it was puked up."

"Are you by the pool?"

"Uh . . . no. The only pools around here are the ones you don't even want to look at."

"Sounds fabulous, Tom. So cosmopolitan compared to Highboro."

"Oh, it's a happenin' place, I can tell you. No tourists, but lots of nice people who want to be your best friend right up to when they rob you or kill you. No sewage, no safe water, no doctors or hospitals, but it does have a cell phone tower and a dinky little airport. And one bar where it's okay to drink if you keep your back to the wall."

"You've been drinking?"

"Not by my standards. You?"

"I'm loaded," she said, examining her half-empty, half-full glass of wine.

"So how's work?" Tom asked.

"Work sucks," Amy said.

"Really? That good? I think that's a new attitude for you."

"Everyone else seems to have it, so why not me?"

"Is that guy still trying to balance the line?"

"Yes. And I feel like a chump. I banked everything on what he was telling me, and we had a crappy year, and now my boss – who made me take him in the first place – is dumping all over me. I don't know how we could have taken such good ideas, and applied them so professionally and so faithfully, and gotten such underwhelming results."

"Yeah, it's like you've got your foot on the gas, and the pedal is to the floor and nothing is happening."

"Yeah, actually," she agreed, "that is kind of what it feels like."

"And he's telling you someday we're going to be perfect, we've just got to put a little more air in the tires, and twist the ignition wires a little tighter."

"Yeah, pretty much. How do you know?"

"Because I used to be that guy."

"And what did you do? I mean, what should *I* do? Because I'm not sure anymore."

"Honestly . . . you've got to be Sherlock Holmes," he said.

"*What?*"

"In the room where I've been staying, somebody left an anthology of Sherlock Holmes stories, and that's all I've been reading lately. But seriously, that's my advice: Be Sherlock. You've got to look at the whole picture, get rid of the red herrings, the things that don't fit or don't work, and figure out logically one step at a time what will work, how one condition leads to the next, how each cause leads to an effect, until you get to where you need to be."

"Is that all?" she said.

"I'm not saying it's simple. It's more than common sense. You have to challenge what seems obvious. And you have to do the math. But, seeing it's the middle of the night here and I'm in the middle of no place I want to be, that's my best advice: think for yourself."

"Great. I'll remember that."

"So are we still quits?"

"Tom, you left. You are in Africa. Yes, we are still quits."

"Well, I just thought . . . you know . . ."

She softened a bit.

"How's your job going?"

"What job?" Tom joked. "That gig didn't work out as planned."

"What happened?"

"The outfit turned out to be crooked. Mostly a bunch of smugglers with a legitimate cover. My buddy didn't know that when he brought me into it. Long story. Anyway, we picked our moment and bugged out as soon as we could. But, um, the people who hired us don't take kindly to quitters. So we've been on the lam for about a month now."

"Tom, are you all right?"

"Lost a lot of weight. But no punctures as of yet."

"Do you need anything? Money?"

"Thanks, but no," Tom said. "It's just good to hear your voice."

He broke away from the call to talk to someone.

"Hey, I've gotta run," Tom said. "My buddy says the landing lights just came on at the airport. This could be the only plane out of here for days, and we're going to see if we can get on it."

"Tom, be careful. Take care of yourself."

"You bet," he said – then, "Amy? No matter what . . . I love you."

"I love you too," she said, reflexively and without even thinking.

Then he was gone.

Just past dawn the next morning, Amy sat in the glow of her laptop display in her kitchen at home, wearing her nightgown and robe. On the screen was a spreadsheet that she had been assembling. Sometime just past 4:00 a.m., she had awakened in bed, and her mind instantly went to work. Unable to get back to sleep, she had decided to make the most of it.

Around 6:15, she finished what she had been working on. She emailed it to herself and to Wayne Reese, and started making breakfast for her kids.

After she got downtown, her first stop was Wayne's office. She startled him. He hastily – guiltily, Amy thought – minimized a window on his computer screen so that she could not see what it was.

"What were you just doing?" Amy asked. "Playing solitaire?"

"No, I was just reading something."

"Did you get the spreadsheet I emailed?"

"Yes, I did."

"And?"

"You're right. Oakton's best years of performance as far as on-time delivery, low expenses, and so on were prior to the Winner acquisition," Wayne admitted.

"My question to you and everyone else," said Amy, "is how could that be? What was different then? And why did it change for the worse? We know now that the Tornado pulled a few stunts to manipulate the numbers in his favor short-term. But why hasn't Lean had more of an impact?"

"I had a long talk with Jayro Pepps, the materials manager, yesterday. He explained some realities that, for whatever reason, I had not come to terms with."

"You want to know what I think?" asked Amy. "I think we should bring back Murphy Maguire. At least temporarily."

"Well . . . I don't disagree with that," said Wayne. "Kurt does seem to be in over his head. And I have to admit that Maguire did somehow get good performance out of Oakton. Although, if he's going to come in and completely undo everything Lean has accomplished –"

"Wayne, *please*. Save it for tomorrow."

"Tomorrow? Why? Tomorrow is Saturday."

"Yes, you heard correctly," said Amy. "I'm calling an emergency management meeting for my direct reports and a few others, like Murphy. I want everybody in one place as soon as possible to take stock of the situation and lay the basis for a turnaround strategy."

Wayne nodded and said, "Okay. I'll be here."

"No, not here," said Amy. "I think I'm going to hold it at my house."

"Your house? Why there?"

"Because I want us to think outside of the box – so I don't want the meeting inside any of the usual boxes. I want the meeting to be off-site, but on such short notice I don't know what would be available – and anyway that's not where I want to spend my energies. Besides, the price is right. My place is free. So what the heck."

"All right. Count me in," said Wayne.

"Good," said Amy, "because anyone who tries to make excuses not to come is fired."

Wayne looked at her and decided she might not be entirely serious, but she also was not kidding.

She left then. Wayne reopened the window he had minimized, and resumed reading about the Theory of Constraints.

Amy sent the email proclaiming the "leadership meeting," as she put it, at her house for Saturday. She sent it to all the senior managers: Elaine Eisenway, Garth Quincy, Wayne Reese, and Viktor Kyzan-ski. But she also included Murphy Maguire and Sarah Schwick – Murphy because she wanted him back at Oakton, and Sarah in hopes that she would be a voice of reason to counter Viktor's obfuscations. She also included Kurt Konani, as the current Oakton manager; and she decided to add Jayro Pepps because of the materials management and inventory issues.

Murphy called her, tactfully inquiring why he was being included in such a group, and Amy simply told him that as the most experienced manager of Oakton, she wanted his counsel for herself and the group. She would wait and listen on Saturday before deciding conclusively whether to bring him back to take his old position.

By midday Amy had heard from everyone except Viktor and Sarah. Just as Amy was about to go to lunch, Sarah called.

"Hi," said Amy, "did you get my email about the meeting tomorrow here in Highboro?"

"Yes," said Sarah. "I'll be there. Murph and I are going to travel together. We'll leave late this afternoon. But, um, Viktor . . ."

"What about Viktor?" asked Amy. "Don't tell me he's out of the office."

"In fact, he is out of the office. And I don't think he'll be able to make it."

"Why not?" Amy demanded, starting to steam.

"Because he's in jail."

A pause followed.

"Did I hear you correctly? Viktor is in jail?" asked Amy.

"Yes. And his bail hearing isn't until Monday," said Sarah. "His attorney is trying to get it moved up, but the prosecutor considers him a flight risk and is trying to hold him. I've been on the phone for hours this morning."

"Why was he arrested?"

"Speeding."

"Speed of other charges."

"And fast was he going?"

"the height of the chase, his Porsche was clocked at being 'in ss' of one hundred and forty miles per hour."

"The *chase*?"

"It began on Interstate Seventy in western Maryland around Hagerstown about one thirty in the morning," said Sarah, "and continued across the border into Pennsylvania. Finally, south of Carlisle, the Porsche ran out of gas and they arrested him."

"Hold on," Amy said. She put her hand over the receiver and called out, "Linda! Linda, find Elaine right away and get her to come in here!"

Then, back to Sarah, she said, "Elaine Eisenway has Human Resources under her – I think you know that, but anyway, I want Elaine to hear this. While we're waiting, what *happened*? Was he drunk or what?"

Sarah sighed and hesitated, then said:

"He had one drink at my place –"

"Your place?"

"He came to me last night. We were married once, you know. And we've been, um, friends . . . off and on, ever since."

"Oh. I didn't know that part," said Amy. She turned from her door and urgently muttered into the telephone, "And, Sarah, try not to tell that to Elaine!"

"Anyway, he may have had a few before I saw him – but that wasn't the issue. The charges don't even include DUI. When he was with me, he was . . . I guess the word is 'distraught.' We've lost Manchester as a client. He learned that yesterday. But it also looks for sure as though DuPont is going to dump us, and General Electric and a few others as well are at least thinking about it. Everything that Viktor has worked for, it's all blowing up."

Amy covered her eyes with her free hand as she held the phone to her ear.

"Even worse," Sarah continued, "the story about Viktor made the

TV news this morning in Washington, so a lot of our clients probably know by now. I'm sure the rest will know soon."

Toward the end of the afternoon, Amy called and spoke to Sarah
again.

"Elaine and I have agreed that we're giving Viktor a leave of ab-
sence until he straightens out his legal issues. But me, I want Viktor gone. Never mind the police chase. Never mind he's gone. the bad publicity. It's the lack of performance and the lost accounts – that's enough. He's done."

Sarah was quiet for a second, then said, "I think that would be for the best. The best for F&D anyway."

"And so, I'd like you, Sarah, to step in and take Viktor's place on an interim basis," Amy told her.

There was silence on the other end as Sarah took in what she was being offered.

"So we'd both be 'interims'?" Sarah asked.

"Yes."

What went unspoken between them, and what they both knew full well, was that Sarah Schwick was no Viktor Kyzanski. She was brilliant technically and professionally – perhaps the equal of Viktor. And she was a competent, disciplined manager – definitely superior to him regarding day-to-day, grind-it-out managerial tasks. What she lacked was his leadership. His panache. His charm. His ability to talk to a roomful of people and after ten minutes have those people believing what he told them and wanting to do whatever he said.

Sarah did not have those abilities. If Sarah spoke continuously for more than five minutes, those listening to her would begin to think about baseball, or just about anything except the subject she was ad-dressing. When Sarah walked into a roomful of people, it could be half an hour before anyone knew she had arrived. If Viktor was pa-nache, she was the antipanache. Both Amy and she knew this, and neither said what they knew.

Instead, Amy said, "Sarah, *don't* be Viktor. Be yourself. Be your best. Find out what the clients really value, give it to them . . . and please, try not to lose another account. Can you do that?"

And Sarah, quiet as a mouse, said, "I'll try."

"See you tomorrow," said Amy.

13

The gloomy and dire circumstances of the hastily called meeting at Amy's own house were nearly matched by the look of the weather outside. The sky was dense gray and even darker to the west, and the winds were gusty and brisk. But Amy of course had many other concerns.

From the office, Amy had brought home a whiteboard and collapsible easel. She erected this nearby, and then set at each place around the table a pad of sticky notes, a pen, and a tablet of paper. Her final touch was to make place cards for each person, indicating where each should sit, and she made sure that Wayne and Murphy would sit next to each other.

By nine o'clock, everyone had arrived, and shortly thereafter all were seated at the table: Wayne Reese, Kurt Konani, Jerome "Jayro" Pepps, Murphy Maguire, Sarah Schwick, Elaine Eisenway, Garth Quincy, and Amy herself.

"Well, let me first of all say that I personally would rather be doing something else on a Saturday," Amy began, "but our financial performance for the past quarter and the past year absolutely stinks. I have been chewed out by Nigel Furst, and in less than three weeks I am going to have to go before him with a plan to reverse the backsliding and get the business out of the dumps. As of now, I frankly do not know what to tell him. So our objective for today is to identify why so many unexpected and unwanted things have happened, why so many desirable things *have not* happened, and what we can do to plot a new course for the company."

Murphy tentatively raised a hand and asked, "May I just say a few words?"

"Go ahead," said Amy.

"If y'all will just let me cut to the chase," said Murphy, "I can tell you what the real problem is."

"*Please.* Please do tell us what the real problem is, Mr. Maguire."

"The real problem is that the analysts in Rockville are overburdened with nonessential tasks."

"*Huh?*" said Wayne. "No, come on! That's *not* the real problem. The real problem – if I had to put it in a nutshell – is variation! Variation in all its many forms!"

"It's not the variation per se," said Kurt, "it's dealing with the variation. It's that we have attempted to instill a Lean Six Sigma culture throughout the company, but we don't have the proper black-belt to green-belt ratio. *That's* the real problem."

"*What?*" asked Garth. "Excuse me, but isn't it perfectly obvious what the real problem is? We're losing customers! Our sales are declining!"

"Look, I don't know if this is the so-called real problem," said Jayro, "but I'll tell you what a big problem is: too many times, we don't have the proper material in stock – while all too often, we are forced by policy to accept material that we don't need!"

"Well, I don't know what anybody else's real problem is," said Sarah, "but *my* real problem is getting data through the testing loop at F&D so that we can get results to customers."

"Which," said Murphy, "goes back to what *I* said was the real problem –"

"Cash flow!" Elaine asserted. "We currently have too much cash tied up in inventory, and we are spending more than we are making. *That's* the problem."

"Ultimately," said Amy, "the *real problem* is that our earnings are not growing! We are not meeting our business objectives!"

"That's what I'm talking about!" said Garth. "How can you increase earnings if you don't increase sales!"

"I'll tell you one way: by eliminating waste!" said Kurt. "If you save money, you make money –"

"No, no, no!" said Murphy.

"– and to save money by eliminating waste," Kurt said, steamrolling on, "we need the proper black-belt to green-belt ratio!"

"To make more money, you have to increase your throughput!" Murphy thundered. "And to increase throughput you have to manage your constraints!"

"There you go with your 'constraints' thing again!" said Wayne. "If you eliminate variation, if you move to one-piece flow, if you –"

"Variation is reality! In some form and to some degree, it will always be with us!" said Murphy.

Amy glanced at her wristwatch. The time was 9:14 a.m., and already everything was out of control.

"Hold it! Hold it! Hold it!" she yelled.

Everyone quieted down and looked toward her.

"I'm glad everyone has an opinion," she said, "but I want to lay out some rules. First, no arguing! Also, no finger-pointing, no blame games, no self-serving speeches, and above all, no excuses! If I hear any of that today, I will cut you off at the knees. What I want are facts. I want to hear clear, objective observations relating to why the business is in the current, undesirable state that it is."

She waited a moment for someone to respond, and everyone was silent.

"All right," Amy said, "I have an idea."

She held up a pad of sticky notes and a pen.

"Let's get some facts on the table – literally," she continued. "I want each of you to take your pad of sticky notes and write down at least one, but no more than three simple sentences that express what's wrong from your functional point of view. Write your name and function at the top of each note, and if your sentence won't fit on one note, then use two and stick them together. Go ahead, let's do that now."

A few minutes later, the table was littered with little squares of paper – several dozen of them, each bearing a simple sentence.

"Let's put them on the whiteboard," said Amy, "so we can all have a look."

They did this, sticking the notes to the surface in no particular order, and the result was a sprawl of comments that resembled utter chaos . . .

Jayro Pepps, Materials:
We have unexpected shortages of various materials at various times.

Amy Cieolara, President:
We are not meeting our parent corporation's objectives for annual growth and other KPIs.

Jayro Pepps, Materials:
Because of corporate policies, we have to accept raw materials from other Winner subsidiaries – whether we need them or not!

Kurt Konani, Production:
Workstations at Oakton work according to takt time, but do not always finish their work during takt time.

Wayne Reese, Operations:
Despite our best efforts, our flow time through production is getting longer, not shorter.

Kurt Konani, Production:
Work flow at Oakton is being randomly delayed at various places in the plant, even though we have improved the efficiency and reduced waste in a number of processes.

Garth Quincy, Sales & Marketing:
The sales force is becoming demoralized and our salespeople are not trying as hard as they should.

Garth Quincy, Sales & Marketing:
Our sales are declining, not growing!

Garth Quincy, Sales & Marketing:
Our lead times for delivery on build-to-order products are long compared to our competition, yet too frequently we are late with deliveries.

Elaine Eisenway, Finance:
Investments in inventories of all types are high compared to historic levels.

Sarah Schwick, F&D:
Our testing loop is complex, making it difficult to predict when results for clients will be completed.

Murphy Maguire, F&D:
Analyst review, approval, and release of designs is erratic, forcing time pressures on operations.

Sarah Schwick, F&D:
Current policy forbids F&D from seeking shortcuts and work-arounds in testing & analysis, due to quality concerns (and hourly billing imperatives).

Elaine Eisenway, Finance:
Cash flow is deteriorating.

Kurt Konani, Production:
Our ratio of LSS black belts to green belts is inadequate.

Murphy Maguire, F&D:
At F&D, I have noticed that professional staff is pressured to maximize hourly billing to clients, causing nonbillable administrative chores (such as routine design approvals) to be neglected.

Amy Cieolara, President:
Our full-time payroll at Oakton has not been reduced, and we are paying relatively high levels of overtime as well as for part-time temporary workers.

The Real Problem

"Okay, so here we have the opinions of what each of us thinks is the real problem – or problems," said Amy. "Now . . . any thoughts on what to do?"

"Excuse me," said Wayne, "but it might help if you tell us where you want to go with this."

"Actually, I don't have a one-two-three process in mind," she said. "I just thought it might help if we laid out all the basic issues and looked at them as a whole."

"Are you saying we have to solve each one of these individually?" asked Garth.

"Individually?" asked Murphy. "I don't believe we can do that."

"Why not?" asked Kurt. "We just have to prioritize them and go at them one by one."

"What I meant," said Murphy, "is that we can't solve one without considering the effect and influence of the others. Because, in many cases, they are interrelated."

"Wait," said Wayne as he stared at the collection of notes on the board. "Is there a cause-and-effect relationship between all of these?"

Amy, too, peered at the board, and said, "Yes, I can see that there certainly could be."

She rearranged a few of the notes so that there was a sequence from one to the next.

"For instance," she said, *"If* 'workstations at Oakton . . . do not always finish their work during takt time,' *then* it stands to reason that 'Work flow at Oakton is being randomly delayed at various places in the plant . . . ' "

"Sure," said Wayne. "It's logical. But I'm still not sure where we're going with this."

"If you solve one – the root cause problem – then you solve the next problem in the sequence," said Amy.

"Or if one solution doesn't completely solve the next problem," said Sarah, catching on, "then perhaps at least you've influenced it positively so you can build on the improvement."

"But how do you know which comes first?" asked Kurt. "It seems like a chicken-or-the-egg kind of thing. Did the inability to finish within the takt cycle cause the delay? Or did some random delay upstream cause the takt cycle to be exceeded?"

"Seems to me," said Murphy, "you've got to find out which rooster has been a-messin' around with the hen. 'Cause lady chickens don't just lay eggs on their own."

```
┌─────────────────┐
│  Wayne Reese,   │
│   Operations:   │
│ Despite our best│
│ efforts, our flow│
│  time through   │
│  production is  │
│getting longer, not│
│    shorter.     │
└─────────────────┘

                      ┌─────────────────┐
                      │  Garth Quincy,  │
┌─────────────────┐   │ Sales & Marketing:│
│  Kurt Konani,   │   │ Our lead times for│
│  Production:    │   │  delivery on build-│
│  Work flow at   │   │  to-order products│
│  Oakton is being│   │ are long compared│
│ randomly delayed│   │ to our competition,│
│ at various places│   │ yet too frequently│
│ in the plant, even│   │  we are late with │
│  though we have │   │   deliveries.   │
│   improved the  │   └─────────────────┘
│   efficiency and│
│  reduced waste  │   ┌─────────────────┐
│ in a number of  │   │  Jayro Pepps,   │
│   processes.    │   │   Materials:    │
└─────────────────┘   │   We have       │
         ▲            │  unexpected     │
┌─────────────────┐   │  shortages of   │
│  Kurt Konani,   │   │various materials at│
│  Production:    │   │  various times. │
│  Workstations   │   └─────────────────┘
│ at Oakton work  │
│ according to takt│
│ time, but do not│
│ always finish their│
│ work during takt│
│     time.       │
└─────────────────┘
```

Everyone else turned to him somewhat agape.

"Well, I *am* just an old country boy at heart!" Murphy said.

"I think what Mr. Maguire is trying to say is that we have to determine the relationships between all of the elements," said Amy, "in order to see which was the cause and which was the effect."

"The affairs of roosters and hens aside," said Wayne, "this could be where DMAIC would very useful, even essential – the process of *define, measure, analyze* and so on."

"Yes, very possibly," said Amy, "but I remind you, we don't have – *I* certainly don't have – months or years to invest in some quest for the perfect process. We need to be right, but we also need to be quick. So

I'm thinking, why not invest the hour or whatever in exploring this cause-effect sequence and see if there is anything to it?"

Which was what they did. They began moving the sticky notes around on the whiteboard, and when they thought they had a correct sequence, they used the colored markers to draw lines between them to indicate the relationship.

There was haggling. Everyone – including Sarah Schwick, for some time – discounted Murphy's assessment of the impact of the Rockville analysts on the entire system of processes.

"How could a relative handful of professional employees choke the entire system?" asked Wayne.

"Mr. Reese, sir, it is because the analysts are so few in number – and yet so essential to so much of what we do as a company – that they are able to be a choke on the entire system," said Murphy.

"You know," said Amy, "it is true that nothing moves at Oakton until an analyst in Rockville has signed off on a production order."

"Is that really necessary?" asked Wayne.

"It's because of liability concerns," said Amy. "About fifteen years ago, Hi-T got sued for hundreds of millions of dollars because of what the plaintiff claimed was negligence in producing a product that failed in its intended use. After that, the only way that we could appease the insurance company was to have a policy in place that all customer orders would be critically reviewed by the F&D analysts prior to production."

"Man, the lawyers sure do run everything, don't they," said Garth.

"That's reality," said Amy. "All orders must pass analyst review. We may not like it, but that's what we have to deal with."

"In fact, nobody likes it," said Sarah. "The analysts do the reviews because they're part of their job description, but most if not all of them hate the process."

"Why is that?" asked Amy.

"Because it's tedious, boring – and yet they're under a lot of professional pressure. If the analyst misses something, and there is a failure in the intended use of the product, it probably means some kind of tragedy has occurred. And on top of those negatives, they don't get anything extra for doing the reviews."

"Extra?" asked Amy. "Why should they get anything extra?"

"Well, let me put it this way," said Sarah, "the analysts *do* get incentives for other aspects of their work."

"Like what?"

"A production design review is just an internal charge-back to

Hi-T. It's treated like an expense. But when the analyst works on a research project for a Formulation and Design client, the analyst's time is billed at an hourly rate."

"Right," said Amy.

"The more billable time the analyst has at the end of the year," said Sarah, "the bigger the bonus the analyst makes."

"So greed rears its ugly head," said Kurt.

"Now, wait," said Sarah. "You have to realize that the analysts all work long hours. Twelve hours a day is the norm, and fourteen and sixteen-hour days are not unheard of. At times these people are working six and seven days a week – for year after year. Believe me, I know what it's like; I used to be an analyst before I – foolishly – thought that moving into management would give me more personal time. My point is that if we don't incentivize the analysts in some fashion relative to the income they're generating, they won't stick around. That's why Viktor coddled them, and fed their egos, and paid them so well."

"They do make very good money," Amy commented. "More than what I make, some of them."

"Like what kind of bucks are we talking about?" asked Garth.

"An entry level analyst makes a hundred and twenty thousand dollars a year, plus benefits and bonuses," said Sarah. "And a senior analyst like Joe Tassoni can earn pretty close to half a million a year."

"Wow," someone muttered.

"But Sarah has a good point," said Amy. "They are bringing in big income for the company, and most of them are at the top of their professions – the best in the world in their fields."

"And it's not just pure greed that keeps them at F&D," Sarah argued. "It's the money *and* the ability to pursue research that is often of deep professional interest to them."

"All right, fine," said Wayne, "but for that kind of compensation, is it too much to ask that they *not* choke the production end of the business? That they give more attention and time to the design reviews?"

"Some of the reviews are cut and dried," said Sarah, "but many are not. They take time. *And* all the while, there is pressure from the project managers at Rockville to give priority to F&D client work. Remember, the analysts are central to everything we do in Rockville. They would be busy even if they did not have to do the design reviews – which are just a huge chore for them. A lot of months we have to prod the analysts to finish up their reviews. It's like we tell them, 'Hurry up! But, oh, by the way, you can't be wrong on anything.' "

Amy cut off the discussion, saying, "Okay, I think I'm beginning to see some of the connections here."

She went to the whiteboard and began trying to diagram the chain of what was going on.

"This is a fact," Amy said, pointing to the bottom note "By policy, and for serious reasons, the analysts at F&D must review and approve all product designs manufactured by Hi-T. We might argue over whether this is necessary, but for now it's a fact this is what is happening. Right?"

"Right," said several of the others in unison.

"At the same time, the analysts have their own research and other duties. That also is a fact. Correct?"

"Correct."

"Thanks to Sarah Schwick, it's been made clear that the analysts are incentivized in a number of ways – ranging from their bonuses to professional interest – to give priority to F&D clients and the hourly billings to those clients that generate income. True?"

"True."

"So if F&D clients get top priority, then design approvals for Hi-T get lower priority. Also true?"

"Yes."

"And if the analysts cannot finish all their work in a given time period, something is going to be delayed. Right? And the work that is put off until tomorrow is almost always going to be the lower priority design approvals. Right again?"

"Yes, I'm sorry to say it, but that's the way it happens," said Sarah.

"If the analysts have to postpone approvals, then when they finally get around to dealing with them, what happens? The approvals are going to be late, and they're going to be released in a big batch."

"Wait a minute," said Wayne. "Why is that? Why the big batch?"

"I'm presuming that's what happens, because that's human nature," said Amy. "It's like email. Most days, because I'm busy, I usually can't deal with each email as it comes in. I wait until I have fifteen or twenty minutes, and then I deal with all of it."

"Yes, and that's what happens in Rockville," Sarah agreed. "When an analyst gets a breather, he whips through all the accumulated designs that have come in, and he signs off and sends them to Oakton. Except that all of these require more than just a token glance. Some can be looked over and approved in minutes, but others may require hours or days of analysis, queries, testing, and so on. And those are going to be held up even longer."

"Therefore, when design approvals finally reach Oakton, they come sporadically and late," said Amy. "And if they come in late –"

"Oakton is always playing catch-up," said Murphy.

With a nod to Murphy, Amy wrote out another sticky note and put it above the others.

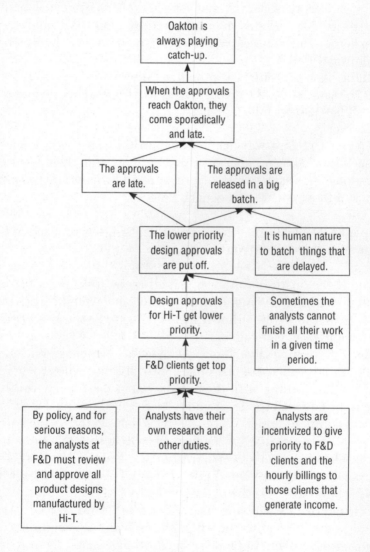

As she did this, Wayne's shaven head turned pinkish and then red. Finally, he spoke up.

"All right, all right," he said, "I have the distinct feeling that you are going to try to pin all the problems on me – and on LSS."

"No, Wayne, I have no intention of doing that, or of letting any-one else do that," Amy said calmly. "As I said at the beginning, there will be no blame games, no finger-pointing, not even any mea culpas, and absolutely no self-serving speeches."

Wayne sat back, but folded his arms across his chest.

"But more than that," Amy continued, "you brought to this company something valuable, something elegant, something that made sense on a lot of levels. I bought in. Many of us bought in. And I've all but staked my career on it. Yet the things we have tried have not delivered – at least not to the degree we expected. So we have to figure out what is really going on and go from there."

She turned back to the white board.

"Now, the statement has been made that Oakton is always playing catch-up. If that is true, the question is, why? What has been going on at Oakton?"

"How far back do you want to go?" asked Murphy.

"I guess as far as necessary," said Amy.

"Well, even before the lawsuit and the F&D approval requirement, it was decided by people far more intelligent than yours truly that Hi-T would avoid high-volume, low-margin production."

"Right, globalization of suppliers was under way," said Amy, "and the conclusion was made – though not by me – that we could not compete against Asian vendors with lower labor costs. Instead, we would carve our own market niche in specialty composites that offered high performance, and for us, offered higher margins."

"But to succeed in the specialty segment," Murphy went on, "we needed flexibility. That flexibility took us into unfamiliar territory, and that in part was what brought on the lawsuit."

"As I understand it," said Garth, "the lawsuit actually had little to do with us. We were caught in a broad net. It was our customer who was primarily at fault for giving us poor specifications."

"Nevertheless," said Murphy, "in order to protect the company, and our customers, and the ultimate consumers, whoever they might be, the design approval requirement was put in place."

"Excuse me," said Amy, "but could we please fast forward?"

"Yes, I know all that seems like ancient history," said Murphy, "but you should understand that one condition begat the next. Every effect has its preceding cause. And because design approval from F&D became mandatory, the effect was that Oakton's ability to produce became *dependent* upon Rockville's ability to approve."

"Dependent? I don't quite understand," said Elaine.

"Yes, dependent. As in, one action cannot proceed until a prior action has been completed," said Murphy. "As in, before you can cook dinner, you must first go to the store and buy the food to be cooked."

"But so what?" asked Elaine.

"When we became dependent upon the analysts, their performance affected ours. If Rockville was late, then Oakton was late."

"Unless you could catch up and get back on schedule," Amy concluded.

"Exactly right," said Murphy. "And the game of catch-up became a game that we at Oakton became very good at playing."

"But if Oakton is as good as you say at playing catch-up," asked Garth, "why isn't it doing more now?"

All eyes turned to Wayne Reese.

"To be honest," said Wayne, "I don't understand it myself. Because LSS has made Oakton more efficient."

"No, sir, I beg to differ," said Murphy. "LSS has not made Oakton *as a whole* more efficient. You have made pieces of the production process more efficient, but you have not made the production system *as a whole* more efficient."

"Wait a minute!" argued Kurt. "Look at all the waste we've removed! We've reorganized the Cooler to get the cold storage materials in and out faster. We've established kanbans. We've lowered the defect rate on the M57 Line by two percent. We've color-coded the resin dye bins so that mistakes are almost impossible. We've shifted personnel between stations to balance staff to workload – and on and on. You can't say that all of that hasn't improved the system!"

"What have you done to improve the performance of Godzilla?" asked Murphy.

"We've reduced the number of people used to load and unload."

"I'm sorry to tell you, but what you have actually done is removed the reserve capacity that was in place for a reason: to allow us to recover quickly when something goes wrong – and sooner or later it always does, or my name isn't Murphy."

Kurt began to defend again, but Wayne put a hand on his shoulder and stopped him.

"No, Maguire has a point," said Wayne. "It's been staring me in the face for months, and I hate to admit it, but until we reinvent the autoclave process technology –"

"We are *not* spending twenty million just to achieve one-piece flow," said Amy. "Not this year certainly, and not any time in the foreseeable future."

"Then," said Murphy, "if you cannot increase the rate of flow through Godzilla . . ."

"Then we cannot increase the throughput of the system as a whole," said Amy, drawing the conclusion.

"I know," Wayne Reese was nodding in admission. "We can improve upstream and downstream, but the flow will not improve because of the autoclave bottleneck."

Amy picked up a pad of notes and a pen.

"This is the cause-effect chain that I think has gone on, that continues to go on," said Amy.

She began writing brief notes describing each link of the chain while she explained the logic.

"The Winner management culture is metrics-driven. That is, the managers with the best KPIs – Key Performance Indicators, as they're called – get the best bonuses and promotions."

She put that sticky note near the bottom of the whiteboard.

"One of the Winner beliefs is that 'maximum utilization' of each and every resource results in 'maximum efficiency.' All Winner managers attempt to make their numbers look like they are managing for 'maximum utilization.'

"The 'maximum utilization' assumption is incorporated in Winner's proprietary WING software.

"If followed unquestioningly, WING results in extremely high inventories, because resource capacities have not been balanced against demand. Everything is running flat out, and inventory is being produced whether it is needed or not."

"I suspect what most managers do is find ways to fiddle with the data fed into WING, and essentially lie to it," said Wayne.

"That's what I did," Murphy said with a shrug of his bearish shoulders. "It's the only way to survive."

Amy rolled her eyes.

"So Winner turns to Lean Six Sigma. Winner's application of
 to reduce capacity and keep the remaining capacity at
 els. Resources, in theory at least, operate at close to one
 – maximum utilization, the ideal – and inventories

 ntinued, "we have reconfigured resources at
 lly we have just enough capacity to meet

 ted 'excess' capacity, we have a real prob-
 uations in workload – especially when pro-

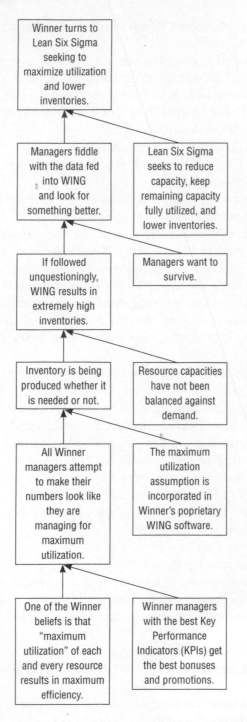

duction approvals come in sporadically and late from Rockville. In other words, we can walk, but we can't run. And if anything trips us up while we're walking, we fall behind.

"Therefore, we cannot play the catch-up game.

"Therefore, if something becomes late, it stays late."

Amy looked over the layout of the notes, and said, "Well, clearly there is an intersection of these two cause-and-effect chains."

"In other words," said Wayne, "If we have only 'just enough' capacity to meet demand, then whenever an unforeseen event causes a delay, we cannot make up for slippage."

"You hit the nail on the head," said Murphy, "and because of slippage, there are temporary bottlenecks caused by the inability to stay within the takt time cycle."

For the twenty minutes or so, with Amy at the board rearranging the notes, writing new ones, and connecting them by drawing arrows from one to the next, they talked and argued and resolved – ultimately created a cause-effect chain that seemed logical and true.

Amy then read through the chain:

"With a balanced production line, Oakton has only 'just enough' capacity.

"Small variations cause temporary bottlenecks in the flow throughout the system.

"Therefore, Godzilla is often less productive than before.

"Therefore, flow time in increasing, not decreasing.

"Therefore, Hi-T is often missing scheduled shipping dates.

"To save customer satisfaction, we now routinely use expensive overnight courier deliveries.

"Even with overnight shipping, deliveries are still days overdue from what was promised.

"Therefore, more and more customers are mad at us.

"Therefore, our sales force is demoralized.

"Therefore, our sales are declining.

"Therefore, cash flow is deteriorating.

"Therefore, the company is losing money rather than making money.

"Therefore, we are not meeting objectives.

"Therefore, Winner management is angry.

"Therefore, the jobs and careers of many at Hi-T are in jeopardy."

Amy turned to everyone else.

"Well," she said, "that is just an amazing chain of undesirable consequences."

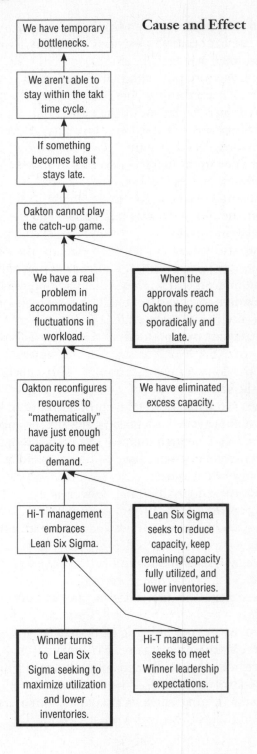

Cause and Effect

We have temporary bottlenecks.

We aren't able to stay within the takt time cycle.

If something becomes late it stays late.

Oakton cannot play the catch-up game.

We have a real problem in accommodating fluctuations in workload.

When the approvals reach Oakton they come sporadically and late.

Oakton reconfigures resources to "mathematically" have just enough capacity to meet demand.

We have eliminated excess capacity.

Hi-T management embraces Lean Six Sigma.

Lean Six Sigma seeks to reduce capacity, keep remaining capacity fully utilized, and lower inventories.

Winner turns to Lean Six Sigma seeking to maximize utilization and lower inventories.

Hi-T management seeks to meet Winner leadership expectations.

"Kind of like a train wreck," said Wayne.

"But it didn't start that way," said Amy. "Look. Down at the base, the intentions were positive."

She wrote one more note and placed it at the very bottom of the whiteboard, below all the others. It read:

"Each of us wants to be successful."

She pointed from the bottom note she had just fixed to the board and the note at the very top.

"We've achieved exactly the opposite of what we set out to do," said Amy.

At the end of the day, Amy was still sitting at her dining room table, studying the whiteboard with its little rectangles of sticky notes and lines and arrows drawn with markers connecting one note to the next. The others had left a short while ago, but a plan had been formed. It was just an action plan, not a solution or a strategy, but it was the next step nevertheless.

"The one thing I do not want," Amy had told them, "is for us to throw together some laundry list of changes only to find in three or six months that we got it wrong or it's been ineffective. We need a well-grounded, logical strategy. Trouble is, we don't have months to put one together. It has to be right, but it also has to be done on the fly."

So it was decided that the first order of business would be to gather and confirm facts, and to assess the situation. Wayne Reese would travel to Rockville, and with the help of Sarah Schwick, would spend the week learning everything he could about the F&D analysts. He would put together a "quick and dirty" value stream map in order to study the work flow to and from the analysts. He would talk to everyone around them, note their work habits, take them to lunch and dinner individually and collectively, and learn the analysts' own thinking about what they did and how they did it. At the end of the week, Wayne and Sarah would return to Highboro with their findings.

In the meantime, Murphy Maguire would go to Oakton, where he would assess what had happened in his absence. He would also do anything obvious that would help bring Godzilla back to better efficiency. But he had solemnly promised not to dismantle the Lean Six Sigma projects – not yet at least, although everyone including Wayne knew that changes would have to be made.

Amy was now gazing at the whiteboard, when she heard herself muttering aloud, "It's that damned balanced line."

The UDE Tree

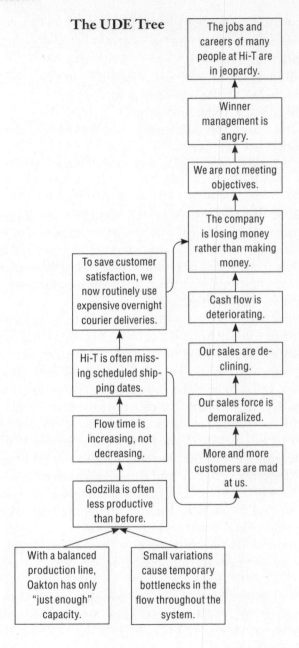

That was certainly a root cause of so much of the difficulty, she concluded. But the analyst issues, too, were a large – and largely hidden – factor in their problems.

She heard the familiar rumble of Harry and Zelda's big Ford as it turned onto the driveway. Seconds later the kids bolted through the kitchen door. Michelle kissed Amy on her cheek; Ben, who was now just slightly taller than his mother, on her forehead. Then they were racing each other for the remote control of the television. In the meantime, Amy went to help her mother get up the back steps. Zelda was having a lot of trouble with her knees. Then Amy had to help her father; he was "stuck" trying to get out of the Ford. Lately, while getting out of the car, Harry would attempt to stand up on the leg that was still inside the vehicle, whereupon he would be unable to sort out what he should do.

Once everyone was inside and the chaos had settled down, Amy poured a glass of wine, much needed, and sat down again at the dining room table. Harry shuffled in and looked at the whiteboard.

"What's this?" he asked.

"It's how the best intentions can end up with bad results."

"Looks like some kind of a tree," he said. "An ugly tree."

"It's the UDE tree," said Amy.

"The what?"

"The tree of undesirables."

"I'm confused," said Harry.

"For once, I'm not."

Then the doorbell chimed.

"Now what?" Amy asked fate.

And when she opened the front door, there stood Tom Dawson.

"Hi," he said, "I was in the neighborhood, thought I'd stop by."

Shaking her head, she smiled, and then said, "Come in."

She slipped her arms around his waist, and was surprised at how thin he was. The fatigue of his journey showed on his face. He was sunburned, yet somehow pale. They hugged each other for some time – before Harry noticed.

"Hey, hey, hey, young man! That's my daughter!"

"Yes, sir, I know," said Tom.

"Dad, do you remember Tom?" asked Amy.

"Pleased to meet you," Harry said, shaking Tom's hand.

"Maybe we could go for a drive," Amy suggested.

"I want her home no later than ten o'clock," Harry said with complete seriousness.

They did go for a short drive. He told her of his ordeals. He wanted to take her to his place, but she wasn't ready for that.

They saw each other again Sunday afternoon. Amy had by then

put her feelings in check. Still, he coaxed her to a walk in the park. Just the two of them in the open. It felt awkward being together. They said good-bye.

They saw each other Monday. He came over after dinner. It being a nice, though cool evening, they sat on the porch together. She began asking a lot of questions. He became impatient at the probing, then got huffy and left. But there were things she felt she needed to know, and satisfied with his answers, she called him an hour later.

They saw each other on Tuesday evening. She went to his place. There was no discussion. Afterward, they talked for hours.

By Thursday, they were able to talk about the mundane. He was unsure whether to restart his aviation business or try to do something else. But he still had a lot in savings, plus his military pension, and he didn't have to decide right away.

"How's work going?" he asked her.

She told him about the UDE tree, and some of what they had learned in the process.

"Well, sounds like you've got your issues," he commented. "You see, in people's minds, 'balance' is good, and 'constraint' is bad. It's not until they see the principles play out that they understand it's actually the opposite in a practical world. That little dice game we played at your house however many months ago? The basis of that is valid."

"I remember you saying there were a couple of other ways to play that."

"Yeah, there's one way that dramatically drops your inventories. And there is a fourth way that gives you fantastic results."

Amy put her arm around his taut waist.

"What are you doing this Saturday?" she asked him.

"I don't know. Why? Do you want to do something?"

"Well, I'm already committed. But I was wondering if you would do a favor for me."

"That depends on what kind of favor." he said.

"I was wondering if you would teach that game to the Hi-T people I'm having over."

"It'll cost ya."

She smiled and whispered, "Then I guess I'll just have to ante up."

14

"The most important finding gained this past week in Rockville," said Wayne Reese, "was that the F&D staff spends a really high percentage of their time – from twenty to as much as forty percent or higher – on tasks that contribute no value from the customer's point of view."

"The *client's* point of view," Sarah said, correcting him. "We generally refer to the customer as a 'client' at Rockville."

"Yes, well, in any case, there is a hell of a lot of *muda* at F&D – no offense to Sarah or anyone working there," said Wayne.

"No offense taken," Sarah said in a listless tone.

It was Saturday morning, just one week after the first meeting around Amy's dining room table. Missing from the first group were Jayro Pepps and Kurt Konani, who were at Oakton sorting some critical inventory issues. But everyone else was there: Wayne, Sarah, Murphy, Elaine, Garth, and, of course, Amy. Her kids had once again given up their house for the day on the promise that this would be the last time for at least a while – and some cash for each of them to spend at the mall.

Unfurled across that dining room table was a long sheet of butcher paper with notes and arrows and stick-on blue dots, orange dots, red dots, and so on showing the general flow of work through F&D. This was Wayne's "quick and dirty" value stream map, or VSM, that he had put together.

"Now, you see the blue dots," Wayne continued. "Those indicate an action in the flow that contributes value. The orange dots add no value, but are necessary – things like regulatory requirements or internal administrative processes. But the red dots are where waste occurs. They add no value, but are part of the total process because

215

of outdated policy or just plain old inertia – just the way things have always been done – and so on. Just look at the number of those red dots. Every one of them represents an opportunity to eliminate waste by applying Lean and –"

"Wait a minute," said Amy. "Where are the F&D analysts in this?"

"Everything done by an analyst is represented by a pink Post-it Note," said Wayne.

"I see there are a lot of pink notes up there," said Amy. "So, where is the value stream for the production design reviews that affect the Oakton plant?"

Wayne pointed to the bottom left corner of the VSM butcher paper where, almost lost in the complexity, a simple line entered from the left and went through a relatively small number of steps, mostly marked with blue dots.

"That's *it*?" asked Amy.

"Well, it depends," said Wayne. "If the analyst approves the design – which happens about eighty percent of the time – then it's released to production planning and goes to Oakton. If the analyst finds an issue – the other twenty percent – then it enters this testing loop, where samples or a full prototype are made up and subjected to a testing cycle. Finally, the results 'loop' back to the analyst, who then either approves the design, sends it back into the loop for more testing, or rejects it and sends it back to the, um, *client* via the salesperson. So it can be simple or complex."

"All right," said Amy, "but that's one corner and one or two loops. What's with the rest of it? Why go into all that detail?"

"Because I felt we needed to see the big picture," said Wayne. "Due to Viktor's lack of buy-in last year, we never really got the chance to map it all out."

"Fine," said Amy. "I can accept that."

"And as I was about to say," Wayne went on, "the full view of the value stream affords us a huge opportunity. Because if we can eliminate waste throughout the F&D subsystem of Hi-T, there should be more resources and time to enable the analysts to do the design reviews."

Amy felt herself getting angry, felt her lips pressing together and her shoulder muscles tensing. But she made herself speak in a low tone calmly and deliberately.

"Wayne . . . I . . . did . . . not . . . send you to Rockville with the expectation of pursuing a full-blown implementation of Lean Six Sigma."

She pointed to the whiteboard, re-erected from the week before.

"Last week we constructed this logical tree that bears rotten fruit. We identified the analysts as being a root cause affecting Oakton's inability to meet commitments, because of the pressures and conflicts surrounding the design approvals. So, while I have nothing against seeing the big picture, it seems to me that it's the design approval part of the value stream where we need to *focus*."

"But, Amy, that's my point!" said Wayne. "Isn't it common sense that if we eliminate the waste *throughout* F&D, at each one of these little red dots –"

"It will take *forever*! We do not have that long!" Amy exclaimed, giving in to frustration. "And common sense, to my way of thinking, says that we focus on what is critical to accomplish the most good right now."

"Okay, okay," said Wayne "I read you loud and clear. We will focus on the analysts."

Amy turned to Sarah Schwick and asked, "What's your take on this?"

"While Wayne was assembling the value stream map – which I do think will be useful in the long run," said Sarah, "I did a more classic time study of the analysts. I went back through three years of time sheets to try to quantify how they spent their time and see if there were any patterns."

"And were there any patterns?"

"No. None whatsoever," said Sarah with a straight face, but then her linear lips cracked a smile. "Sorry. Just trying to keep things light. Yes, there *were* patterns. For instance, there were far more design 'clearances,' as they are officially called, at the end of the month, when there is pressure to clear them out, along with other administrative chores. And there were also more when the number of projects going on was low – or in other words when the analysts had nothing better to do."

"If I may comment?" asked Murphy. "I never had the luxury of being able to quantify it, but based on my observations, the analysts are a true, but intermittent bottleneck."

"What do you mean by that?" asked Amy.

"A bottleneck, by most accounts anyhow, though not necessarily mine," said Murphy, "is a resource that cannot consistently or reliably meet the demands placed on it. So its output is typically less than demand. This is in contrast to a primary constraint, which is the resource most likely to become a bottleneck if not properly managed. But as for the analysts at Rockville, I think that they are equal to the demands placed on them maybe just sixty percent of the time. What that means is that forty percent of the time – four out of every ten days – they can't keep up. Things like design reviews get pushed to the back burner, or completely off the stove. Then when things cool down a bit, they catch up on whatever was put off. Because design reviews are, for them, a pain in the neck of low priority, there is usually a big backlog at that point – and the analysts just churn them out before the next high tide of test results or whatever comes in."

"I didn't quite know how to say it," said Sarah, "but, yes, I think that's very much what happens."

"So the analysts are a true bottleneck," Murphy concluded, "but only intermittently and mainly with whatever work they don't want to do. But let me tell you, that plays hell with trying to schedule production in a manufacturing plant."

"Yes, but Murph, for years Oakton did well with on-time shipments and turned in very respectable numbers," said Amy. "How did you do it back then?"

"Back in the good ole days? Well, I always did everything I could to be sure that Oakton had a healthy backlog of cleared design reviews," said Murphy. "But if the backlog of approvals ran low, I would feed in some build-to-stock product refills – just to keep everybody in Highboro happy, so they didn't think we'd all gone to the beach. And if the supply of approved build-to-order runs did not recover, then I would just get on the phone to B. Donald Williams, and B. Don would call Viktor, and Viktor would go and rattle the analysts' cages, and lo and behold, a few days later a new batch of approvals would magically appear. It was all very informal – yet effective."

Wayne was shaking his head; Elaine was shuddering; Garth was chuckling; and Sarah was looking amused and peeved at the same time.

"You know," Sarah said to Murphy, "I was one of the ones in those cages."

"Sorry," said Murphy. "We all do what we must to get by!"

"And how is Oakton?" Amy asked him. "What is your assessment?"

"I must admit, in all honesty, that I am impressed with some of what has been accomplished in my absence," said Murphy. "The M57 Line in particular, with its new configuration, is downright slick – not that that improvement or any of the others will provide the increase in throughput that we desperately need. Nevertheless, I think that Oakton can be made profitable, from an operating standpoint, in fairly short order. *If*, that is, we jettison the notion that the plant must have a balanced line."

All eyes turned to Wayne.

"I thank you for the compliment," he said to Murphy. "On the other hand, I've given everything we talked about last week a lot of thought, and I really do *not* think that we should give up on the balanced line just yet."

"Just yet?" challenged Amy. "You think we should wait another year until everything is all that much worse? Or what?"

"No! Look, the main issue is variation! If we continue to work to reduce variation, everything should be fine!" Wayne argued.

And when skeptical or blank looks came from the others, he added:

"I just don't think we should run away from everything that we've accomplished."

"Well, in the interest of resolving this," said Amy, "I have invited someone to join us today. Sort of a special guest."

"Who?" asked Elaine.

"Nigel Furst," Garth guessed.

"No, definitely not Nigel," said Amy.

"Peter Winn," suggested Sarah, as a joke.

"Oh, yeah, right," said Amy. "As if Mr. Winn would deign to come to my house in Highboro. No, our mystery guest is known to some of you, but not to others. Let me see if he's ready."

She turned on her cell phone and pressed a speed-dial number.

"Hi, it's me. Ten minutes? Great."

By the time Tom Dawson arrived, Amy had everything in place – dice, pennies, and tally sheets. She called everyone back from their break, introduced Tom, and then seated everyone around the table.

Amy was at the head of the table, in the position of the penny vendor, representing raw materials. Wayne was to her right, with Sarah to his right. Murphy Maguire sat opposite Amy at the far end of the table. To Murphy's right was Garth, then Elaine in the final position. Tom took a chair from the kitchen and squeezed between Amy and Elaine at the corner of the table. With pen in hand, he would keep score on the tally sheets.

"In this first round," Tom said, "we are going to simulate a balanced processing line."

And he explained the rules, which were the same as when Amy and her kids and her parents had played months before: everyone had one die and four pennies to start. Everything was "level." Each person, however, could only move the number of pennies rolled with the die, and only if there was a sufficient number of pennies in queue in front of that person. A roll of six, in which only four pennies were in queue, meant that only four could be moved to the next person, and so on.

The targeted expectation for output was sixty-five pennies. This was to allow some slack below the seventy-cent average of three-point-five extended over twenty turns.

They played those twenty turns. The pennies crossing the finish line as Elaine's long white fingers with their red-painted nails swept them into the clear, numbering at the end: forty-six. The inventory of pennies in process had nearly doubled by then from twenty cents to thirty-nine. Clearly, this was below expectations with respect to output and far above with respect to the symbolic investment in penny inventory.

"Should we play it again?" asked Amy, looking at Wayne. "Maybe we can do better next time? Maybe we can meet the sixty-five-cent target?"

"I don't see what the point is," said Wayne. "I mean, yes, I am a little surprised we didn't come closer to achieving the average. But clearly the expectations were too high. We should have been shooting for what we can actually deliver, not some pie-in-the-sky number."

"Suppose that sixty-five represents the actual market demand," said Amy. "Now what are you going to do?"

"I'm going to commit to the number I can actually reach," Wayne asserted.

"And give up a third of the market that's there for the taking?" asked Amy. "Fine, Wayne. *You* go to Nigel Furst and tell him that. I'm sure he'll be very understanding."

"Now wait a minute!" Wayne protested. "The rules are against us. We're always hamstrung with the lower number. Either the inventory isn't available, or the ability to process isn't what it should be. The whole idea of Lean –"

"We're not demonstrating Lean," said Tom, "we're simulating a balanced line."

"But you're using dice! A one to six spread! *That* is variation!" Wayne complained.

A deep chuckle emerged from Murphy at the end of the table, after which he said, "Hey, I am here to tell you that there have been months when I would have been happy with that range of variability. I have seen it all: material not showing up because vendors went bankrupt. Skilled people in the hospital. Lightning strikes blowing out transformers. Equipment overheating and catching fire. And then the mere every*day* randomness!"

"Wayne, let me tell you," said Tom, "we could eliminate the dice in this simulation. If you had enough people – twenty or thirty – all just passing pennies from one to the next, you would still have variation. You'd have people screwing up and passing three pennies or two instead of four, then the next person trying to cope with five or six on the following turn, and on down the line. You would end up with waves, not a smooth flow.

"Then think about each person having to actually do a processing step. Like one person has to turn the pennies heads up, and the next make them all tails up, and the next in a square, and the one after – I don't know – put them all in line with one finger's width between. Whatever. Think of all the fluctuations that would happen when you add complicated tasks to all that dependency from one person to the next, to the next. Even without the dice you're going to get ripples and waves."

"That's why we have takt time!" Wayne said. "We calculate takt and balance the line so that everyone has sufficient time to complete whatever tasks have to be done."

"But, Wayne, you're loading every workstation to run at ninety-three or ninety-four percent of its capacity," said Murphy. "What happens when somebody isn't ready at the end of the takt cycle? When somebody drops the ball? Something just doesn't show up when the clock strikes?"

"Then we're late!" Wayne admitted. "And if it happens consistently, we make adjustments."

"The problem," said Murphy, "is that you never know who's going to have a bad day. And if you constantly keep making adjustments based on temporary bottlenecks, then the workforce doesn't know which end is up."

Wayne tried not to scowl, but he knew there was truth in this because he had seen the confusion at Oakton when Kurt had been forced to scramble employees from one area of the plant to another for exactly that reason.

"Well, I don't know that much about production," said Sarah, "but if a balanced line is problematic, what's the alternative? An *un*balanced line?"

"Yes, an unbalanced line," said Tom. "And the way you unbalance the line is through the use of a constraint."

"Now I know where you're going – to the Theory of Constraints," said Wayne. "I've been reading about it, but . . . I don't know. I'm just not convinced."

"All right, I hear you," said Tom. "But let's just give it a try."

And they did. The setup was the same as in the round before, with four pennies in queue in front of everyone except Amy, who had the penny jar. But this time everyone would use two dice – except for Murphy, who would only have one. Murph would represent the constraint.

After the twenty turns, simulating a month's output, they had moved an impressive eighty-six pennies through the system. This was obviously well above the sixty-five-cent target.

"Excess finished goods!" Wayne carped at the end.

"All right, Mr. Wise Guy," said Amy. "We are assuming plenty of demand and a profitable market for everything we process. The point is that we not only met the low target, but we beat the expectation handily. *With* a constraint in place."

"And with doubled capacity everywhere else!" Wayne countered. "Seriously, look at how you got there! Twice the capability for four out of the five of us doing the processing. In the real world that would be very expensive."

"On the other hand, look at your throughput," said Murphy. "Output has nearly doubled. We're selling everything we make. Customers are happy because they're getting their products. I say that higher throughput – the rate of making money, I'm talking about here – more than offsets the higher inventory and expense!"

"Does it?" asked Wayne. "I'm not so sure. Look at all that inventory still on the table, especially in front of you, Murph. That's got to be forty to fifty pennies stuck in front you."

"But remember," said Amy, "that buffer is in place so that the constraint always has enough to work on, and keeps chugging along. Everywhere else, inventory levels are fairly low."

"He does have a point, though," said Tom. "The overall inventory number is high – sixty-one pennies."

"Yes! You see! This would be a very expensive system to run!" said Wayne.

"I have to take Wayne's side on this one," said Elaine. "From an accounting point of view, I'd be wondering about costs and investment."

"That's why in Round Three, we're going to improve it," said Tom. "We're going to run things the same way, with a constraint in place, but we're going to make a couple of changes. First, we're going to take away Amy's dice. Whatever Murphy rolls with his one die, he will call out that number to Amy – and Amy will feed that same number of new pennies to Wayne and into the system.

"Second, we're going to set up Murphy with a large buffer of pennies so that even with high rolls of his one die, he should have a large enough backlog to be able to process whatever he rolls. So pass twelve pennies down to Murph. Everyone else starts with the standard four."

The Third Round began – and when the little die left Murphy's big hand, a measly single dot was the result. So Amy removed one penny from the jar, and with a look worthy of Ebenezer Scrooge, slid it across the table to Wayne Reese. For his part, Wayne rolled a four with his two dice, and so emptied his entire stock to Sarah, leaving him at the end of the turn with that one penny in queue from Amy.

On the second turn, Murphy rolled a boxcar – six – and Amy drew six from the jar to pass to Wayne. At the same time, Wayne rolled a four, but could only pass that single penny in queue on to Sarah.

And so it went, turn after turn. By the end of the twenty-turn month, the results were clear: inventory had fallen dramatically – choked by the rolls of the constraint – yet output was still quite high. The pennies moved across the finish line by the sweep of Elaine's hand numbered seventy-four. Yet work-in-process inventory was nearly the same as at the start: thirty-one at the concluding turn, as opposed to twenty-eight at the beginning.

"Look at what happened," said Tom. "You exceeded the expectation of sixty-five by nine cents. That's what? More than ten percent."

"About fourteen percent," said Elaine.

"And you kept inventory at quite manageable levels," Tom said. "Ending inventory was about the same as the starting inventory, and was way below the ending levels of the two previous rounds. Everything flowed quickly to the constraint, and quickly away from the constraint toward the finish line. If you think about it, Wayne, you're actually abiding by Lean principles better with a constrained system than you are with a balanced line."

Wayne nodded, but kept quiet. The lightbulb had not quite been switched on in his mind, but he was beginning to see the light.

"What you have at this point," Tom went on, "is a system that is stable and robust. You have enough processing speed that if one of the workstations goes down for a day – goes to zero output – that station, once it's restored, could catch up again quickly, and your month wouldn't be ruined."

"Unless *I* am the one who goes down," said Murphy.

"Yes, that's right. In this configuration, if Murphy gets knocked out for a turn or more, you've lost whatever he would have rolled in those turns from your month. So you want to protect the constraint above all. But actually there is a way that Murph could take a day off or go off-line for maintenance or whatever, and yet it wouldn't ruin you. Or more important, you can increase your output, yet keep the system stable. I'll show you that, and then I have to go. I'm off to the Florida Keys."

Amy looked at him. This was news to her.

"Now we have a stable and robust system," Tom continued. "What do we want to do next?"

No one answered.

"The market its growing," Amy prompted. "The minimum demand is now in excess of seventy-five cents, not sixty-five. Or the market is asking for new offerings or more flexibility in options in what we currently offer."

"They don't just want pennies anymore," said Garth. "They want nickels and dimes, too."

"Something like that," said Amy.

"So think," said Tom. "We have a good system, but we need more from it. What do we do?"

"Improve it," said Wayne.

"Yes, but how? And where?" asked Tom. "Do we improve Sarah? Do we give her three dice instead of two? If we did, what would we gain from that? Nothing. She already does everything as fast and as perfectly as we could want."

"That's what I've always thought," said Sarah.

"Or do we give everybody three dice – everybody except Murphy, who stays with one die?"

"No, that doesn't make any sense," said Elaine. "What would be the point? And now you really are talking about excess capacity."

"You have to improve the constraint," said Wayne. "Logically, that would be the thing to do."

"Right!" said Tom. "To improve the system, you improve performance with respect to the constraint. You do what they call 'elevate' the constraint. You fine-tune Murphy's performance, so that he yields more of what you want."

"How?" asked Garth. "Give him two dice like the rest of us?"

"No, you don't want to do that, because then you're back to all the issues and problems of a balanced line."

"Give Murphy two dice and everybody else three dice," said Sarah.

"You could do that," said Tom, "but Elaine and Amy would freak out."

"That would be very expensive," said Amy, "and we would have to be absolutely sure that the long-term market would support that investment."

"You improve Murphy's yield," Wayne suggested.

"That's it!" said Tom. "You focus all your Lean and Six Sigma techniques on the constraint. Not necessarily on the constraint *itself*, but on things that improve the constraint's operations."

"Okay, I see," said Wayne, with a note of enthusiasm.

"Instead of trying to eliminate waste everywhere, you target the waste that most affects the constraint's performance. Instead of improving everything, you improve whatever improves the yield of the constraint."

"Which would be generally, I think, much more affordable than adding capacity everywhere and improving everything," said Amy.

"To do that in terms of the dice game," said Tom, "we're going to symbolically improve Murphy in Round Four, but improving his one die. In this round, everything stays the same as in Round Three – twelve penny buffer inventory for Murphy, no dice for Amy – but when Murphy rolls a one or a two, it's going to equal a four. If he rolls a three or a four, it's going to equal a five. And if he rolls a five or a six, it will be the equivalent of a six."

"So you're eliminating all the low rolls," said Wayne. "In a sense, you're eliminating the rolls that waste a turn on low output."

"Exactly," said Tom. "All right. Pass the pennies around. Everybody set?"

The fourth round was by far their best. In the first "week" of the round, they moved twenty-three pennies across the finish line. In the second, twenty-four; then another twenty-four cents in the third game week. And during the fourth week, a fabulous twenty-six cents were swept into the finish pile. The grand total: ninety-seven cents.

As for inventory, they began with twenty-eight pennies in all the queues, and they finished with thirty-two pennies in process. The queue in front of Murphy dropped to six for two turns in a row – during their fourth week, their most productive – but never went below.

"By the way," said Tom, "there is a name for what we did in the Third and Fourth Rounds. It's called Drum, Buffer, and Rope. The Drum is the system constraint – Murphy, in this case. The Buffer is the time required to deposit materials in queue for the constraint to process. And the Rope is the communication connection to the gate that releases those materials for processing. So Drum, Buffer, Rope – or DBR, as it's known."

As everyone else pondered the implications of what had been demonstrated, Tom got to his feet.

"So . . . I hope that helped," said Tom. "Sorry, but I've got to run. I've got a hot date with a fishing boat down on the Gulf."

"I'll walk out with you," Amy said.

Outside, as they went to his car, she slipped her arm around his.

"Where you going?" she asked.

"The Keys. A Marine buddy of mine called. Said he's taking his boat out, doing a little fishing, and wanted some company. I knew you'd be working, so . . ."

"I thought you'd be around tonight," Amy said, disappointed. "When will you be back?"

Tom shrugged his shoulders. "A couple of days. I'll call you."

Then a quick kiss, and he was in the Mustang and gone.

Inside, Amy tried to clear Tom from her mind. The others had used the interlude to take a break; the dining room table was deserted when she returned. She went to the kitchen where she had set up refreshments, and was pouring a glass of ice water when Sarah appeared at her elbow.

"Tom seems like a good man," Sarah said quietly.

"He is," said Amy. "When he's around."

Elaine gravitated toward them.

"Does he always go off like that?" she asked.

"He has a restless streak," said Amy.

"If Bill did that, I'd kill him," said Elaine.

Poor Bill, Amy thought.

Then she added, "It's not all bad that he likes his freedom. Gives me lots more time to work."

Sarah caught the irony and sniggered.

"Well, let's get back to it," said Amy.

As she went to round up the others, she discovered Wayne and Murphy in the backyard – and they were talking to each other. Just as she was about to hail them to come back to the table, Wayne cracked a smile at something Murphy had just said. This was a good sign, Amy thought.

The whiteboard on which they had constructed the logic tree of undesirable consequences – the UDE Tree, or "Oodie" Tree, as Amy pronounced it – was set up in the dining room and next to this was a second whiteboard that Amy had brought home from the office.

"Last week," she said when everyone was seated, "we assembled this . . . well, this ugly chain of events that digresses from good intentions to dysfunctional results. Today, for however long it takes, we are going do the opposite. We are going to start with the foundation of undesirables and build skyward to create a logical chain of events that takes us from our current reality to a future reality some months from now. In that future reality, we will have turned performance around, become profitable, and good things will be starting to happen again. But before we go any further, I am going to announce some decisions I've reached."

Amy looked from face to face.

"The first of these is that we have to give first priority to turning around Oakton. F&D has overall better profit margins – or used to – but quantitatively, F&D makes a much smaller contribution to the bottom line. Therefore, Oakton comes first. Sarah, I want you to know that this is not a reflection on you or anyone else in Rockville."

"I understand," said Sarah. "It's one set of numbers against another set of numbers. I just hope that our issues are not ignored."

"F&D will not be ignored, my word on that," said Amy. "In fact, we will be dealing with at least one of the F&D issues right away – because it seriously affects Oakton. I'm talking of course about the analyst bottleneck with respect to design reviews. That's my second policy decision. In the past, the analysts have tended to sit on the production design reviews."

"True, and actually they've been incentivized not to deal with them," Sarah interjected.

"Well, that has to change," said Amy. "Instead of being low priority, the reviews have to become top priority. Instead of being finished in batches when there's nothing better to do, they have to be dealt with on a daily basis."

"I can tell you now," said Sarah, "that's not going to be popular with the analysts or probably anyone else at F&D."

"We'll explain it to them," Amy with a bit of edge in her voice.

"Just remember," Sarah warned, "that the analysts in particular have options, and they are hard to replace."

"Yes, well, we'll work on it," said Amy. "And that brings me to my third and maybe the most important decision. I think we need to unbalance the production line at Oakton."

She turned to Wayne Reese, who was trying to appear impassive.

"Wayne, can you abide by that?"

"In the interest of achieving quick results," said Wayne, "I suppose I'll have to go along."

"This is not just for the sake of quick results," said Amy. "I believe this has to be permanent."

Wayne clammed up, but clearly wanted to speak.

"Go ahead," Amy said. "Tell me what you're thinking."

"I know what the dice game shows," said Wayne. "But you're not going to base a policy decision on that, are you?"

"Excuse me," said Murphy, "but I can tell you that while the dice thing might be simplistic, it does accurately depict what goes on in a system with variability and a series of interdependent process steps. In fact, what happened in Round Three was pretty much how I was running Oakton until a just few years ago – before Winner and the WING terminals telling us how to be more productive. Trouble was, we never – I never – made it to Round Four. We kind of allowed inertia to take over. B. Donald Williams tended to be a president who left well enough alone, and I . . . well, I suppose I could see no reason to rock the boat if B. Don was happy."

"B. Don was always intimidated by Viktor," Sarah murmured.

"Ancient history," said Amy. "The point that I think Murphy was trying to make is that we had a system that worked well – and it was a constrained system, not a balanced system. I've gone back and looked at the metrics and I know that it did work. Look, I will never know as much about manufacturing as you, Wayne, or Murphy. But everything I've learned says that a constrained system is faster and easier to establish, and yields better results. Therefore . . ."

"All right, I have to admit, maybe the balanced line has skunked us," said Wayne. "But here's my other problem: we went around last year telling everyone about Lean Six Sigma and takt time and why they were so important. What happens *now*? What happens, for instance, when we tell them takt time doesn't matter?"

"What matters more to them? Takt time or a paycheck?" asked Amy.

"Excuse me once again," said Murphy, "but I have to agree with Wayne on this one. Employees will generally do whatever you tell them to do for the sake of that paycheck. But if you want them to care about their work – and more than that, about the larger mission – then you have to have credibility. We need to be careful that people don't get the idea we're just feeding them a new flavor of the month."

"You know, I personally dropped out of Lean Six Sigma for a number of reasons," said Sarah. "But Lean especially was very popular with the employees at F&D – not so much the analysts, but the technical staff. If we abandon Lean and Six Sigma and introduce something else, they're going believe it was all just a bunch of . . . you know . . ."

"Bull twinkle," suggested Murphy.

"Well, wait a minute. Are we?" asked Amy. "Are we abandoning Lean and Six Sigma? Because I never said we were."

"I hope not," said Wayne. "My whole life has been transformed by Lean thinking. I can't throw away everything I've learned."

"Amy, as I told you before I went to Rockville," said Murphy, "there is a lot of overlap between Lean, Six Sigma, and the Theory of Constraints. The question is in how they are applied."

Amy sat back and thought silently for a moment.

"Here is what we are doing," she said. "We are going to integrate Lean, Six Sigma, and the Theory of Constraints. And we will use the appropriate parts of all three to increase and sustain the velocity of the business."

Amy looked from face to face around the table.

"How's that?" she asked.

"In physics," said Sarah, "velocity is speed with direction."

"Isn't that what we want?" asked Amy.

"Lean and Six Sigma," said Wayne, "are both about speed – eliminating waste and reducing variation so the flow is faster and costs less."

"And the Theory of Constraints shows where to focus the improvements so that they have a real impact," said Amy.

"Sounds right on the money," said Murphy.

The discussion that Saturday – and, indeed, the debate at times – was long and intense, though not without harmony. By the middle of the afternoon they had created a tree of arrow-tipped lines connecting a progression of sticky note "leaves" on the previously blank whiteboard. In general form, this tree resembled the tree of Undesirables on the neighboring board, but this new tree rose to a happy outcome, and showed every condition that would have to occur in order for that outcome to become real.

Each rectangular note on the tree stated – in present tense, typically, although the progression implied the passage of time – something that had to be in place before the next, higher event on the tree could occur. The tree was read from bottom to top, with a terse statement of the "current reality," as they called it, written on a trio of pink-colored notes at the very base:

Hi-T's performance is declining.

Corporate objectives are being missed.

Our management mission: a performance turnaround bringing operational stability & financial growth.

From this declaration of the issues were what Amy called "injections" – changing actions that were to be injected into company policies and operations to turn Hi-T around. Three of these were based on the non-negotiable decisions that Amy had made:

Injection: Our turnaround strategy gives Oakton first priority.

Injection: We unbalance the production line at Oakton, and have all personnel complete their work quickly, but consistent with quality & safety requirements.

Injection: Autoclave (aka Godzilla) is recognized as the production system constraint (the Drum).

A fourth injection came out of the team's general discussion:

Injection: Professional incentives at F&D are linked to overall performance (not hourly billings).

What flowed from these injections were desired outcomes, stated in concise wording and connected by arrow-tipped lines. The injections were written on green-colored notes; the outcomes on canary yellow notes, to differentiate the changes from the effects. And the arrow-tipped line implied a qualifying phrase such as:
"With the foregoing accomplished . . ."
Or, "Because of this . . ."
Or, "As a result . . ."
Or, "Therefore . . ."
Or any other appropriate wording.
So by that afternoon, with the tree complete, it could be read from bottom to top essentially this way:

Injection: Our turnaround strategy gives Oakton first priority.

And . . .

Injection: Professional incentives at F&D are linked to overall performance (not hourly billings).

Therefore . . .

F&D policies give production design reviews top priority.

Therefore . . .

F&D analysts and tech staff clear most designs very quickly.

As a result . . .

Design clearances flow smoothly to Oakton at predictable time intervals.

Because of this . . .

Oakton has an ample supply of orders to produce and production planning/ scheduling is simplified.

Then, as a separate, though related progression, starting at the bottom of the board:

Injection: We unbalance the production line at Oakton and have all personnel complete their work quickly, but consistent with quality and safety requirements.

And . . .

Injection: Autoclave (aka Godzilla) is recognized as the production system constraint (the Drum).

With these in place . . .

Godzilla is staffed and scheduled to maximize its capacity.

And . . .

All non-Drum resources have protective capacity and are synchronized to the Drum's schedule.

As a result . . .

Protective capacity downstream from Godzilla assures finished product quickly reaches Shipping.

And . . .

Protective capacity upstream and the synchronized release of materials assures fast processing so that a timely buffer of material is always ready for Godzilla.

Here, the chain was connected to the F&D design-clearance sub-chain, and continued:

With this in place . . .

New materials enter production at the rate Godzilla processes them.

Because of this . . .

Production flow time decreases.

Therefore . . .

Our lead times are competitive.

**Turnaround
Strategy**

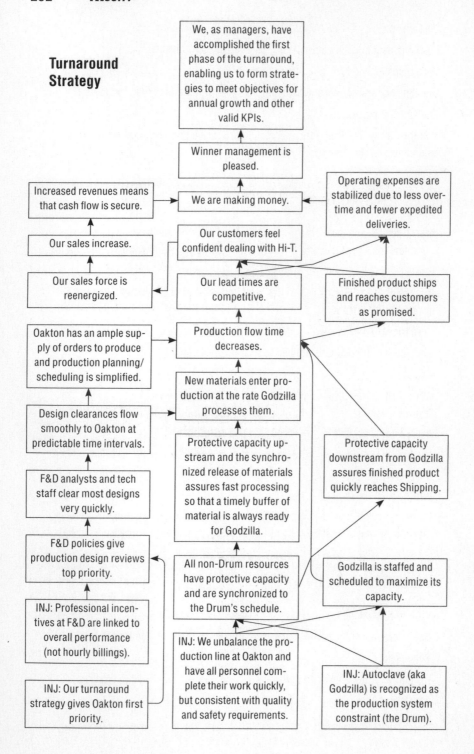

And . . .

Finished product ships and reaches customers as promised.

With these in place . . .

Operating expenses are stabilized due to less overtime and fewer expedited deliveries.

And . . .

Our customers feel confident dealing with Hi-T.

Because of this . . .

Our sales force is re-energized.

Therefore . . .

Our sales increase.

And . . .

Increased revenues means that cash flow is secure.

With the foregoing accomplished . . .

We are making money.

And . . .

Winner management is pleased.

And . . .

We, as managers, have accomplished the first phase of the turnaround, enabling us to form strategies to meet objectives for annual growth and other valid KPIs.

Amy finished reading aloud the logical chain of conditions.

"All right, I think we have the essential strategy in place," she said to everyone. Then she joked, "So why are all of you just sitting here? Get out there and make it happen!"

Amy overslept – perhaps deliberately – on the morning of Winner's fourth quarter earnings release. When Amy finally made herself open her eyes, the time was 6:39 a.m. For a second she debated whether to turn on the small television in her bedroom. On most weekday mornings, she would listen to one of the business channels while she was getting ready for work so as to catch the major n stories. Today she debated and finally decided it would be l know rather than not know what was being said.

Her bedroom filled with the light of the TV, an came a talking head with a headline capt Misses Big!"

Amy groaned.

"Our top story," said the head, "Winner Corporation reports earnings for the quarter and the year that miss analyst estimates by a mile – seven cents below consensus for the quarter and a huge fifteen cents a share below *their own* estimate for the year. On a year-over-year basis, Winner is actually *flat* with the previous year, contrary to Peter Winn's pledge to investors at last year's annual meeting that he would restart the growth engine that this venerable company once was. Already reflecting the news is the Winner stock price, plunging twenty percent in European trading, and almost certain to go lower."

Amy scurried into her bathroom. By the time she got out of the shower and had wrapped herself in her robe, there were three commentators on screen – two guys in suits, and a woman with big, honey blond hair – all dissecting Winner's performance.

"So is Winner turning into a loser? I mean, will they even hang on to the name?" one of them joked.

"The big question," said the woman, "is what went wrong? How did this so-called growth company stumble so badly?"

"Well, the release that Winner put out lays most of the blame on the Hi-T Composites acquisition. Clearly, Winner overpaid for that business. But the Hi-T subsidiary has just been going nowhere for more than a year. Obviously, whoever is running Hi-T really dropped the ball."

"*You jerk!*" Amy screamed. She threw her towel at the screen.

Her bedroom door flew open, and there stood her son, Ben, with his baseball bat, ready to take on the intruder he assumed had broken into the house. Behind him was Michelle.

"Mom? Are you *all right?*" she asked.

"No," said Amy. "I mean, *yes*. I'm fine. Please, I need to listen to this."

"But wait, guys," the big-hair woman was saying, "if you look at the numbers, they're lackluster almost across the board at Winner – the chemicals business, industrial equipment unit, the technology group – they're all unimpressive. It's not just the Hi-T subsidiary."

"Yeah, I thought the whole idea of a conglomerate, which is what Winner is, was that if one business was down the others would be ~~~~ing ahead. But you're right; all of the Winner businesses are ~~~~ in performance."

"~~~~ exception," said the woman, "that being the Winner fi-~~~~ oup. Between the mortgage-backed securities and ~~~~ures trading, they're really raking it in."

"~~~~ at this once was a company that beat the

estimates with great regularity. And now they can't even live up to their own guidance."

"Well, I'm sure Mr. Winn is feeling the pain this morning. Let's check the stock price again . . . Wow! Look at that! Down ten points in the premarket since yesterday's close!"

Amy pressed the power button on the remote and the screen went dark. Her kids were huddled around her, hugging her.

"Mom, are you going to get fired?" asked Ben.

"I don't know," she said quietly. "Don't worry. We'll be all right, one way or another. Go get ready for school."

Every day leading up to the Crystal Ball had seemed to put another twisted knot of dread in Amy's stomach. To her it was not a question of whether Nigel would seek to humiliate her in some fashion, but a question of how many times and in how many ways. Would he make her wear a pointy dunce cap? Would he insist that she sit in the corner with her face to the wall? How many snide remarks would he make? And how would she respond? How *should* she respond? That was the issue that above all invoked the most dread in her. Should she just take it? Should she fire back? Attempt to trade barbed witticisms with him? Should she just quit?

"I'm not quitting," she told her mother as they got dinner ready the evening before she left for New York. "I will not resign. If Nigel wants me out, he's going to have to take whatever action to . . . to do whatever."

On the appointed day late in January, Amy arrived at the Winner corporate offices in Manhattan only to discover that Nigel's Crystal Ball had already taken place – so far as everyone else was concerned. The other presidents had made their presentations the day before. They were already at some exclusive club in Texas for a few days of hunting, fishing, and golf – flown there in Winner's fastest plane, a Citation X. Nigel would join them that evening. He had stayed behind so that Amy could make her presentation to him – alone. This was not a good sign, Amy feared.

Nigel kept her waiting in his conference room for what seemed like hours. He finally arrived – with two of his staff, who were superfluous; they said almost nothing. Amy greeted him with upbeat cheeriness. He responded with stone-faced grumpiness.

"I want you to know," Nigel said, "that Peter and I have had several discussions about you. It is safe to say that Peter is not your biggest fan these days – if indeed you have any fans at all. Really, does anyone believe in your leadership anymore?"

"I think my staff believes in me, more so now than ever," Amy said.
"Really?"

"Yes. And I think that most of Hi-T's customers still believe in me."

"Customers, right," said Nigel. "Those are becoming fewer in number, are they not?"

"We're making changes. We'll get them back," she said.

"How?"

Amy gestured to the Reality Tree.

"Good Lord, what is that?"

"It is a logical map showing what has gone wrong, how we intend to address the issues, and exactly what must happen in order for us to get back to profitable growth."

Nigel sighed.

"All right, proceed," he said. "However, I am sure you are aware that your future with Winner will be decided by what you are about to say."

She began with background and then delved into the misconceptions and events that made up the chains of "undesirables" – the UDE Tree. At first, Nigel interrupted her every few minutes to complain about lack of foresight or to scold her for not being more vigilant. But Amy kept her cool, and as she began to describe the elements of the Turnaround Tree, Nigel listened more carefully, hand on his chin as he concentrated and grunting every so often to acknowledge a point she had made.

In the end, after more than an hour, he sat there skeptical, but intrigued.

"It seems simplistic," Nigel said. "It's . . . too easy to understand."

"Oh. Well, would you would prefer a convoluted plan that's incomprehensible?" Amy asked.

Nigel frowned.

"Listen, I know you have your doubts," she said seriously. "But you understand the bottom line. Why not just judge us on that basis?"

Nigel pinched his lower lip with thumb and forefinger as he mulled over what his decision should be.

"All right," he said at last. "I will give you three months. One financial quarter. If you can effect a quick and clear turnaround in that amount of time, we'll let you continue. But the reversal of trend has to be unmistakable. There must be no further backsliding – on any of the metrics."

15

So the race was on. Back home in Highboro and exhausted, Amy went to bed right after dinner – only to wake up at three o'clock in the morning as if some menacing phantom sent by Nigel had come into her bedroom to torment her. She turned on the light next to her bed, and she was alone, of course. Yet the phantom was real and it was in her bedroom; it was the fear and worry over how she could possibly accomplish what had to be done to effect the turnaround in three months. Three months, that was all the time she had. After an hour or so lying there, her mind spinning, she gave up on sleep, put on her robe, went down to the kitchen, and brewed coffee.

By 5:00 a.m. or so, she had made the decision to have a small management team. All functions were essential, and all had contributed to creating the Reality Tree. But now it was time for action – and there was no time for long or superfluous discussions. So she decided that the core turnaround team would be a foursome: herself as über-boss, Sarah Schwick handling F&D, Murphy Maguire back at Oakton as production manager, and Wayne Reese remaining as ops manager, but with some limits.

By 6:00 a.m., Amy had written an email explaining this, and by 7:30 she was on the phone with Murphy talking about the issues.

"I want to put you in Oakton with the title of production manager," she told him, "with Jayro Pepps and Kurt Konani both reporting to you. Jayro would keep his position as materials manager. Kurt would be plant manager – if he wants to stay. How do you feel about that?"

"Jayro and I work very well together. No problems there," said Murphy. "As for Kurt, I guess I'm all right with that, as long as he understands and supports what we need to accomplish with unbalancing the line and making Godzilla the system constraint."

"Kurt is going to need some coaching," said Amy.

"True, although I am not sure Kurt will accept me as a mentor. He's even more dedicated to Lean than Wayne is. And, to be honest, I am a little nervous about having Wayne looking over my shoulder."

"You will report on a dotted line directly to me," she said. "I want us to stay in close communication. And I will make sure that Wayne gives you a free hand to do what has to be done."

"All rightie then," said Murphy. "Let me get things tidied up here in Rockville and I'll be on my way as soon as I can."

Just past 8:00 a.m., Amy was on the phone with Wayne. She braced herself, because she was not sure what his reaction was going to be. And she needed Wayne; Murphy could not run all of operations by himself, and this was no time to be looking for Wayne's replacement if he chose not to be sensible. Soon into the call, though, she felt that she could be direct with him.

"Wayne, I really need you to give Murph a lot of leeway. He should be judged by results, and by progress toward the conditions we stated on the logic tree for the turnaround."

"I'm fine with that," said Wayne. "I'm planning to stay out of his way. My only worry is that he will dismantle something valuable just because it's Lean or Six Sigma and not what he had in place."

"Murphy is too sensible for that. And for me, it doesn't matter whether something agrees with Lean or Six Sigma or the Theory of Constraints or any particular doctrine. If it works within a constrained, unbalanced line and it's helping move us toward the conditions stated on the logic tree for the turnaround, then we keep it. If not, we have to move on."

"Fair enough," said Wayne.

By nine o'clock, Amy was on the phone with Sarah in Rockville.

"Well, here we go," she told Sarah. "Now, your first mission is to set up a simple system to get the analysts to give priority to the production design reviews and feed the cleared designs to Oakton on a fast track."

"I'm already on it," said Sarah. "But I can tell you I'm going to get push-back from analysts and possibly a lot of other people as well."

"You've got to make it happen, Sarah."

"I'll try."

"No, seriously, you have to get it done – and soon."

"You have to understand, Amy, that morale here is very low right now. Everyone knows we are not doing well. They know Viktor is gone, and he's probably not coming back – and Viktor was the heart and soul here."

"That's not true," said Amy. "You and all the other brilliant people are the heart and soul of Formulation and Design. Viktor was just the face, and he failed because he refused to change. For F&D to survive, there has to be change. You have to get that message out there."

"My strength is chemistry," said Sarah. "And once in a while, I can tell a good dirty joke. But I am not much of a motivational speaker."

Amy snickered, and said, "Tell you what, get the priority policy set up and I'll come up for a day and help you walk the talk. Call me when you're ready."

Murphy Maguire stopped by to see Sarah before he departed to brief her on where things stood with various projects he was leaving behind.

At the end of that, Sarah said, "So you're going home."

"Yes."

"I'll miss your veggie atomic buffalo turds."

"I'll email the recipe," said Murphy. "And I wish you well with getting the analysts to prioritize. That is very important. If Oakton can depend upon even a wavy, but steady flow of clearances – never mind smooth – why, that is going to be just as important as any materials we use."

"Yes, well . . . I understand. Tell me, since you've been here for a while, do you notice anything that would help? If you were in my position, is there anything you would do?"

"Me? I don't understand all of the intricacies of what y'all do here. But . . . well, one thing I have noticed is that y'all – er, that is, the average person – have fifty things going on at the same time."

"Oh, tell me about it!" said Sarah. "Fifty things at the same time, that's conservative."

"But y'all are trying to do fifty at the *same* time. Or at least twenty-five."

"What else can we do?"

"Focus on *one* at a time."

"No, that's impossible," said Sarah. "I mean, there are fifty!"

"One of those has to be the most important," said Murphy. "I mean, in the plant, what I tell people is: as soon as work comes your way, get on it, heads down, and get it done. Then do the next thing, and the next."

"But we don't have that luxury."

"Why not?"

"Because there is so much. It's just overwhelming. And, just using myself as an example, there are so many times when I can't finish because I'm waiting for someone else to supply something – or I'm just plain interrupted!"

"Interrupted due to something of higher priority? Lower priority?"

"No priority!" exclaimed Sarah. "I'm sure that's at least part of the problem."

"Maybe this is just my Southern sensibilities, but if you were in a private conversation, I wouldn't think of interrupting. Unless, say, the building was on fire – a higher priority. Perhaps you could devise some kind of signal?"

"Possibly. But it's going to take time."

"One last humble suggestion from an old factory hand," said Murphy. "If you were to stagger the workload so that higher priority work is released first every morning or on some kind of time frame, that might help. At Oakton, what we'll be doing is what's called 'gating the materials' – or putting them onto the plant floor – in the priority that we want them to arrive at Godzilla, and then from Godzilla to the shipping dock. Maybe something like that would work for you, with respect to projects being buffered to the analysts?"

"I don't know," said Sarah. "As I said, it's going to take some time. But thanks, Murph. Have a safe drive back."

"You're welcome. See you in a few."

The following week, Amy flew to Rockville – paying Tom Dawson out of her own pocket – for a day of town hall–style meetings with F&D employees, lending her weight as president to add impact to the changes that had to occur.

In the first meeting, with F&D employees assembled in the auditorium of Building One, Amy stood on the dais looking into the rows of grim, serious faces. There were whispers going on, and comments made behind the cover of raised hands. The rumors, she knew from talking to Sarah, had been whirling all through the buildings, with people claiming crazy things that they knew "for certain" were going to happen – everything from 50 percent across-the-board staff cuts to an announcement that the F&D business had been sold off or that the whole operation was being moved to India or would simply be shut down altogether.

As Amy picked up the microphone, she heard someone in the back rows mutter, "Hold on tight . . . here we go, down the toilet."

Amy fought the urge to laugh.

"I think everyone knows who I am," she said, "so we'll skip the introductions. What you don't know is why I am here. I'm aware that there have been all kinds of rumors circulating. So let's get this out of the way. I am *not* here to announce layoffs or staff reductions. Nor is F&D being sold or moved or outsourced or any of that. So all of you can breathe a sigh of relief. None of those things are happening today – and hopefully not ever, although I cannot guarantee that. Much depends on what happens in the next three to twelve months, and much of that depends on you.

"All of you know that two major clients have recently walked away from F&D, and a number of others are less than happy. Through the efforts of Sarah Schwick and others, a portion of the business that was lost has been recovered, and the project managers are working their contacts to bring in new accounts. However, F&D cannot survive by doing things exactly as they have been done before. No one on the client side argues with the quality, accuracy, or reliability of the work done by F&D. Where we are getting serious push-back from the clients is with respect to high cost and slow performance. We take too long and we cost too much. Which brings me to the reason why I am here today.

"We urgently need to change a number of policies and procedures that affect work flow. I am here to impress upon you the importance of these changes and help answer any questions you may have. You may or may not be pleased with these changes, but I assure you they are absolutely necessary.

"The most important change might not seem that relevant to you individually, not at first, but I want you to know about it anyway. Last year I stood here and talked about Lean and Six Sigma. We – or at least *I* – thought that these were a complete answer to improving our operations and our business overall. As it turned out, that expectation was optimistic. Who knew?

"But we are not backing away from Lean or Six Sigma. Both offer powerful toolsets of great value and we will continue to embrace the virtues of those disciplines. What we are going to do that is different is to apply Lean and Six Sigma within the context of a third discipline known as the Theory of Constraints. Instead of trying to improve everything, and remove waste everywhere, we will be applying Lean and Six Sigma in ways that increase the throughput of the entire company and deliver the financial gains necessary to sustain and grow our business.

"Now, let's get to some changes that are going to affect your work on a daily basis. We have determined that at F&D, the efficiency of the business depends upon the efficiency of the analysts. You'll learn why later. Just remember that while all functions are important, here at F&D, the analysts are the most important resource. The role of everyone else is to ensure that the analysts always have what they need *ahead* of when they need it – and to process what they produce as quickly as possible.

"And for the analysts themselves, there are going to be changes. I am told that design reviews in the past have been considered by many to be a chore and handled with a kind of 'we get to them when we get to them' attitude. From now on, design reviews – and speedy clearances where warranted – must be at the top of every analyst's to-do list. In order to accomplish the turnaround in performance – not just at Formulation and Design, but for Hi-T as a company – and achieve the gains we need to be successful, we need those clearances to be reaching Oakton as soon as possible.

"F&D has had a great legacy in materials research and engineering. I firmly believe that if you embrace the changes that need to be made and we work together, F&D will climb to a new level of greatness in the years ahead. Sarah . . ."

The analysts, not surprisingly, were less than thrilled with Sarah's priority system. For years they had been calling their own shots, using their own discretion as to what to work on and when to work on it. They had managed their own time, but they had managed it pretty much for their own interests and purposes. Now – the outrage! – they were being told what to do, and of course they didn't like it.

"I do not work here to do clerical work at the bidding of lawyers!" one of them said pompously. "I am here to do advanced, meaningful research!"

Amy, standing to one side, backing up Sarah, wanted to tell him, *If you want to work here at all, you need to do things our way.* But she held back.

"You've always had to do these design reviews," Sarah pointed out. "All we're doing is having you deal with them sooner rather than later. You shouldn't be spending any more time on them than before. We just want you to get them out of your hair – and out of the building – in a few days rather than in a few weeks."

Sarah's system was utterly simple. There were two kinds work: 1) design review clearances, and 2) everything else. The clearances were first priority; everything else was second priority. The analysts were to spend most of their time in the coming days eliminating whatever design review backlog they currently had. After that, they were to check each morning for new, incoming reviews. If there were any, they were to do the reviews first, then they could pursue their client projects for the balance of the day.

"Our objective," Sarah told them, "is to clear out the vast majority of reviews in less than three days – either clear them for production and send them on to Highboro and Oakton, or reject them and send them back to Sales with an explanation."

"What about the reviews that require lab testing or computer modeling or some kind of extended analysis?" someone asked. "Are we supposed to not work on anything else until the results come back?"

"The first thing every day," Sarah explained, "you work on whatever reviews have been sent to you. Most will take fifteen or twenty minutes; complicated designs, maybe an hour or so. Clear all the designs that merit clearance and send them on. For those few that require some kind of testing or modeling, as soon as you've written the technical instructions, you're done *for that day*. You can now turn to your project work. But the next day you have to follow up and check the status of the designs that didn't get out of the building the day before. And you do that until each design is either cleared or rejected."

"I just want to know one thing," said Joe Tassoni, standing up as if he spoke for all the analysts, "what's wrong with how we did things in the past?"

"I'll take that one," said Amy, stepping forward. "What's wrong with how we handled design reviews in the past is that it was always a problem – just not for you. Taking two, three and four weeks for a design review became so normalized that it was a hidden problem. But for Oakton and for the salespeople who had to explain to customers why things took so long, it was a real difficulty. Now, it's clear that for competitive and all kinds of reasons, we have to change."

On the subject of change, there was one other topic that had to be dealt with that day: the analysts' annual bonuses. Sarah approached it tangentially, first giving them news she thought they would like.

"Starting now," she said, "time spent on production design reviews will be treated the same as client-billable hours, and will count toward your annual performance assessment. We are changing the

policy because these reviews are s~~...~~
begin to see them as mo~~...~~

There were i~~...~~
applau~~...~~

"Are they still around?"

"All but one or two."

"Then you'll get 'em," said Murphy.

Within the week, a number of the veterans who had serviced Godzilla prior to balancing the line were back in place. Over Kurt's objections, the Lean pacemaker scheduling practice on the M57 Line was discontinued. Godzilla was designated as the Drum for all operations. And Murphy soon had a task group working to peg inventory planning, scheduling, and shipping dates to the rhythms of Godzilla's output.

Almost immediately after assuming the mantle of production manager, Murphy began organizing meetings for all of Oakton's managers and supervisors, and soon, with Wayne Reese's cooperation, every manager within the Operations sphere. Murphy had everyone play the dice game simulation learned from Tom Dawson, so that they would understand the practicality of a constrained, unbalanced line. Afterward, they would talk about how their individual functions could best serve the flow to and from the Drum.

From a production standpoint, the turnaround began to happen with surprising speed. The wandering bottlenecks that had plagued the balanced line largely disappeared. Just as in the dice game, materials were released to production only at the rate at which they actually went into and came out of Godzilla. And under Murphy's experienced eye, staffing reassignments ensured that there were enough hands available in unconstrained processes to move work-in-process quickly to the autoclave Drum and away from it, through Final and Packaging and into Shipping. Gone were the Lean supermarkets, as these temporary storage areas for work-in-process were no longer needed – the reason being that WIP only accumulated where it was supposed to, which was in front of the Drum.

In the end, many of the changes brought about by Lean and Six Sigma were kept. Murphy even went out of his way to compliment Kurt Konani and the Lean Green and Black Belts for their efforts – though he soon put on hold the large number of LSS projects that were scheduled until their effects could be evaluated. Some took from this that the days of Lean Six Sigma were over, that the noble experiment had run its course and management was no longer interested. But these cynics would find their disgruntlement to be premature. For as Murphy himself would later state it: "Even an old dawg like me has new tricks to learn."

• • •

Murphy entered the Oakton toolroom with a cast-iron kettle in hand – only to find Jayro Pepps carefully heating the bottom of a large skillet with a propane torch. In the skillet, something was crackling.

"Jayro, what are you up to?"

"What's it look like?" asked his materials manager. "Makin' lunch."

"And what sort of lunch might that be?"

Jayro tipped the edge of the skillet to afford Murphy a better look.

"Trout," he said to Murph. "Fresh caught, about six-fifteen this mornin' on my way to work. Might share, if you got somethin' to trade."

"I got somethin'," said Murphy. "Somethin' good."

He lifted the lid on the kettle and wafted some of the aroma toward Jayro with the back of his hand.

"Oh my. What is that?"

"Osso buco," said Murphy.

"Huh?! Osso *what*?"

"Veal shank. Braised Eye-talian veal shank. Learned it from one of the Geniuses up in Maryland, a gen-u-wine Eye-talian by the name of Joe Tassoni," said Murphy.

"You mentioned him," said Jayro. "He's the bottleneck in Rockville."

"Not just him personally," said Murphy, "but Joe and all the other analysts. Looks like something may actually be done about that, however, and Oakton might just start getting a steady flow of clearances."

"All right, these beauties are done," said Jayro, shutting off the torch. "Let's eat."

They ate quietly for a few minutes, the only utterances passing between them being the murmurs of appreciation for the goodness of what they were eating. Murphy at one point looked around the drab, windowless room and realized how much he had missed these lunches.

"So, from your standpoint, how are we doing?" Murphy asked.

Jayro let out a sigh of frustration, and said, "I've got more headaches than I got aspirin to make them go away."

"How so?" asked Murphy. "Bring me up to date."

"I think that when you left," said Jayro, "we were putting the kanbans in place."

"Kanban. Why don't they just call it the *card* system? That's all *kanban* means. It's a Japanese word for 'card,' " Murphy grumbled.

"Well, it's not usually a card anymore," said Jayro. "It's whatever signal triggers the order to replenish the material."

"I know. I'm just being grumpy."

"Anyway, we were putting the kanbans in place. And then Kurt wanted us to do POUS – you know what that is?"

"Point of Use Storage," said Murphy.

"Right. So now we've got all these racks with bins for various parts and materials, placed right on the plant floor so that inventory is close at hand and the operator can just pull whatever is needed without having to go get it from storage, or wait for someone else to bring it."

"Yes, I've seen what you're talking about. So where's your head-ache?"

"First of all," said Jayro, "we don't make just two or three kinds of widgets here; we make thousands of different kinds of widgets. We make widgets and *bidgets* and *tidgets* and every other *idget* that's out there – standard and custom, too."

"Yes, you don't have to tell *me* that."

"So with all that complexity –"

"Different racks," Murphy concluded.

"Right! And they won't all fit! There's only so much space," said Jayro. "Then Kurt got the idea to put casters on them, so that we can swap out the racks faster."

Murphy rolled his eyes, and said, "That sounds like Kurt. Once that guy gets an idea in his head, he's going to make it work no matter what."

"Anyway, we've got all these racks being rolled in and rolled out – only the trouble is that there are times when an operator goes to pull materials, there's nothing to pull. Some of the bins are empty."

"Completely empty? Totally out of stock?"

"Yes, empty! Or not enough to run the order that we need to produce. I mean, usually it's only a few bins, but it happens. Then we have to juggle the orders, and call up the vendors, get on the internet to find other sources, all that."

"Now tell me something," said Murphy, with a nice flaky chunk of trout on the end of his plastic fork, "whether it's a kanban or whatever, it's still a min-max kind of thing, right?"

"Right. When the quantity gets down to the min level – the minimum safety stock quantity – that triggers a buy signal and a replenishment order goes out."

"Well, is somebody forgetting to reorder?" Murphy asked.

"Rarely. No, what's been happening is that the reorder signal is sent, but the stuff – whatever it is – isn't here when we need it."

"And the reorder point is fixed? The same every time?"

"Uh-huh. Like let's say the bin holds one hundred pieces at the max level, and fifty pieces is the min level. Once we use fifty of them, it triggers a reorder for another fifty to replace the fifty we've used. But sometimes we go through the remaining fifty before the new fifty shows up."

"Huh," said Murphy.

"And then sometimes if we see that we're getting *really* low, we'll place a bigger order," said Jayro, "only to have everything show up – and sit there month after month above the max level. Most of this of course is on computer – on WING – so it's automatic for the most part."

"On WING?" Murphy asked suspiciously. "What version?"

"WING four-point-seven. The Lean version."

"Is it playin' games with us?"

"Not supposed to be. I've asked Kurt, and he says, no. It's a pull-through inventory model – nothing is produced until a customer asks for it."

"And what does Kurt say about the out-of-stocks?" asked Murphy.

"He says that we – meaning me and my materials people – must have miscalculated the reorder quantity. Then, kind of out of the side of his mouth, he says to make the reorder a little bigger next time – but not *too* big."

"Of course not," said Murphy. "Inventory has been 'leaned' down, because we don't want too much sitting and doing nothing. That would be waste."

"Anyway," said Jayro, "that's what we've been doing. We bump up the reorder quantity, or we play with total min-max ratio, and sometimes it works, sometimes it doesn't. Sometimes we go out of stock like lemonade on a hot day, and sometimes the bumped-up quantity just sits there month after month, barely touched. And it's not like a winter-summer thing that you can predict we'll use less or more. It's . . . well, it's unpredictable."

Murphy held up a short length of the hollow veal bone and peered through it like a telescope.

"Well, let's clean up and get back to it," said Murphy. "By the way, the trout was fantastic."

"Skilled preparation," said Jayro, holding up the propane torch. "That's the key."

"That and fresh fish. And as for the inventory issues, we have to get this solved. Assuming we soon start getting a steady flow of clearances from Rockville, we cannot afford to drop the ball. Let me think and do some checking, and you do the same, and we'll talk again in a few days."

Some days later, Murphy walked into the Oakton plant early in the morning and found Jayro at his desk next to the Cooler. He poured a steamy cup of coffee into a Hi-T mug from Jayro's pot, pulled up a chair, and sat down. Jayro gave him a nod in greeting, but was absorbed with some graphs before him on the screen of his terminal, and held up the index finger of his left hand indicating he would turn his full attention to Murphy in a moment. When he did, Murphy was staring at him with a silly grin on his face.

"Yes?" asked Jayro.

"Time," said Murphy.

"Time?"

"Time is the invisible resource required in everything we do here," said Murphy.

"Is that a fact?" Jayro chided.

"Perhaps, Jayro, you would like to write that down for posterity."

"Well, I would, Murph, but I'm running low on paper."

"Time to reorder then," said Murphy. "Which brings me to the purpose of my visit. Your unpredictable out-of-stocks that we talked about a few days ago. I think that *time* may hold the answer."

"How so?"

"With a min-max system, the order is triggered once the minimum safety stock level is reached. Now, the minimum reorder size is a fixed quantity, but the time between reorders is variable. It could be five days or five months or far longer between reorders – the timing between the purchase events varies."

"Just for the sake of argument, what's wrong with that?" asked Jayro.

"What's wrong is what you described over lunch a few days ago. The time it takes to replenish may not be quick enough to cover demand. You follow me?"

"I think so. In fact, I think that is what has been happening."

"So in periods of peak demand there may not be time for a reorder to be filled before the safety stock is exhausted. And by the same token, if you bump up the quantity to compensate and demand then falls, then we could be sitting on that stock for a very long time."

"It's been known to happen," said Jayro.

"But suppose the order trigger was not based on having used up a fixed quantity; suppose the timing was fixed and the quantity was whatever was used during the fixed-time interval? Suppose the re-order trigger was a regular time period – like every day, every week, every two weeks, every month, or whatever? The demand will vary – as it always does – but the reorder trigger will be a fixed time interval that provides a reliable time frame to replenish what has been consumed."

"And prevent an out-of-stock," added Jayro. "What made you think of this?"

"A number of things. One of them, truth to tell, was that I was downtown talking to Garth Quincy," said Murphy. "And I asked Garth about this matter, because Garth of course sees it from the other side. We had just started talking when Amy Cieolara happened by, and she told us the story of her grandfather, who was a candy salesman in Ohio, what they call a 'route salesman' who represented a wholesaler, and if it was Tuesday her grandfather would be in Akron, and if it was Wednesday he would be in Canton or someplace else, selling candy to the corner stores and newsstands and so on.

"Well, the rule – set by the wholesaler – was that all sales folks were only supposed to sell by the sealed box, containing twenty chocolate bars, or by the case containing many boxes. But this was in the Depression. These little mom-and-pop stores couldn't pay for a whole box of Hershey bars or gumdrops or whatever, never mind a whole case. So Amy's grandpa would open up boxes, and sell to his customers only what *their* customers had actually bought during the past week. So the candy case was always stocked, Amy's grandpa always had a sale of some sort from everybody every week, the wholesaler forgot about his ironclad rule, and everybody lived happily ever after – until the big chains came along, when everything changed. Anyway, I mention it because time-interval sales with no minimum quantities – that stuff has been around for a while. But the main reason why I think it especially makes sense for us is that it is similar to DBR."

"Drum-Buffer-Rope," said Jayro. "How does that figure in?"

"Ordering by time and with no minimum quantity is closely re-lated to how we are managing Godzilla, and thereby, Oakton. The buffer? The cushion that we acknowledge, and that we use to accu-mulate a ready supply in front of Godzilla, the constraint? Took me a while to realize this, but that buffer is actually based on time, not physical quantity. How much *time* does it take for work-in-process to reach Godzilla? The exact quantities are less important than the supreme importance that there is always a reservoir of material ready for Godzilla to process. The reservoir rises and falls, but the time to refill it – and that indeed it is continuously refilled on time – is what matters."

Jayro considered this. He then turned his computer monitor so that Murphy could see it better, and said, "Look here at what I've done."

Murphy put on his reading glasses, peered closely at the screen, and said, "Why, Jayro, it's a masterpiece."

"No, it's a bar chart."

"Still, the bold use of color, the greens, yellows and reds – you should be in Paris painting the Eiffel Tower!"

"True, but instead I'm here putting up with you," said Jayro. "Now, what I've done is taken some historical data showing demand patterns for a particular material – one that's given us problems."

"And these tall bars?" asked Murphy. "These are spikes in demand?"

"Yes, and some of them are huge, as you can see," said Jayro. "So I'm trying to figure out if there is any regular or meaningful pattern in the timing, but so far the demand seems random and unpredictable, and a few times a year it outstrips our ability to restock given the lead times of the supplier."

"That's using min-max, correct?"

"Correct. If I overlay the order and fill dates – here they are in Gators orange and Tar Heels blue – you can see that the order dates at any rate are also random."

"Yes, interesting," said Murphy. "You know, I was joking about your artistic ability, Jayro, but this may indeed turn out to be some of your best work."

"How's that?"

"Well, here are the really important questions, I think, relevant to what I said to time triggers for reordering," said Murphy. "What is the reliable replenishment time for the material? And what is the peak demand pattern for that time period? Above all, we want to keep Godzilla supplied with a ready inventory of material to consume."

"So you're looking for an equation," said Jayro. "An equation, or set of equations, that will calculate the time to reliably replenish and whatever quantity is needed for the material buffers feeding Godzilla."

"Yes, that's the size of it."

"And of course this has to be calculated for every material we use," said Jayro.

"Start with the troublesome ones first," Murphy suggested.

"Well, it looks like I do have exciting challenges ahead of me," said Jayro.

"If you would like, I can probably get one of the Microbursts – the IT fellas – downtown to help out," said Murphy. "But I don't want to steal any of your fun."

"Oh, that's all right. I'm sure there's more than enough fun to go around," said Jayro. "And I'm serious, Murph, if this helps my supply headaches to go away, it will be well worth it."

Everybody liked Joe Tassoni. But there were times when he could be a real pain in the neck. After the meeting, the analysts began to focus their efforts on a one-time, all-out attempt to eliminate the design review backlog – and within a week, they had largely succeeded. They then began to abide by the morning routine for reviews. When new review requests came in from Sales, they would deal with them first thing in the morning, and if possible issue the clearance that same day. Even Joe was doing this at first, but after three or four days, he just plain began to ignore the reviews. This came to Sarah's attention, and she went to see him.

"Joe, what are we going to do with you? Just look at this!"

From the edge of Joe Tassoni's office, Sarah stood aghast, surveying the piles and piles and piles of lab reports, program folders, sheets of handwritten notes, compact discs, professional journals, and email printouts. Yes, email. Joe fundamentally despised computers, and so he printed everything. And then there were all of Joe's personal amenities: his cappuccino maker, his pots of herbs, his tomato trellis, his little refrigerator, his Limoges china and his Tiffany silverware kept stored in the same safe along with heaps of classified documents. Sarah regarded this array of chaos – an oxymoron, yet applicable, because the general chaos was ordered into groups of chaos.

"I use the pile system," said Joe, seated at his desk.

"I can see that," said Sarah.

"But I know where everything is. Just because something doesn't use electricity does not mean it doesn't work."

"Right," said Sarah, having her doubts. "Well, as Murph Maguire might put it, at least your inventory is visible."

"What you mean by that?" asked Joe, curiously.

"Your inventory – what you have to work on – is out in the open. With the other analysts, it's mostly hidden away on hard drives and servers. They probably have just as much as you do, but no one can see it."

Joe brightened at this, hearing the comment as a positive, which in one way it was.

"Tell me," said Sarah, "in these piles, how many different projects are in progress?"

Joe shrugged, and said, "It depends. Maybe a few dozen."

"A few dozen? And how long would it take to finish any single one of those projects?"

"It's hard to say. Some a few months, some a few minutes."

"A few *minutes*?" asked Sarah.

"Yes. It depends."

"The ones that could be finished in a few minutes," said Sarah, "why don't you just take those few minutes, like right now, and finish them?"

"Well, again, it depends. For some, I am waiting for one or two things – tests, documentation, other opinions, what have you – before I can finish them. For others, I just haven't gotten to them yet because I am working on something else."

Sarah nodded. "I see."

Whenever Sarah Schwick wanted to talk about something nontechnical, she always went to Brenda.

Brenda was in charge of client billings and had been with Formulation & Design since the very beginning. She knew the corners of every closet in the place, and the bones of every skeleton. During the breakup of Sarah's marriage to Viktor, Brenda had become Sarah's confidante. While others had speculated from time to time, Brenda was the only one who knew for certain that Sarah and Viktor were still sexually intimate on occasion. Brenda could be trusted with a secret, and she always gave Sarah straight answers.

The two of them sat on a bench outside the building at noon that day, eating their lunches from paper sacks and talking about the prosaic matter of work flow.

"We're all so much into multitasking, doing fifty things at once," Sarah said.

"Everyone wants to look busy," Brenda said, "especially these days with clients leaving. People are scared."

"What, of layoffs?"

"Sure. If you have a lot of work waiting to be done, it feels more secure. On the other hand, if you don't have much to do, maybe you're expendable."

Sarah picked at her bulgur wheat salad as she considered this.

"Look at Debby Henson, " said Brenda. "She hoards her work. She obsesses about everything. She only lets go at the very last minute. And it's always like she's *so* important, because she's got so many things going on. Like the more out of breath she is because of all this work she has to do, the more vital she is."

"I know. She's kind of an extreme case, but we're all like that around here," said Sarah. "I mean, I'm like that. I admit it. What's frustrating is we do a little of this and a little of that, and nothing ever seems to get done."

"Until it's overdue and everyone is yelling for it," said Brenda.

"Well, you know, Viktor always encouraged multitasking. It was like if you could juggle twenty or thirty balls in the air, you met with his approval. He wanted to load people up with as much as they could handle – sometimes more than what they could handle – and then spread things out."

"It wasn't bad for billings," said Brenda. "I mean, if you pace your work, it's a lot easier to fill your time sheet."

Behind the huge lenses of her glasses, Sarah's small brown eyes blinked as she realized something.

"So, in other words, we're always rewarding the plodders and the slowpokes," she said, "and penalizing the fast and the efficient."

"Yes, you could say that," said Brenda. "And I do think a lot of it is because of fear – fear that if you finish early, the same will be expected next time, even though the project may be more difficult. Fear that you might not have enough to do. Fear that you might not look busy enough."

Sarah blinked again.

"You know," she told Brenda, "when you're juggling, you're really only dealing with one ball at a time."

Her tone was so serious that Brenda laughed.

"What's that supposed to mean?" she asked Sarah.

"The speed of your hands is what matters."

"And not dropping the ball."

"Right, speed and accuracy. Maybe we should be working that way. One ball at time, but transfer it fast and move on."

Murphy Maguire had a dental appointment one morning, causing him to arrive at the Oakton plant some hours later than usual. As he entered the plant, the security guard, Suggins, flagged him down.

"The prez is here," said Suggins.

"The *who*?" asked Maguire.

"Miss Amy. From downtown. And she's got two visitors."

"Where?"

"They're over by Godzilla."

Murphy hurried in that direction. As he came down the long aisle, he indeed spotted Amy Cieolara near the huge autoclave. With her were two men dressed in jacket and tie; one had a tape measure and the other was jotting down dimensions on a pad of paper.

Filled with apprehension, Murphy put on a cheerful face as he approached.

"Good morning!" he said to Amy.

"Oh, great, I'm so glad you're here," she said.

She introduced him to the two fellows, who were salesmen with an exhibit company located in Raleigh.

"Well, it certainly is a surprise to see you here!" Murphy said pleasantly.

"Surprise? Didn't you read my email about the conference room from last night?" she asked.

"Uh . . . no. I just came from the dentist –"

"I'm moving in!" Amy said with a grin.

"Excuse me?"

"Not permanently," she assured him. "And I won't be here all the time. But if you have no objections, I'd like to conduct most of my meetings from here at Oakton – from next to Godzilla."

"May I ask why?"

"Dramatic effect," said Amy.

"I'm not sure I understand."

"We've decided that Godzilla is the bottleneck – the primary constraint – that will determine the throughput of the Oakton plant."

"Correct," said Murphy.

"And we want – we need – everyone to recognize this fact. We want everyone to subordinate all other operations to servicing the demands of the system constraint, and to synchronize their actions with Godzilla. Right?"

"Yes, also correct."

"So," said Amy, "it hit me last night that one way to get people to pay attention would be to move my meetings out here to Oakton and hold them right here on the plant floor. We already have a portable conference room that's part of the trade show display we used at the Composites World Expo. Have you ever seen it?"

"Just pictures," said Murphy.

"It's nice. Carpeted, recessed lighting, inlaid hardwood ceiling –

and big glass windows, so everyone can look out at Godzilla. So I'm thinking what better way to signal that this, right here, is the center of the company?"

Murphy nodded thoughtfully, chuckled, and said, "Well, it's a bit unusual. But actually I rather like the idea."

"I promise we will not interfere with anything. And it won't be forever," said Amy. "I think that after a month or maybe six weeks, people will have gotten the message."

"I cannot promise you, Amy, that it will be entirely comfortable for you here," Murphy warned. "It can get quite hot in this area."

"We can install air-conditioning," said one of the salesmen.

"And Godzilla makes a lot of noise during the venting procedure," Murphy added.

"For how long?" asked Amy.

"A few minutes."

"All the better. It'll make everyone pay attention," said Amy. She turned to the salesmen.

"How soon?"

"We can have it set up by tomorrow afternoon if you want."

"Does that work for you?" Amy asked Murphy.

"Yes, ma'am, that works just fine for me."

A little more than a month after Oakton went to an unbalanced system with a constraint – a description certain to chill the blood of most corporate executives, at least the uninitiated – the midquarter metrics for all Winner businesses were posted. Within twenty-four hours after this event, Amy Cieolara got a phone call from a livid Nigel Furst.

"What in the world are you DOING down there?!" Nigel demanded.

"Nothing!" Amy said reflexively. "Wait! Sorry, I mean, we're doing lots of things! We're implementing our turnaround tree! I mean, our turnaround *plan!*"

"Peter Winn called from Rio de Janeiro. He wants me to terminate you – *right now,*" said Nigel.

"But why?"

"Because he's been on the WING and he's seen your numbers! And frankly, I'm not sure I disagree. Amy, you promised me during our little talk that you would not allow the situation at Hi-T to get any worse."

"Well, it hasn't! In fact, it's getting better! We're really turning the corner, moving the needle in the right direction!" she insisted.

"Oh, really? Then how do explain – just to pick a few items from the WING report summary – that resource utilization at your Oakton plant was down from ninety-four percent to a depressing seventy-eight percent? Average productivity per line employee, down eleven percent. Direct labor, up twelve percent. And work-in-process inventory, up *fifteen* percent! Oh, wait. Sorry, WIP was down fifteen percent. Anyway, you get the point. Amy, performance is clearly deteriorating. I'm afraid that –"

"Hold it, hold it, hold it," said Amy. "This is all from WING, isn't it?"

"That is what we use within the Winner Corporation, yes."

"Then I know what's happened," she said. "Let me grab my copy." She did this while composing her thoughts for a defense.

"I'm waiting," said Nigel.

"Right, got it. Now, let's look at the larger picture. Look for instance at the output of the Oakton plant *as a whole* for the most recent month. That metric has gone up. We're shipping more, which is why WIP is down, and just as important, if not more so, we're shipping on schedule. And look at the uptick in cash flow. That's happening because we're getting paid for those shipments. The full impact hasn't yet hit because of the accounting lag between billings and receipts, but it will become obvious in the next month and longer. Check out accounts receivable; they too are up – do you see that, Nigel?"

"Hmm, yes. Yes, I do see it now," he mumbled.

"Oh, and look at Oakton's operating expenses," Amy continued. "Overtime has come down, because we're expediting less. Shipping costs, too, are less – because we're not having to pay for hugely expensive overnight shipping to make up for production delays."

"But then how do you explain the precipitous drop in resource utilization?" asked Nigel.

"Resource utilization is looking at each and every individual workstation in the plant, not at the production system *as a whole*. You see, what we've done, in effect, is we've added what we call 'protective capacity.' And we've done that in a couple of ways. One is that the release of materials into production is such that every resource is not being used to the max, but only to the extent that *the system* can utilize what is produced. And we are no longer working to takt time. We have reconfigured to achieve the fastest flow through the nonconstraints, which means that not everyone will be working to the max *all* the time."

"The nonconstraints?"

"Yes."

Nigel sighed and complained, "You're confusing me."

"I'm sorry, it is somewhat counterintuitive. Let me try again. You see, going for the fastest flow means that once a workstation has finished its processing, and passed on its WIP to the next station, there may often be a brief idle period, because more materials have not yet been gated in. That's going to cause the utilization metric to fall."

"Well, why wouldn't you want all equipment and workers to be busy all the time? It just doesn't make sense!"

"Sir, it does makes sense. You want the speed to the system constraint to be fast so that Godzilla never starves. And after Godzilla you also want speed so that you don't miss your shipping window."

"*What?! Godzilla? Starving??* What are you talking about?"

"Mr. Furst, please, never mind. It's technical," said Amy. "Just look at the bottom line. Look at Hi-T's operating income. It's turned! It's on the increase – and that growth will continue. Right now we're in the middle of the quarter and it doesn't look like much, but as it goes on our operating profits *will* accumulate."

Forty-five minutes later, and after reaching Peter Winn on his yacht in Rio de Janeiro harbor so that she could explain the bottom line improvement to him, Amy had defused the crisis.

But the experience had unnerved her. She was immediately connecting by phone and email. There was a scheduled meeting of what Amy was now calling the Velocity team, but she moved it up by a week. What if the corner had not yet been turned? She needed assurance that the turnaround plan was really working, that everything that could be done was in fact being done.

The portable conference room from the Hi-T trade show display had by now been erected on the plant floor near Godzilla – and had become quite a conversation piece among the employees with its carpeting, fabric-covered walls, plush chairs, and its huge and beautiful high-strength light-weight carbon-fiber conference table that could be easily lifted by two people yet could withstand a direct hit by an artillery shell. The inevitable joke that followed, delivered ad nauseam at trade shows, was that those around the table might not be so lucky.

Gathered around that high-tech table forty-eight hours after Nigel's call were the members of the Velocity Team: Elaine, Wayne, Sarah, Murphy, Garth, and Amy herself. Outside the windows was a splendid view of Godzilla.

"When one's head is on the chopping block, it can be a little unsettling," Amy said, having described her conversations with Nigel and Peter. "Therefore, that's why I moved up our meeting. I really need to know, first of all, if everyone is completely confident that the turnaround is on track. So . . . is it?"

"I would never say that we have nothing to worry about," said Elaine. "But I am seeing real improvement on the operating side. Everything you told Winner is taking place."

"I might mention here, since we're touching on finance," said Murphy, "that there are three measurements that come from TOC that have served me well in my own thinking about money: throughput; investment, including inventory; and operating expense."

"And you want to increase throughput, while reducing in a relative sense the investment and inventory, and obviously operating expense," Wayne Reese inserted, wanting to show that he was on board. "I've been doing a little reading, doing my homework."

"Well!" said Amy with a sweep of her hand. "Please continue!"

Wayne turned to Murphy, as if deferring, and said, "I don't want to steal your thunder."

"It is not my thunder to steal, sir. This has been around for a while. I just apply it."

"All right . . . feeling like a student at an oral exam," said Wayne, "throughput is the rate at which inventory is converted into completed sales – cash, in other words. Investment and inventory – and of course inventory is a shorter-term investment – is the money that has purchased both the means of production and whatever is to be sold from that production. And operating expense is the money spent to make the system work."

Wayne stood, went to the whiteboard, took a marker, and wrote some letters and arrows.

"So, over time, we want throughput – T – to be increasing, while capital investment and inventory – I – and operating expense – OE – are declining in a relative sense."

"In other words," Sarah said, getting the gist of it, "if we're converting sales orders into paid receipts faster and faster, and operating expenses and investment and inventory stay the same, then I and OE are lower and T is higher relative to each other."

"But how can inventory be lower if sales are going higher?" asked Elaine.

"We're talking about inventory held *within the system*," said Wayne. "It's moving through faster, but the amount held is lower, because we've 'leaned' it to only what is required. We're buying raw materials based on demand patterns and time to reliably replenish."

"So as a business," Amy said, "the goal is to make the most, the quickest, with the least."

"Yes, ma'am, that's the idea," said Murphy. "The most money by the quickest path with the least investment."

"Basic capitalism," said Wayne.

"But I do use that general concept whenever I evaluate the choices of a major decision," said Murphy. "I think about what the effect of the decision will be on T, I, and OE. If I increase investment and it does not proportionally increase throughput or reduce operating expense, then that's a bad decision. Likewise, for example, if I increase operating expense by hiring more workers or whatever and the result is a large gain in throughput – more sales with faster turnover of inventory – then that's a good decision."

"All right then, by those measures, how are we doing so far?" asked Amy. "It seems to me we've improved."

"Definitely," said Wayne. "Throughput is increasing because we're shipping on time and getting paid faster. Inventory is lower because we've been working off WIP. And expenses are down due to, among other things, less overtime – as well as fewer mistakes and less scrap, if I may put in a plug for Lean."

"Well, that's great," said Amy. "However, I know that Nigel Furst will always want more. And I certainly think that we can do better, that there are more than ample opportunities for improvement."

"I think we would all agree with that," said Wayne.

There was general assent around the table, with Sarah adding, "It's been a good start, but we really need a few more policy injections onto that logic tree we've created."

"How well is the priority system working?" Amy asked her. "Are the analysts doing the design reviews the way they're supposed to?"

"We still have some issues," said Sarah, "but basically the priority system has been doing pretty well. Some of the analysts still moan and groan that the reviews are beneath them. And there are a couple of analysts – Joe Tassoni, to name one – that I have to keep an eye on. But we're now at the point that more than eighty percent of all incoming reviews are cleared within forty-eight hours."

"That, ma'am, is *a lot* better than it used to be, let me tell you," said Murphy. "We have a good, healthy buffer of clearances at this point."

"And it's done wonders from an operations standpoint," said Wayne, "to have more flexibility in production planning and scheduling, as well as purchasing and just about everything else. So thank you."

"You're welcome. On the other hand," she said, "there is that twenty percent that do not get cleared in forty-eight hours. Whenever we have to do some kind of involved verification of the design in order to grant the clearance – destructive testing, extended computer modeling, that kind of thing – then the process can become protracted."

"I can second that," said Garth. "We have customers who can get huffy over what they see as unnecessary delay. They say things like, 'Why are you challenging the professionalism of *our* engineers? We've already verified this design!' "

"I can see how that would get under their skin," said Wayne. "And to me, as a Lean guy, it does seem wastefully excessive. So assuming it's really necessary –"

"It is," said Amy. "According to *our* lawyers we have to observe due diligence."

"So the question becomes, how can we do it faster?" Wayne finished.

"I think I may have at least a partial solution," said Sarah. "Just before Murphy left Rockville, we were talking about, for the lack of a better term, single tasking. These days everyone seems to take such pride in multitasking – having a zillion things going on and trying to do half a dozen of them simultaneously. But the more I've thought about it and looked into it, single tasking is the better way to go in terms of system output – and throughput."

"Why is that?" asked Amy.

"Because of dependency. If I'm trying to do six things at once, and I'm switching back and forth, doing a little on this one and a little on that one, I'm holding up at least one of them from being passed on to someone else who has to do the next step. Whereas if I focus and finish whatever I've started, then it can move on. And if everyone abides by single tasking, there should be an increase in speed."

"But if you're truly multitasking," said Garth, "aren't you opening two or three channels so you can do that many more things? I mean, if I'm driving, I can still carry on a conversation with a customer."

"Everyone uses that example," said Sarah. "Okay, so you can drive and talk at the same time. But can you write a report while you're driving?"

"I hope you don't try!" said Amy.

"And anyway, I object to multitasking in the office or in the lab for the same reason that driving with a cell phone pressed to your ear isn't a great idea – because it can lead to mistakes. Which is the last thing that F&D can afford right now."

"That's a good point," said Wayne.

"I've figured out, though, that people are not just multitasking; they're accumulating and pacing their work. Some of them actually hoard their work. They're afraid of looking like they don't have enough to do. Or they're perfectionists and don't want to let go. Or they want to feel like they're ultra-important because they have so much going on."

Amy rubbed her chin and said, "I'd never thought about it, but I can see this being a significant problem, especially in an office setting."

"Well, I've found a remedy – if I can get people to do it," said Sarah. "There is a technique called Relay Runner. It's a single-tasking work policy – or work ethic, really – and it has just a few simple rules."

"You mean someone like me can understand it?" Murphy joked.

"Actually, it's very similar to what you already are doing at Oakton," Sarah said. "Once you're handed a task, you take it and run with it. And you keep running fast as you can – consistent with requirements for safety and quality – until one of three things happens. Number one, you finish the task and hand off the assignment to whoever gets it next. Number two, you're blocked and have to stop because you have to wait for something you can't supply. Or, number three, a task with a higher priority is given to you – at which point you pause what you were doing and run with the higher priority assignment."

"Yes, that is very similar to what we do at the plant," said Murphy. "But the struggle is to not allow the second and third conditions to occur. Once a job is in production, we don't want work-in-process to wait because something isn't available. And the specifications and materials are already prioritized as they are released onto the plant floor. To interfere with that is usually what we call expediting, and that is something we prefer to avoid."

"The prioritizing," Wayne added, "is done in the planning and scheduling phase. And that's where, if Garth or one of the salespeople alerts us to some special need, we can juggle the schedule to please the customer. Or if we're low or out of stock on some material – assuming we know about it – we can rearrange the sequence so that we produce an order for which we have all the materials."

"By the way," Murphy said to Wayne, "I have progress to report on that last matter."

investment," said Elaine, "then with this we can lower the magnitude of the investment while still getting the same return – our net profit on sales. So our return on investment – our ROI – for our inventory improves by a lot."

"Hey, you know what? I love it, too!" said Amy. "Let's add that to the tree and think about what it does."

Injection: We establish time to reliably replenish (TRR) and use peak demand patterns to set stocking levels for raw materials.

And . . .

Injection: We replenish what's been consumed during each fixed time interval.

As a result . . .

We improve our material buffers' ability to prevent out-of-stocks.

Therefore . . .

ROI increases.

And this state leads to the higher condition . . .

Winner management is pleased.

"Great. What else?" Amy prodded. "What else speeds us toward those happy days when both our profit centers – Hi-T and F&D – are making gobs of money, customers are lining up to do business with us, and Nigel Furst is thrilled to have me be president?"

After the smiles and chuckles, it was quiet for a moment. Then Wayne Reese spoke up:

"You probably know what I'm going to suggest."

"Haven't a clue," said Amy.

"Lean Six Sigma. It's been on hold at Oakton, and it's fallen by the wayside in Rockville. But I for one think maybe it's time we revived that effort."

"We are not going to revive what didn't work," Amy said bluntly.

"All right," said Wayne, "I grant you that the balanced line did not function all that well for us. And takt time may be overblown. And a few other things. But let's not forget that a number of projects accomplished by LSS *did* work. For instance, the ability of Six Sigma techniques to solve the cracking problem in a number of the Navy components."

"And I have to give Wayne and Kurt and LSS their due," said Murphy. "Oakton is a better manufacturing plant due to Lean and Six Sigma. No question in my mind about that. The reconfigured M57

Line in particular. I have to say that the new M57 is – why, it's just slicker than a greased pig at the county fair."

This broke up everyone at the table.

"What? Y'all've never wrassled a greased pig?" Murphy asked. "Well, I can tell you, they're pretty slick!"

Shaking her head, but with a smile on her face, Amy said, "Wayne, this is nothing against you, because I know you were sincere. And if you'd rather I talk about this in private, I'll be happy to do that."

"No," said Wayne, "I'm from South Boston. I can take it. Let's get it out in the clear."

"My problem with Lean Six Sigma is that, while it did make improvements, it did not accomplish what we needed – what I expected – from a business and financial standpoint. The improvements tended to have local benefits rather than systemic impact."

"But we shouldn't throw the baby out with the bathwater," Wayne argued. "After all, we – or I should say, the company – has made the investment. Why not capitalize on it?"

"The employees at Oakton, I have to say," said Murphy, "love Lean. It helps them feel more in control, empowered, engaged – whatever the current buzzword. They like it."

"In Rockville," said Sarah, "it's the same way. The trouble in Maryland is that a small contingent – the Lean Greenies, who have idealistic and wonderful reasons that I personally sympathize with – was allowed to hijack the LSS program. Before it got off track, LSS was doing at least a few things of real value. . . . Well, actually, no, I take that back. Or maybe I don't."

"Make up your mind," said Elaine.

"The standardization of report formats," said Sarah. "That was worthwhile. But did it increase throughput for the business? Did it reduce our project backlog – which for us is our inventory – or lower our expenses? Not significantly, if at all. There were – and are – too many other factors that outweigh that little improvement."

"Like the analysts," said Murphy.

"Here is what I feel did not work with Lean Six Sigma," said Amy, "and what I do not want to revisit: the 'N over ten' ratio of activities that we are supposed to have going on to bring on the Lean culture. The obsessive-compulsive need to have the orthodox proportion of black belts to green belts – and the long list of LSS projects that we are supposed to have going to certify people as having Lean and Six Sigma training. And, above all, trying to make *reality* fit Lean, rather than the other way around."

Expanded Turnaround Strategy

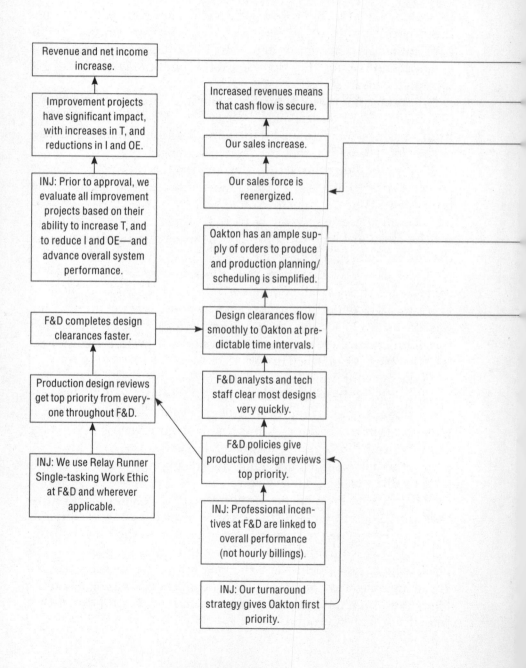

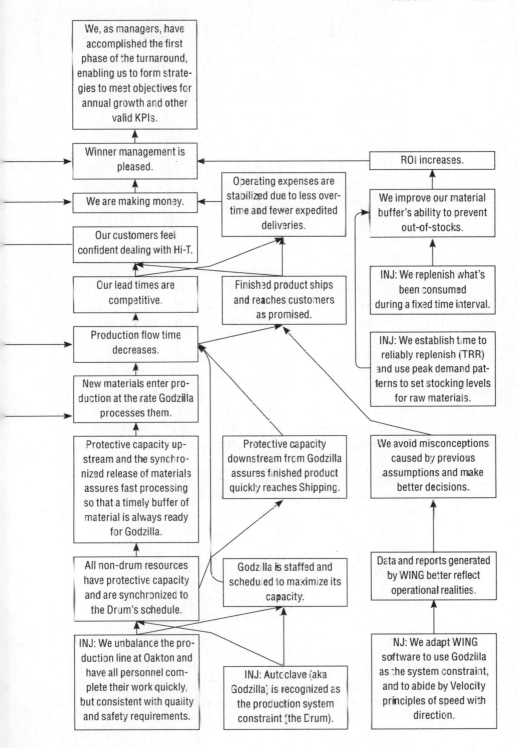

Wayne, who had been taking in all of this with a sober and poker face, now said, "I understand what you're saying, and I agree with most of it. But don't you remember the fourth round of the dice game that Tom Dawson showed us? In the fourth round, we simulated what would happen if we elevated the performance of the constraint, and that was when we got our best numbers."

Amy shifted her gaze to Murphy, as if to coax a comment from him.

"The main reason we halted LSS at Oakton," he said, "was because we needed to stabilize the production system. Until you have a stable system, it makes no point to try to improve it. But we are now very close to having that stability, and I think that as soon as we put in place the things we were talking about today, we will have achieved it. And that will be the time to start improving what we have with Lean and Six Sigma and any other means at our disposal."

Pursing her lips as she considered this, Amy then said, "So much depends upon the choice of what to improve. Where do we focus? What are we going to change? What are we going to change *to*? How do we identify the changes that truly will accelerate the velocity of the business?"

"Logically, the place to focus would be the constraint," said Wayne.

"The *performance* of the constraint," Murphy emphasized, "and the system overall. It's the flow that matters – the flow to, through, and away from the constraint. If you just keep improving the constraint, then it's no longer a constraint, and you've lost your control point. *And* you've probably got a bottleneck somewhere else where you don't want it."

"Okay, I get your point," said Wayne. "But as far as evaluating improvement candidates, we have to take into account their effect on the constraint. It could be a quality issue upstream from Godzilla that affects the overall performance – like the cracking problem in the Navy components."

"Absolutely," said Murphy.

"Throughput, investment, inventory, and operating expense," said Amy. "What if we evaluated all proposed improvements based on how they influence those measurements? Instead of evaluating based on waste elimination or doing something just because it seems like a good thing to do, we choose the improvements that really are going to accelerate the velocity of the business."

"So if we identify something that is really going to boost throughput," said Wayne, "and/or reduce the others, then that's the project we pursue."

"And if we have five candidates," Sarah added, "then we go with the ones we expect to have the most positive effect on T, I, and OE."

"I think that works," said Wayne. "I think that's on the money."

"Done!" said Amy.

And this, too, was added to the tree:

Injection: Prior to approval, we evaluate all improvement projects based on their ability to increase T, and to reduce I and OE – and advance overall system performance.

With this in place . . .

Improvement projects have significant impact, with increases in T, and reductions in I and OE.

Therefore . . .

Revenue and net income increase.

This statement then links to the higher condition . . .

Winner management is pleased.

There was one more item that was necessary. The WING software that Hi-T was still obligated to use was generation 4-L. It still contained the assumptions of a balanced line, takt time, and other vestiges of Wayne's original LSS efforts. Needless to say, this was causing confusion and problems, both operationally and in the reporting. So they added one more change to the tree:

Injection: We adapt WING4-L software to use Godzilla as the system constraint, and to abide by Velocity principles of speed with direction.

The result is . . .

Data and reports generated by WING better reflect operational realities.

And . . .

We avoid misconceptions caused by previous assumptions and make better decisions.

17

Joe Tassoni, who was skeptical of all organizations and suspicious of all managers no matter who they were, was unconvinced of the efficacy of the Relay Runner work ethic – even though Sarah, Wayne, and Amy had met separately with all the F&D analysts to explain the special status the analyst function held as being a system constraint. Joe, who had almost nodded off sitting in his seat, didn't get that "constraint" part either. So he had requested a private meeting with Sarah Schwick in order to gain clarification – although, really, he just wanted to complain.

"I do not understand why you now want people to do . . . what is it called? *Single* task?"

"Yes. Single tasking," said Sarah. "Do the most important thing, one thing at a time. Focus. Get it done. Then move on to the next most important thing."

"How can this be better than multitask?" asked Joe. "It does not make any sense! With single task, one thing gets done. With multitask, many things are being done."

"Yes, exactly, many things are *being* done. With multitasking, many things are being worked on, but it takes longer for any one of them – usually all of them – to be *finished*."

"I am not sure that I agree," said Joe. "Whenever I am driving, I am always multitasking – eating my breakfast, dictating my letters, talking on my cell phone, whatever."

"And, Joe, don't you slow down? Don't you arrive later than you otherwise would because you are multitasking?"

"Slow down? Why would I do that?" asked Joe.

"Joe, as someone who commutes on a bicycle in suburban Washington traffic . . ." She stopped herself. "Never mind. What you do while you're driving is between you and law enforcement. But here at work, we need you to play by the rules . . . the *new* rules. Look, Joe, you're overworked. We're all worried about losing you – either to another job or, frankly, to the grave."

Joe lowered his head. He was all too aware of these fears. Another job would probably pay much less; the grave would pay nothing.

"All right, all right," he said, "I can try. Tell me again; what do you want?"

"Single task," said Sarah. "Do you know what a relay race is?"

"Yes. I have even been to the Olympics one time."

"Good. Imagine a relay runner on the track."

Sarah struck a pose like a runner, trying to humor him.

"You and everyone here at F&D are going to be like that runner – ready and waiting. When you're handed the project – the baton – you take off running down the track . . ."

She demonstrated, running in place.

"And you run, run, run . . ."

"Okay, yes, I am running already," said Joe.

"Until one of three things happens. You're finished – you've designed your testing schedule, you've rendered your evaluation, whatever is called for."

"All right."

"Or you're blocked – you can't finish because you need a second opinion or something from somebody else."

"Or third?"

"You have to stop to do something of a higher priority."

"Ah, you see! I predict that is going to happen all the time!" Joe protested.

"No, the way we're setting up the priority codes, it should not happen very often to you or the other analysts," Sarah assured him.

"What happens when I need to think about something?" he asked.

"Go ahead and think! It's part of the analyst process!"

"Suppose I need to think about it for a couple of days? A week?"

"Then consider yourself blocked," said Sarah. "Look, I recognize there is a creative aspect to your job. But you need to focus on one thing as much as possible. Once you have a baton, run that race; don't wander all over the track trying to run six or seven races at the same time."

Joe sighed and looked around.

"What about my pile system?" he asked.

"You can keep your pile system," said Sarah, deciding to fight only one battle a time.

"*Molto bene*," said Joe.

The continuing struggles at F&D that spring were metaphorically more like guerilla ambushes and impromptu insurrections than pitched battles. One afternoon a lone analyst – not Joe Tassoni – threw a tantrum when asked about a design that should have been cleared three days prior, and the analyst stormed out. Happily for all, he returned the next morning and signed off on the clearance. That was about as dramatic as it got. But there were all sorts of little resentments and confusions and passive resistance, and these often hidden skirmishes went on through the summer and into the fall.

The most difficult thing, Sarah found, was getting people to subordinate their own needs, their own inclinations, their interests, their convenience, their predispositions, and so on to the needs of the system and the constraint – aka the analysts. Only if they did that would the system yield greater flow and become less chaotic. Even some of the analysts had trouble with this, brilliant though they were.

Most managers, especially the ambitious ones, want to show how good they are, want to show off, and they tend to do this by optimizing performance for whatever is under their own individual responsibility. Viktor Kyzanski was one to try to exploit this natural competitiveness – not the first executive to think of this, certainly not the last – often using billings as the overriding metric to bring it out. He would make it a game, as in which lab could be the most billable? This drove up billings; it also drove away all value-conscious clients. This had once been fine with Viktor; he wanted only the clients with the deepest pockets and the organizational largesse to spend freely. But now Viktor was facing time in the slammer, due to his personal despair over the backfiring of his winning strategy.

Yet Sarah was now faced with the burn-in of Viktor's culture – as well as plain old human self-centeredness. Through these times, she found herself going head to head with those who didn't get, or didn't want to get, the new priorities. Part of the problem was that for the longest while she had trouble stating the priorities succinctly in public; she would bury them in rationality, and by then everyone forgot what she was saying.

At last, after a lunch with Brenda, she came up with some simple watchwords:

"Oakton First. Analysts First."

That had a certain ring, and sort of caught on. Still, Sarah seemed to be forever going head-to-head – and she was usually a head shorter – with those like the kinetics lab manager who really didn't like her priorities because they interfered with *his* schedule. After all, he'd been doing his own schedule for years; why shouldn't he be the one to determine the order in which tests should be done?

"Your priorities are simply not efficient for *my* technicians!" he told Sarah.

And if it was not some headstrong go-getter with tunnel vision, it was the laid-back, vapid-minded techies on cruise control:

"I don't see what difference it makes. It all has to be done anyway, so, like, if I'm doing centrifuge, why not do all the centrifuge? You know? Like, why do you want me to stop doing centrifuge and go do elastometer?"

Or:

"Oh, I forgot. You needed that today, didn't you?"

These were often the smart people, too. Sometimes the less intelligent – the ones who did not question – got it quicker.

For Sarah Schwick, organic chemistry had always come easily. Human chemistry was much more challenging. She learned in this time that she had to be strong, yet gentle. She could not be a diamond; she had to be more like graphite.

It was easier at Oakton. Murphy Maguire had experience on his side, not only in an intimate knowledge of the plant itself, but with respec to running it successfully as an unbalanced system with Godzilla the constraint. The major failing of the pre-Winner era – and it hardly Murphy's alone – was that inertia had become the lim continued growth.

As one might expect, there was some confusion – an carping – on the part of the workforce over the seeming w tween the two messages. For years, during Murphy's fi they had been told that Godzilla's schedule was law, and thing else revolved around it. Then Kurt and Wayne t Godzilla had the same status as all other equipment i that the M57 Line was setting the pace. Now they dzilla was back on top.

I thought we wasn't spozed to pay no m la. Spozed to be like ever-thang el

"Now, Tee-Jay, you just do what you're told. It's real simple. Even you can get this. We empty the 'Zilla; we fill the 'Zilla. Empty the 'Zilla, fill the 'Zilla. Fast as possible. In and out, in and out, in and out, real quick. Got that?"

"Sounds X-rated to me. But whatever y'all want."

The Godzilla pit crew – of which Tee-Jay was a member – was back. And those boys were soon at the top of their game again. Turnaround time between emptying what had been processed, filling it again, and getting the big autoclave back into operation was reduced to single digits – less than ten minutes. This reduction meant that Godzilla, instead of doing eleven soaks per day, on average, could now do twelve. And this multiplied by six or seven days a week – every other Saturday was set aside for maintenance – meant that the single-digit changeovers were like gaining an entire production day extra every month. On an annual basis, with strong demand and full production, this was roughly equivalent to an extra two weeks of throughput.

One of the best things that happened due to Murphy Maguire's sojourn to Rockville was that he could get on the phone to Sarah Schwick any time and she would take his calls. That had not been the previously, as Murphy had no rapport with Viktor. If Murphy special requests, the only way that they would be honored Don made the call. After B. Don departed, that channel , whereupon most requests made by Murphy were Murphy could get through any time he so de-

told Jayro, "is never underestimate the s."

led and said, "Hey, Sarah, got a ques- be done from a technical stand- enty-three-hour soaks in the hedule and we've got seven get but one or two in a ust going to kill us."

e some of them?"

got seven full-capac That's like a w thing else."

"I have, and Garth says the dates have been promised. They are high priority. These batches have to go in."

"Email the details and I'll get back to you," she said.

The next day Sarah called back and told him:

"On four of the seven, there is nothing that can be done. On the batch at the top of the list, it's the design spec. The chemistry and the applications require a full twenty-one hours at the specified temperatures and pressures.

"The next three – you'll love this – there is no compelling technical reason why those composites have to be in the autoclave for twenty-three hours. But they are government contracts, and twenty-three hours is contractually specified. I was told that it would take an act of Congress to change that."

Murphy groaned and said, "Don't you just love bureaucracy?"

"But here, maybe, is the good news," Sarah said. "The remaining three batches are such that we might be able to play with the time-temperature-pressure ratios. Usually, the composites that have the long soaks in the autoclave are low temp and low pressure. But if we go to a higher temp and higher pressure, maybe adjust the ambient atmosphere, we can reduce the time spent in Godzilla."

"Reduce by how much?"

"Don't quote me yet," said Sarah. "We have to do some testing. But we think we might be able to get it down into the six-to-eight-hour range."

"That would be like going from three days down to one day," Murphy said with exuberance. "That would help tremendously."

"I've got Joe Tassoni on it. If Joe says it can be done, you can take it to the bank."

"Um . . . hmm, you've got Joe on it? My only question is, when are we going to get it?"

Sarah laughed and said, "He's much, much better these days. I mean, he's still same old Joe Tassoni, but we've got him abiding by the relay runner rules. And his piles are smaller. Plus, I've got a new assistant helping him stay organized and on track. I think he likes her; she's gained five pounds."

"All right, we'll remind Joe that any improvement to Godzilla helps his bonus," said Murphy.

"He knows that. All the analysts know that Hi-T's performance affects their bonuses."

"Then you might add," said Murphy, "that the next time I come to Rockville, I'm bringin' ribs – Memphis style, the way he likes 'em."

On a rainy Saturday, Amy walked into her kitchen and heard a kind of whirring-buzzing sound issuing from the basement. She descended the steps and peered into the laundry room, and there was Michelle. The washer was running, the dryer was spinning, but Michelle had also strung clotheslines wall to wall and she was hanging wet laundry on these. To speed the drying process, Michelle had set up a variety of electric fans, and the laundry was billowing in the breeze of these. Amy came in and at first just stared.

"The dryer can't keep up," Michelle explained in a deadpan tone, "so I am elevating the constraint."

"What a smart young lady you are," Amy told her.

"Well, I have to be, or I'll be stuck down here all day and all night. Since we have to do Grandma and Grandpa's laundry as well as our own, it's almost twice as much."

Zelda had had knee replacement surgery a week before and was recovering. Therefore, all laundry was being done at Amy's house.

"If only my brother would help out," Michelle grumbled.

"... watching your grandfather, which is no

"I have, and Garth says the dates have been promised. They are high priority. These batches have to go in."

"Email the details and I'll get back to you," she said.

The next day Sarah called back and told him:

"On four of the seven, there is nothing that can be done. On the batch at the top of the list, it's the design spec. The chemistry and the applications require a full twenty-one hours at the specified temperatures and pressures.

"The next three – you'll love this – there is no compelling technical reason why those composites have to be in the autoclave for twenty-three hours. But they are government contracts, and twenty-three hours is contractually specified. I was told that it would take an act of Congress to change that."

Murphy groaned and said, "Don't you just love bureaucracy?"

"But here, maybe, is the good news," Sarah said. "The remaining three batches are such that we might be able to play with the time-temperature-pressure ratios. Usually, the composites that have the long soaks in the autoclave are low temp and low pressure. But if we go to a higher temp and higher pressure, maybe adjust the ambient atmosphere, we can reduce the time spent in Godzilla."

"Reduce by how much?"

"Don't quote me yet," said Sarah. "We have to do some testing. But we think we might be able to get it down into the six-to-eight-hour range."

"That would be like going from three days down to one day," Murphy said with exuberance. "That would help tremendously."

"I've got Joe Tassoni on it. If Joe says it can be done, you can take it to the bank."

"Um . . . hmm, you've got Joe on it? My only question is, when are we going to get it?"

Sarah laughed and said, "He's much, much better these days. I mean, he's still same old Joe Tassoni, but we've got him abiding by the relay runner rules. And his piles are smaller. Plus, I've got a new assistant helping him stay organized and on track. I think he likes her; she's gained five pounds."

"All right, we'll remind Joe that any improvement to Godzilla helps his bonus," said Murphy.

"He knows that. All the analysts know that Hi-T's performance affects their bonuses."

"Then you might add," said Murphy, "that the next time I come to Rockville, I'm bringin' ribs – Memphis style, the way he likes 'em."

18

On a rainy Saturday, Amy walked into her kitchen and heard a kind of whirring-buzzing sound issuing from the basement. She descended the steps and peered into the laundry room, and there was Michelle. The washer was running, the dryer was spinning, but Michelle had also strung clotheslines wall to wall and she was hanging wet laundry on these. To speed the drying process, Michelle had set up a variety of electric fans, and the laundry was billowing in the breeze of these. Amy came in and at first just stared.

"The dryer can't keep up," Michelle explained in a deadpan tone, "so I am elevating the constraint."

"What a smart young lady you are," Amy told her.

"Well, I have to be, or I'll be stuck down here all day and all night. Since we have to do Grandma and Grandpa's laundry as well as our own, it's almost twice as much."

Zelda had had knee replacement surgery a week before and was recovering. Therefore, all laundry was being done at Amy's house.

"If only my brother would help out," Michelle grumbled.

"Ben is helping out. He's watching your grandfather, which is no easy task these days."

Amy reached for the basket of wet clothes and began to help her daughter.

"Elevating the constraint," Amy said, "what a great idea."

"See, you think I'm not listening when you talk about work," said Michelle, "but I'm soaking up every word."

"Right," said her mother.

• • •

278

A full year and more had passed since that spring day when they had added a few new "leaves" and branches to the Turnaround Tree. And the tree was now full grown.

At Oakton, their chronic production problems were entirely behind them. With Godzilla identified as the system constraint and designated as the Drum of operations, and everything else synchronized to its performance, the system had become reliable and predictable. Once materials came onto the plant floor, they flowed quickly to the queue within the Autoclave area, the time buffer that Murphy and crew had calculated always ensuring that Godzilla never starved and was always full. When time inside the giant autoclave was finished, the WIP would flow through downstream processing with speed similar to the upstream end, and the time buffer to Shipping enabled finished inventory to be there when the trucks arrived. Only an equipment outage or some equivalent mishap could seriously disrupt the system, and with the preventive maintenance schedules that Kurt Konani established, with Murphy advising him where to focus, that was a rare occurrence.

The fixed-time-interval inventory system, based on a reliable time to replenish what had been consumed by actual demand, was in place. Advocated by Murphy Maguire, modeled and implemented by Jayro Pepps, and perfected by Wayne Reese and his Highboro staff, it had pronounced effect on both operations and finance. Inventory stocks were high enough to protect production – and Godzilla, the Drum, in particular – but low enough that the cash required to maintain them was way less than it had been. Depending on the material, the reduction averaged about 30 percent – and Wayne was working to further improve this on some of the more expensive materials. In times when credit became pricey and even difficult to obtain at all for other businesses, this would prove to be a tremendous advantage.

At Formulation & Design, under Sarah Schwick's direction, the relay-runner work ethic meant faster flow. There was far less "pacing" as people, for whatever reasons, sought to stretch their workloads, and the hoarding of tasks for individual aggrandizement was severely frowned upon. In principle, the single-tasking discipline was similar to what was done in production at Oakton, but the simple priority system that Sarah had put in place enabled flexibility. At first the priorities were set mainly to speed design clearances to enable production. But Sarah then improved upon the system so that there was a prioritized pipeline of projects that were gated to the F&D work staff in a way that would limit concurrent demand for critical resources during the same window of time. The sequencing allowed projects that were coming due sooner to have priority over others in which time to report to the client was more ample.

And she now had a free hand to do what she had long thought was necessary, which was "fixing the loop." However, she and her people at F&D did it not the way she would have done it a few years before – fiddling with this, and tinkering with that – but by establishing Joe Tassoni and the other analysts as the Drum of F&D and then buffering whatever would serve them best so that it would be in queue when they got to it. They had worked hard to be sure that when an analyst opened a project folder, everything the analyst needed to render an evaluation was right there. The analyst then did not have to send the project back into the labs for some missing test or a faulty array of data. As promised, they had removed from the analysts' duties anything that an analyst did not have to perform. All of this combined meant that the analysts became several times more productive than they had been, even as the quality of their work improved due to fewer distractions, better input, and more time to focus on what was important.

Then in the second half of the year, Sarah found a rainmaker – a replacement for Viktor Kyzanski. He was Dr. Marvin Crest, a brilliant and distinguished scientist, and a failed entrepreneur. A small company he had founded had gone under, and he had taken refuge in academia. But Dr. Marv, as he soon became known informally, not only knew his science, he also knew how to close a sale.

Amy Cieolara gave Dr. Marv the title of president of Formulation & Design, as this was practically a requirement for dealing one on one with higher management in other organizations. But Amy kept Sarah Schwick as the operational head of F&D, and gave Sarah the title of director. Marvin and a small staff would get F&D in the door of potential clients, bring home the business, and then Sarah and the project managers would take it from there. Within months Dr. Marv had brought in three multiyear, multimillion-dollar research contracts from Fortune 500 clients.

Therefore, for all of those reasons, throughput had gone up. On the production side of Hi-T, there had been an upward spiral, as predicted by the Turnaround Tree: improved operations had pleased the customers, and pleasant customers had re-energized the sales force, who in turn had delivered more sales. Indeed, Oakton was converting sales orders into delivered goods at a faster rate than at any time before, and revenues ramped upward.

The same was true at F&D, with Sarah delivering faster and better fulfillment of obligations, and Dr. Marv being the catalyst to bring in new accounts to drive revenues. Given the vastly improved efficiency of Joe Tassoni – and the other analysts as well – they were able to get results "out of the building," which had become Sarah's mantra, at a faster rate, yet with superb quality and creativity. Again, throughput had increased.

At the same time, inventory and investment had been declining in a relative sense. Inventory in production had contracted thanks to the time-based reordering and the faster, smoother production output. At Rockville, the project inventory – the billable or logged hours against a given project, which could not be billed until certain payment conditions were met – was also down in a relative sense, because the flow was better. Reports were leaving the building quicker, and so were the invoices. As for investment, in both segments, no significant new plants or equipment had been added, so the business was earning more with the same investment – a thing of beauty in the eyes of any capitalist.

Operating expenses: also down in relative terms. Overall expense on the manufacturing side had actually risen slightly, mainly because payroll was higher, as Oakton had hired a few extra hands to protect speed. But in proportion to throughput, the increase was, in relative terms, a net decrease – which is to say that the gains in revenue and income far exceeded the amount added to payroll. And in Rockville, the elimination of Viktor's salary alone brought down current expenses, as Dr. Marv was a fraction of his price. And no other significant expenses had risen because of what they had done.

So Hi-T had fulfilled its purpose. It was a money-making machine, a money-*growing* machine. In standard accounting terms – by generally accepted accounting principles, or GAAP – the picture was quite pretty. Revenue was up; cash was growing. Long-term debt was being paid down; short-term liabilities were down overall, as well as down relatively. And in the equity portion of the standard accounting equation, net income was gloriously blossoming.

At the end of the year, Hi-T had had the third best year of its existence, despite the slow start in the first quarter. The first quarter of the new year was recorded as the best single quarter *ever* in the company's history.

And was Nigel Furst appreciative of these accomplishments? Well, he was not unappreciative. With almost no fanfare, he finally and officially deleted the *interim* from Amy Cieolara's title, which was now "President, Hi-T Composites, Inc., a wholly owned subsidiary of Winner Corp." Of course, the *interim* had never been there on her business cards or stationery or anything public. Still, she felt better having it gone from the internal files.

Plus, there was more! Nigel gave her a 5 percent raise. He was also charming and nice as he did so, saying he wished it could be more but that new austerity measures approved by Peter Winn forbade any executive raises above 5 percent. Amy just looked at her pay stub after the raise took effect, shook her head, grumbled to herself, and said nothing to anyone else.

Tom Dawson, perhaps, did better by her. The weekend after Amy was no longer "interim," Tom gassed up his plane and they flew to North Carolina's Outer Banks. He flew near Kitty Hawk and they landed on a little strip – a somewhat tricky landing due to the gusts that day – and he pulled two bicycles from the back of the plane for them to ride to the beach. And something else.

"Here," he said, handing it to Amy, "you might need this down by the water on a day like this. Besides, you got that company of yours to fly; you might as well have the jacket."

It was his Marine pilot's flight jacket. Amy held it up and looked at the patches, the squadron patch on the right shoulder, American flag on the left, some garish other ones, and high center in the back: the U.S. Marine Corps mascot bulldog with jauntily tilted World War I helmet and a smoking cigar clenched between jaws.

"Wow, I should wear this to the office," Amy said.

"They'd better get out of your way."

"Ooo-rah!!" she yelled, putting it on.

He placed both hands on her shoulders to steady her, took something brassy from his pocket, then began to pin it to the jacket over her heart.

"Your wings?" she asked.

"My naval aviator's insignia," he said.

"Does this mean we're going steady?"

"It might."

19

"So the perennial question," said Amy, "is, what do we do for an encore?"

The second quarter was drawing to a close, and Amy was holding a meeting of the Velocity Team minds – the usual crew: Sarah, Wayne, Elaine, Garth, and Murphy, plus of course Amy herself. As had become customary, they were meeting in the Hi-T trade show display conference room, which still stood on the Oakton plant floor next to Godzilla. Erected here the year before, it was never the original intent to keep it in the plant this long. Certainly Amy was no longer holding regular staff meetings here. But it had proven to be so handy for production meetings that it had never been taken down. Then someone had backed a forklift into it, severely denting one of the walls, and the industrial smell of the plant had gotten into the draperies and carpet – so it was never going to see a trade show again and Amy just said, "Keep it."

So for the Velocity meetings, when they discussed how to keep the Reality Tree growing from a current reality to a stronger, better future reality, they always came to Oakton. Amy thought it worthwhile to keep reminding herself and everyone else that Godzilla was still the Drum of the business.

"We're about to go into the second half of the year," Amy was saying, "and I think that this could just be the best year Hi-T has ever had. We had a fantastic first quarter. The second quarter, based on the numbers I've been seeing, looks strong. If we can continue the velocity we've achieved – just to use my new favorite word again – we are going to be the best business in Nigel's group. And wouldn't that be sweet? So our objective today is to add some new branches to the old Reality Tree, and – what's the matter?"

She was looking directly at Garth Quincy, who was squirming and frowning as Amy talked.

"You look like you've got indigestion or something," Amy said.

"Well, we all know first and second quarters have been strong pretty much across the board," said Garth. "But I have to caution you that my salespeople are reporting some softness here and there. This is particularly true in certain segments, like the construction and maritime markets."

"Interest rates have been rising," said Elaine. "So it's obvious that the economy will cool down at some point."

"How bad do you think it could be?" Amy asked Garth.

"Of course, I don't really know. Probably not that bad. But I hate to see us get our hopes up and then the market won't let us accomplish what we set out to achieve."

"You know, Garth, we're calling it the Reality Tree," said Amy, "because we're trying to keep a realistic link between the current state and the future state, whatever direction we decide is the best for the company and everyone associated with it."

"My suggestion," said Wayne Reese, "would be to look at our future from our customers' points of view. We need to ask questions as if *we* were them. Questions like, 'Why do I want to keep dealing with Hi-T?' And, 'Why is Hi-T the best choice?' or, 'Why is Hi-T the only choice worth considering?' Then when we have the answers, we just have to do it. We have to make it real."

"And we verify what we think, right?" asked Garth. "I mean, we verify as best we can that what *we* think they value and what they really *do* value – and will pay for – are the same. Because I know from bitter experience that what they *say* they want and what they really do lay down money to buy can be two different things."

"Sure, but my point," said Wayne, "is let's align our future with the future of the customers and markets where we want to be."

"Because it's not going to happen any other way," Murphy added.

"Exactly. The customer is always right, good times, bad times, no matter what the economy is doing at any particular moment."

"Yes, I totally agree," said Amy. "That's a smart thing to do. So let's look out into the future and I'll play customer and pose a corn-ball question: 'Amy, why is Hi-T the only good choice as a supplier to my company – Customer, Incorporated – for composite materials?' "

"Because," said Garth, speculating, "I can get the best, high-performance composites designed, manufactured, and delivered in less time and for less money than it takes to get them from Asia or anywhere else in the world."

There was a split second of silence followed by a chorus of hoots and howls.

"Right!" said Elaine. "Only when pigs can fly!"

But Amy wasn't laughing.

"Now, wait! Think about what he just said!" Amy called out. "Take the first part – we already do that! We can debate what 'best' or 'high-performance' means, but let's not quibble. The fact is we do design, manufacture, and deliver – on time! – quality composite materials that meet or exceed the performance expectations of our customers. And that's a fact!"

"Excuse me, but I think it was the second part that tickled the funny bones around the table," said Murphy. "The delivered in 'less time' for 'less money' than 'anywhere else in the world' – it was that part. Not that I wouldn't love to have that happen, but I think that's what got the rise out of us."

"All right, let's take that apart," Amy challenged. "What about 'less time'? Does a vendor with Asian-based manufacturing really have an advantage over us? Let's just take transportation time and North American customers for starters. How long does it take a container ship to cross the Pacific?"

"I don't know exactly," said Wayne, "but Shanghai to Los Angeles? Last I looked it was around twelve days for a typical ship, not counting harbor or weather delays."

"So we have a twelve-day, maybe a two-week headstart with all customers in North America, for anything coming across an ocean by ship. And for customers in Europe and South America, and every place *except* Asia, we're more or less on equal footing as far as transport time. Do you see what I'm saying?"

"Sure, but what about everything else?" asked Elaine.

"Everything else? Okay, what about a vendor that does its engineering in Asia? What advantage do they have? They have email . . . but guess what? We have email, too. They have computers; we have computers. They have smart people; we have smart people. Where is their invincible advantage?"

"Well, payroll, of course! Salaries, wages!" said Elaine. "It's all cheaper in Asia!"

"So they pay their people less. Why is that an *invincible* advantage?"

Elaine appeared to be about to have a conniption.

"Well . . . because! Lower wages mean lower costs! Higher margins!"

"Automatically? Just because you pay less in labor?"

"Everything else being equal! Of course!"

Amy, who was normally quite composed, was on her feet, pacing, those light brown curls of hers flying about her shoulders and green eyes flashing.

"Everything else is *not* equal, and it's *never* going to be equal! And that is good, not bad. Because it means that if we do it right, we can stay in the game long into the future. There are many components to cost; there are many aspects to value; and there are many ways to compete. This business is based in Highboro, and while I'm president, at least, it will live or die in Highboro. Therefore, it is our job as managers to find the 'inequalities' that give us a strong advantage in the marketplace. If we have a competitor with low labor costs, then we have to create an advantage to counter that. And I commend Garth for giving us a goal that is, in my opinion, not unreasonable: doing what we do quicker and for less money than any other supplier in the world – with quality, with safety, with prosperity for everyone associated with this business. Now . . . how can we make it happen?"

And so they settled in for the day. By the end, they had another whiteboard covered with sticky notes and arrows – and there was hardly a doubt in anyone's mind by then that if they advanced, leaf by logical leaf, branch by structured branch, they would create a sturdy future for Hi-T and everyone connected with the company.

The starting strategy was simple. In Amy's words, "We will start by using our new strengths and speed in production and inventory management as a platform to build marketplace advantages for ourselves and our customers."

Next, they conceived of their customers as being in three general groups: existing accounts, lost accounts that could be regained, and new accounts that had not yet done business with Hi-T. They then designed offers and capabilities that would appeal to any or all of these groups.

From these basic strategic decisions flowed a variety of specific initiatives:

Injection: We build supply chain alliances to help our customers win against their competitors.

Because of this . . .

We gain special, strategic relationships with our best customers.

With their new expertise in time to reliably replenish, they could create working relationships that could tremendously increase the value to the customer in ways that traditional sales and purchasing could never achieve. They would look into the markets that their customers faced, and help those customers increase their own velocity toward their goals.

In related fashion, they would offer vendor-managed inventory services, either free, for the biggest accounts, or for a modest charge. Rather than the customer having to devote resources to keeping track of consumed stocks, computer linkups would accomplish that and automatically trigger the necessary orders. This would be less strategically intimate than the alliances – although it could also augment them – but it would still help build a close and secure relationship.

Injection: We use our new inventory management skills to offer vendor-managed inventory to customers.

As a result . . .

Mutually advantageous customer relationships build long-term sales.

Unfortunately, the effects of the Winner acquisition had been such as to drive away a number of accounts. The long lead times, the missed shipping dates, and other aggravations had caused some customers to express their displeasures with their feet – and leave. But Garth and a number of the salespeople in the field felt that some of these lost accounts could be brought back, given that the causes that had brought about their departure were now remedied. The problem was, how could they convince them? And so . . .

Injection: We offer "promise kept or the penalty is on us" types of guarantees.

As a result . . .

Customers believe in our sincerity and place orders, which leads to repeated, long-term sales.

The idea was that there would be guarantees offered to these lost customers that would inflict a substantial penalty on Hi-T if shipping dates were missed or if a quality issue caused dissatisfaction. Amy was nervous about this one, but when Murphy and Wayne agreed the risk could be minimized, she signed off on it.

Then there were potential new customers. Garth's sales force would of course continue to make presentations and seek relationships with the larger users of composites – the "biggies," as Garth called them. But there were plenty of potential customers that the sales force could never get to. Most of these were smaller companies and distributors, and a lot of them were offshore in faraway markets. So the question became how to reach them, draw them in, and then service them efficiently. The answer was to create a buy-direct presence on the internet.

Injection: We create web-based mechanisms for buy-direct purchasing offering incentives and do-it-yourself inventory control.

Because of this . . .

We bring in smaller-volume customers at low cost to us.

But what could not be neglected was the matter of good ole innovation – finding new offerings in composite materials that could be patented by Hi-T, would offer razzle-dazzle in the marketplace, and might be difficult for competitors to knock off and create generic equivalents. Sarah Schwick championed this injection, and she tried to do so tactfully, because in fact it had been neglected. B. Don had been conservative in the innovation realm, content to grow slowly with existing and conventional offerings. The Tornado, in his fixation on the short-term pop, had killed most of what B. Don had going. And until now Amy herself had had too much to deal with to give serious thought and investment to pioneering tomorrow's cutting edge, whatever it might be.

However, it was Sarah's opinion that buried in the scads of archives at F&D there might already be a few candidates. These consisted of research and development conducted years ago – promising stuff, some of it – that had been shelved and forgotten about because Viktor, for all his lip service to Science, was more interested in current billings, or there was no client available interested in forward-going funding to finish development, that kind of thing.

"But," said Sarah, "if we find even one worthy candidate that opens up a whole new market for us . . ."

"We'd be golden," Amy said, finishing the sentence.

"And for a fraction of the cost of starting from scratch," Sarah added.

"Let's do it," said Amy.

Injection: We seek "hidden assets" in the form of past proprietary research that can be used to bring impressive new market offerings in shorter time and smaller investments.

With this accomplished . . .

We know whether to fund advanced new research or develop promising new products for future sales.

Yet one of the most effective initiatives – in terms of a quick, positive, and lasting effect on the bottom line – came in the form of *disincentives* for certain types of products. That is, getting customers *not* to buy products that robbed Hi-T of throughput – while providing them with good-value alternatives that did contribute to much higher throughput, that is, of course, the rate at which orders became transformed into cash.

This came about due to those twenty-one and twenty-three-hour processing soaks in Godzilla. If there were just a few of them, they would be scheduled for a weekend, when the effect of Godzilla being tied up for an entire day with a single batch would have minimal impact on the total production system. But if there were a lot of these coming in the span of a few weeks or a few months, as Murphy pointed out, it just played hell with Godzilla's output and therefore the throughput of the system.

"And the crying shame is," said Murphy, "that our wonderful customer who specifies these long soaks is paying just pennies per pound more than composites requiring only a two-hour soak. Some cost engineer years ago figured out that the customer ought to pay more due to higher energy consumption over twenty-plus hours versus two hours. But that is almost completely beside the point! The real issue is that these long soaks are tying up Godzilla, and therefore the entire Oakton facility, and the throughput of the entire company! And what do we get out of it? A couple hundred bucks extra! That's it!"

"And there is no need for it in a lot of cases," said Sarah. "Years ago, there might have been value added from a practical or technical side of things. But with advances in resin chemistry, fiber, and so on, most of the time, with our knowledge anyway, we can accomplish in the autoclave whatever has to be done in a lot less time."

"Honestly, the ones who insist on the long soaks should be paying,

Growth Strategy

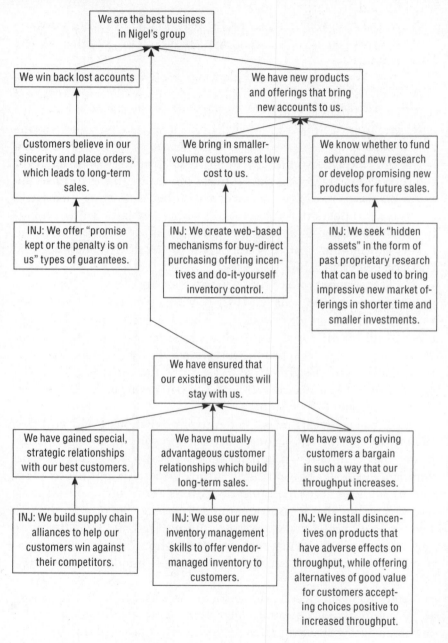

like, ten times what everything else with shorter soaks are priced at!" Murphy said.

"Um, the trouble," said Garth, "is that one of the major customers that insists on the long soak happens to be our good friend, the United States Navy."

"Hmm. Yes, I'd say this is a dilemma," said Amy. She thought for a moment, then concluded with, "Let's do this: let's revise or create a new standard that uses up less Godzilla time. And we will give anyone switching to the new standard a nice discount for some reasonable time. I will then personally talk to Admiral Jones and give him a heads-up. And I suspect it really won't take an act of Congress to get the spec changed. If nothing happens, then we do have to raise the price. Because a full day of system time is phenomenally expensive."

Injection: We install disincentives on products that have adverse effects on throughput, while offering alternatives of good value for customers accepting choices positive to increased throughput.

With the result that . . .

Customers get a bargain and our throughput increases.

20

For Wayne Reese, seeing was believing. What he saw over time, and concluded to be true, was that Lean – and Six Sigma – functioned better within the framework of Theory of Constraints than without it. This was because the tenets of TOC could quickly establish a stable system, which Lean and Six Sigma could then improve – but with a perspective derived from the system constraint. With that guiding, "true north" sort of perspective, there was a more meaningful context for deciding which points of the improvement compass mattered most. Lean and Six Sigma could then be – and were, under Wayne's new handling – focused upon what would deliver the best *system* results. It was no longer a matter of eliminating waste for the sake of eliminating waste. It was no longer a matter of finding the "biggest" wastes, because without the concepts of a system constraint and the money-making measurement of throughput, it was hard or impossible to know what the biggest wastes truly were. It *was* a matter of looking at the system constraint, and what affected its output – which determined throughput, and thereby the operating profit of the company – and making the LSS choices based on what would yield the best results.

So while Murphy Maguire, Kurt Konani, and Jayro Pepps were working mainly from an agenda centered on Oakton, Wayne was working in concert with them, but rather from a concentric circle one magnitude larger. He was working on things outside the Oakton circle, like finished products storage and ordering – optimizing the replenishment of stocks so that orders for these would flow within the stream of custom composites. He was integrating the new web-based ordering so this new river of orders – well, more like a creek at first – would automatically take account of Godzilla's processing abilities before promising a delivery date. And any number of other things in addition to merely dealing with the administration of the overall operations function.

One day, an email came to Wayne:

From: Kurt Konani
Subject: Baby 'Zilla

At the top of the message, Kurt had written the single line, "Isn't it so cute!"

Below this was a photo of a decidedly uncute, perhaps anti-cute, ugly, cylindrical piece of industrial equipment. It was an autoclave, perhaps a third to half the size of Godzilla. As it turned out, some glass-products maker in Chattanooga was closing down and selling off its equipment, and the autoclave, which was fairly new and in good condition, was for sale. Below the photo, Kurt had listed the specs, and then asked the question:

"What do you think?"

Wayne picked up the phone. What Kurt wanted to do was install this second autoclave – "Baby 'Zilla" – next to the humungous Godzilla so as to add capacity to the Drum and system constraint. What could be wrong with that? But fearing that Murphy Maguire might cut off the discussion before it even got started, Kurt had sent the photo to his old ally, Wayne, first.

Of course, Wayne knew that Murphy ultimately would have to be included in the decision. And Amy Cieolara as well. Amy insisted on being involved in any decision that directly affected Godzilla and the performance of the production system.

So the four of them met soon after the photo made its rounds. Kurt laid out his case. The technical merits of the proposed Baby 'Zilla were good. It would not do all of the exotic and proprietary things that the larger Godzilla would do, but as an auxiliary, it was acceptable. The price, too, was a bargain. Yet Murphy was reluctant to give the green light.

"Come on, Murph! What's wrong with some extra capacity on the Drum?" Wayne asked. "You say we need protective capacity everywhere else; why not add to Autoclave?"

"I'm not absolutely saying, no," said Murphy. "But I am asking, what is the effect on the system going to be? We definitely know that buying this equipment is going to add to investment, and if we use it, it's going to increase operating expense. What is it going to do to throughput?"

"Obviously," said Kurt, "it should increase throughput."

"Why?"

"Autoclave can process more!"

"So you are planning to use the Baby 'Zilla?" asked Murphy.

"Duh?! Yeah! Of course we're going to use it!" said Kurt.

"Well, that's what concerns me," said Murphy.

Amy jumped in at this point, saying, "Garth Quincy has been telling me that the marketing-sales injections we came up with are having the desired effect – even in what appears to be a softening marketplace. Don't we need to increase the capacity on the system constraint – the Drum – in order to reap the benefits of those new sales? And if we don't, aren't we going to risk disaster if we can't deliver on those commitments?"

Murphy nodded, and said, "Yes. There is a risk. No question. However, there is also a risk if we add capacity to the Drum to the extent that Godzilla is no longer the system constraint."

Kurt was now confused and frustrated.

"All right. Time out," Kurt said. "Pardon me, but I don't get it. We want growth, right? So we need to elevate the system constraint to accommodate the growth. At some point, yes, there is enough capacity in Autoclave that Godzilla is no longer the system constraint. I've got that much. Isn't that necessary and good? Shouldn't we be *trying* to do that?"

"Let me tell you a little story," said Murphy. "Back in the days of yesteryear, when B. Don was president, we both read that book called *The Goal*, and we figured out a plan. In those days, like most people, we thought that constraints were fundamentally bad. They had to be recognized, but then they had to be eliminated. And we realized that if we did that and continued to push production, a new constraint or bottleneck would occur.

"Now, in *The Goal*, there is a Boy Scout hike that is an analogy for a system with a purpose to achieve. And there is a chubby kid named Herbie who is the bottleneck to the progress of the Scout troop trying to reach its campsite for the evening, because Herbie is the slowest kid and determines the speed of the hike. Anyway, B. Don and I came up with a strategy called Herbie-busting. We would elevate the constraint, and as a result the Herbie would move somewhere else. And then we would bust open the new Herbie, and the system constraint would again move, and so on and so on.

"Well, every time we did that, undesirable things would happen. In those days, the Herbie – or the Drum as we say now – was not in Autoclave. Back then we had four other autoclaves in addition to Godzilla. And we would stagger the processing so that one autoclave would be being emptied while another was being filled and the others were running. The Herbie at that time was in Coatings. So, we go in and we add capacity to Coatings, ramp up production, and the production constraint then shifted to Lamination. What did we do? The same thing. We added some dandy new equipment to Lamination, ramped up again, and then the constraint went to Final – and so on.

"Each time we busted the Herbie, we gave ourselves problems. There was confusion on the floor, and in scheduling, and even between B. Don and me. And there was a always a period of chaos until things got sorted out – any number of unwanted consequences. When the constraint shifted to Final, that was a nightmare, because of the complexities of setting up the equipment in Final.

"So at long last, B. Don and I put our heads together and we said, 'We're going to nail the Herbie down in one place, keep it there, and run everything else accordingly. And that's what we did. We specifically picked Autoclave because the length of the process time made it a natural constraint – and it is relatively simple. Once the stuff is inside, it cooks for a specified length of time, and not much can go wrong. Trust me, because my name *is* Murphy, never choose to locate a system constraint where lots of things can go wrong.

"Once we'd picked Autoclave, we deliberately began shutting down the other autoclaves to limit capacity. Everyone thought we were nuts, but it worked. Eventually, we got completely rid of three of the autoclaves – because we had optimized Godzilla so that it could do everything we needed. For a while, we kept one other autoclave as a backup, in case Godzilla was out of service for some reason. But then the Tornado made me get rid of it. 'You're only using one! Why do you need two! Sell it!' O-kay. That's what we did."

"It's funny," said Amy, "but I remember B. Don telling me, 'We nailed the Herbie.' At the time, I had no idea what he meant."

"And so the moral of the story," said Wayne, "is keep the Drum in one place."

"Yes," said Murphy. "If at all possible, make sure the Drum stays put."

Kurt cleared his throat and said, "I understand now where you're coming from. But doesn't it make sense to get this used autoclave and at least have it on hand if we really need it – as in, if it will increase throughput?"

"Kurt – and Amy – your points about being able to service increasing sales are compelling," said Murphy. "So my suggestion would be, yes, let's install the Baby 'Zilla. But let's also be very careful about when and how we switch it on. Because if the Drum starts emptying the Buffer, so there is waiting for something to process, then we're back to making trouble for ourselves. The Drum must stay the Drum, and the Rope – the release of materials in synch with the rate of the Drum – and the Buffer must always supply full loads for the Drum to process."

"Everyone agreed?" asked Amy. "Then let's do it."

"All right," Wayne said to Kurt, "looks like you're on your way to have a look at Baby 'Zilla."

Admiral Jones had a bearing that could suddenly become as intimidating as forty-foot whitecaps in a heavy gale. But on that day in October when he came to Highboro, North Carolina, to ceremoniously award to Hi-T Composites a multiyear contract renewal, the Admiral was as ripply and bright as the Caribbean on a sunny day. For Amy Cieolara, it was a tense, yet happy occasion as she guided the entourage through the Oakton plant tour, then to a catered lunch where Nigel Furst joined them, then to a brief press conference outside Highboro city hall.

On the business page of the *Highboro Times* the next morning, above the fold was a photo of Admiral Jones shaking hands with Nigel Furst, the two of them flanked by a United States congressman and the mayor of Highboro. At breakfast, Amy showed the picture to Ben and Michelle.

"Mom, where are you?" Ben asked. "Weren't you there?"

"I was there," Amy asserted, pointing at the picture. "See, that's the top of my head just on the other side of Mr. Furst's shoulder."

"Well, that's not fair," said Michelle. "You did all the work."

"No, sweetie, lots of people did the work to get that contract. I'm just happy we got it."

"Is it for a lot of money?" asked Ben.

"Yes, although it's actually less in total dollars than the contract before this one."

"Does that mean your company makes less?"

"If all goes to plan, we'll make slightly more money, in what the accountants call net income. But the dollars the government spends will be less than before. It's a good deal for everyone," said Amy.

"How can you do that?" asked Michelle. "How can you make more on less?"

"Haven't you noticed?" her mom said. "I'm getting smarter every day."

On January 3, 2008, the price of Winner common stock closed at $82.02, the highest it would ever be for the coming year. From then on, the price began a descent that was nauseating for any brave investor stubbornly holding Winner shares. By early April, it was hovering around $57 per share; by late April, the price would not rally above $39 – a drop of 50 percent in four months. And it would get worse.

Through the spring and summer, the full exposure of the Winner financial services group to mortgage-backed securities and other derivatives became known, and the stock continued to tank. But the financial services mess, though the main cause of the decline, was not the only cause of Winner's misfortunes. All those years of borrowing to finance expansion and to cover up mistakes had saddled the corporation with debt, and servicing this debt was now like a poor swimmer being caught in an undertow, as cash flow fell and cash reserves were drained. This was, after all, the same management culture that had produced Randal "the Tornado" Tourandos, master of the short-term pop. There were other, less-gifted tornadoes spread all through Winner. When faced with anything short of a bullish economy, they had little idea what to do. For 2008, the business strategy of nearly every Winner company seemed to consist of across-the-board layoffs, ever more draconian cost reduction, and wait it out. Hope for better times, like, *soon.*

It was in this environment that Hi-T Composites turned in one of its best years ever. While all the other Winner executives by midyear had slashed their forecasts – and were joking darkly about slashing their wrists – Amy Cieolara modestly reduced the forecast for Hi-T, and then beat it handily.

"How?" Nigel Furst asked her at the end of the third quarter. "How are you doing it? These numbers are on the up and up, are they not? Every other president in my group is either declaring losses or in any case is way behind in comparisons with other years. Here you are, slightly ahead of where you were this time last year, in a much better economy, and a mile ahead of where you were a few years back."

The answer, as Amy explained, was not one-dimensional. But the

Reality Tree strategy for the future that she and others had put in place was still working. The alliances Hi-T had forged with certain of its customers to help them beat their competitors were now paying off on both sides – enabling the best of Hi-T's customers to gain share as their competitors withered in the bad times, and strengthening Hi-T's own sales. Likewise, any customer who had taken advantage of Hi-T's vendor-managed inventory capability was in a stronger position because of it. Hi-T's own time-based inventory replenishment was keeping its own inventories quite low compared to historic levels – a key advantage in these recessionary times. Encouraging customers to opt for standardized products had helped reduce costs on both sides of the buyer-seller fence. All of those were working well.

And then there was dumb luck. Or more to the point, there was capitalization on dumb luck. Sarah Schwick had had a few trusted people at F&D go through the research archives, and among the few gems in the rough they had turned up was an old, yet innovative design from the 1980s for a composite with photovoltaic properties. The design had been shelved back then due to high manufacturing costs and minimal market appeal due to the then-low costs of fossil fuels. Times had changed. Amy ordered a manufacturability analysis, and the Juicebug, as it came to be code-named, was now much cheaper to manufacture and the potential market, for the price, absolutely huge. F&D's Dr. Marv had a test quantity manufactured, then took this to a solar company in California, which ultimately ordered 1.7 million of them from Hi-T to be used in a pilot project.

Garth Quincy and the rest of the Hi-T sales force scored their sales gains. Even in a recession, there are secular growth trends – and, just as with the Juicebug, renewable energy was one of the themes that was working. There were the composite airfoils for wind turbines, the composite casings for electric vehicle batteries, and composite components for a new "sea engine" that used wave energy to make electricity. And there were orders for composites going to, for example, pipelines in extreme environments. Sales and stock prices might be down, but there were those with money to invest for tomorrow, and they were still judiciously spending. The ability of the customer to buy merely in the quantities needed, and still get quick fulfillment, was a key factor in Hi-T being chosen for all of those.

At Oakton, in the meantime, Baby 'Zilla had been delivered. And installed. But except for a few test runs, "BZ" was being kept nonoperational until the production constraint – still Godzilla – truly had to be elevated. As a result, the system was running well, with the Drum-Buffer-Rope of TOC giving framework for Lean Six Sigma improvements – in production and throughout the company.

Thus, as 2008 progressed and the heads of most Winner businesses myopically pored over measures of cost cutting, Amy Cieolara and her crew actually grew the business. At the highest levels of Winner, there was indeed praise for her and Hi-T's accomplishments. Peter Winn, confronted daily with an abysmal stock price – a low of $6.13 in October of 2008 and a rally to $12.57 by year-end (Gasp! It doubled in just three months' time!) – as well as abysmal headlines, was keeping close watch on Amy Cieolara. He needed her.

So it happened again. It was late in January 2009, and this time Amy Cieolara was not snoozing on a meetingless morning. She had slipped out of the office and was picking up Girl Scout Cookies for Michelle's troop. The world economies were still reeling; even cookie orders were down from the year before.

Still, the entire backseat and trunk of Amy's BMW were filled with boxes of Tagalongs, Thin Mints, Trefoils, Samoas, and every other Girl Scout Cookie variety. She just was about to drive away when her cell phone played its little jingle.

"What's up, Linda?"

"Peter Winn's office just called. He wants you to come to New York right away, and he'd like you to stay and have dinner in Manhattan tonight."

"Oh, for crying out loud," Amy said. "Doesn't this guy ever plan anything in advance? I should get him a calendar for his birthday."

"They've offered to send a plane to pick you up. So I guess it's pretty important."

Amy sighed as she thought this over, then said to Linda, "All right. You know what to do. Cancel everything for this afternoon and tomorrow. Get me a hotel, nothing ridiculous, but not next to the boiler room – or the elevator."

"They say they've taken care of all that. Their only question was, when would you like the plane to arrive?"

Amy drove home and moved all the cookies out of her car and onto the dining room table. As she was packing for New York, she called Tom Dawson.

Since his African misadventure, their relationship had been stable, more or less. But Tom was forever flying off to hunt elk in the Rockies or go fishing in the Gulf – typically with one or more of his

Marine buddies, not with her – and in between he was running his aviation business, which also took him out of town for a day or two at a time. And she was forever working into the evenings and weekends, or traveling on business, or doing something with Ben and Michelle, or helping with her parents' medical issues. Yet somehow in the past year or so, she and Tom had settled into a comfortable pattern that almost resembled domesticity – whenever they were both in town, that is.

"Hey, are you going to be around tonight?" Amy asked him over the phone.

"Why? You're looking for some hot romance?"

"Unfortunately, no. I have to go to New York on short notice."

"So you're looking for a pilot?"

"Um, no. I'm looking for someone to stay with my kids. I'd ask my mom, but she's been having a lot of problems with Dad at night. Can you do it?"

Tom sighed. "Sure. Gotcha covered."

"And could you and Michelle deliver Girl Scout cookies tonight?"

"No problem. Anything else?"

"That's it. I've got to run. *Thank you.* We'll do something fun this weekend, I promise."

"Yeah, I've heard that before," he said – as in fact, he had.

When Winner's sleek, ultrafast Cessna Citation X landed in New York, there was a silver Mercedes with a driver waiting for Amy. The driver was a fit young man wearing a jacket, white shirt, and tie – and he was not only polite, he was cheerful, making pleasantries with her on the drive into the city. The Mercedes used the private entrance; an ordinary-looking, heavy steel, garage-type of door rose as they approached from a side street, and the driver took them straight into the building. Riding the mahogany-paneled executive elevator to the fifty-ninth floor, Amy said to herself, *I could get used to all this.*

No, responded an inner voice, a deeper voice. *It's nice, but it's really not me.*

Amy had by then phoned Peter Winn's office, and had been put directly through to him. In their brief conversation, his tone was gregarious, even gracious, but he would divulge absolutely nothing about the reasons for her summoning. So here she was.

Mr. Winn's assistant presented confidentiality agreements for Amy to sign. Once Amy had done this, she was ushered into the chairman's inner sanctum, where Peter Winn awaited and greeted her as she walked across that enormous oriental carpet. Peter was looking rakishly handsome as always, and yet Amy detected traces of fatigue in his face. His trimmed red blond hair was decidedly more gray than Amy remembered.

"How was your trip in? Everything enjoyable, pretty much, wasn't it? You know, the X is my favorite of all the air fleet, really is. Others are bigger, and you know, plusher, roomier, but nothing is faster than the X. I should have had the pilot do a high-performance takeoff for you. Have you ever experienced a high-perf takeoff? Really something. You can feel yourself being just, you know, almost slammed into your seat – the power of those twin Rolls Royce engines just spooled up and released, you know. But times being what they are, you know, price of jet fuel and noise regulations and all that . . . well, another time."

All the while they had been chatting – that is, he had been chatting, Amy essentially just saying, "Hello!" – Peter Winn had been leading the way through his office and into a smaller side room, more intimate and more casual than his stately main office. The decor in here was more like an upscale suburban living room, with comfortable loungelike furniture and a huge flat-screen plasma TV, and – Amy noticed, her son having educated her – all the serious video-game machines of the day: PlayStation, Xbox, Wii, and a Falcon Northwest Fragbox. This, she sensed, was where Peter Winn came when he just needed to shut it all out.

Yet there was someone else here. Rising to greet Amy was a mature, elegant woman, perhaps sixty years of age. She was tall, thin, wore a tweed, yet also rather formal, suit with a light salmon blouse beneath. With a sincere and great smile, she came toward Amy, extending a hand with long white fingers and perfect nails.

"Mrs. Diana Boule," said Peter, introducing them, "this is Ms. Amy Cieolara."

"Amy! So very good to meet you," said Diana.

"Thank you, and very nice to meet you as well, Mrs. Boole," said Amy.

"Wonderful, and please, by all means, call me Diana."

Amy was connecting name and face as they spoke, and the memory flashed upon her of this woman being on the magazine cover of *Fortune* or *Forbes* or maybe both. But Amy could not recall immediately the reason for Diana Boole's celebrity.

"Well!" said Peter, having introduced them. "I'll just let you two get acquainted."

And with that, Peter Winn departed back into his main office, closing a door behind him.

"Please, Amy, have a seat," said Diana. "I am sure you are wondering what all the fuss is about."

"Yes, well . . . Peter – Mr. Winn – has told me nothing."

"Good. That's as it should be. So let me fill you in," said Diana. "I am the head of a private equity concern called Boole Group Partners. The partnership owns outright, or has a controlling interest in, a . . . well, I wouldn't call it small, but a limited portfolio of companies. Which is all to say, we invest. We are investors; we are not traders; we are not flippers; we are not a hedge fund. And we are not vultures; our purpose is not divestiture. None of that. Rather, we simply invest in successful companies with superb management – making the investment when the right opportunity presents itself, and when the terms for us are favorable."

"I see," said Amy, wondering what Peter had set up here, wondering if this was just a pleasant trap of some sort.

"Peter assures me there are no microphones in this room," said Diana. "No bugs of any sort. So feel free to speak freely at any time."

"I will, but I'm just trying to sort things out," said Amy.

"Of course you are, and you have nothing to fear," said Diana. "Boole Group Partners has honed its investment philosophy along the lines of Warren Buffet and Benjamin Graham. We are in for the longer term. We do from time to time sell businesses, if we sense their business models have lapsed and cannot be repaired. But we prefer to avoid selling. And we do not meddle. We do not micromanage. We listen; we state our expectations; and then we get out of the way and let that superb management, that we nurture and prize so dearly, go do the job."

"That sounds very . . . wise," Amy said.

"I am glad you think so," said Diana. "Because the Boole Group Partners has made an offer to purchase Hi-T Composites. The price is a good one for Winner, a realistic price, not the premium that Peter would prefer, but these are not the times for that. Anyway, the mechanics of the deal are straightforward. Winner desperately needs cash to recapitalize its financial services unit and Hi-T is about the only Winner business anyone with a brain might want to buy. And I have the ability to write a check for the whole amount – not that I would, of course – which puts me at the head of the line."

"Has Mr. Winn agreed to the sale?" asked Amy.

"Yes. Winner and Boole Group Partners have reached an agreement in principle – on one condition, *my* condition: that you, Amy, remain in position as president of Hi-T and as its chief executive officer. Hence, our private conversation here today."

Diana and Amy spoke with each other for an hour or so, then met with Peter and his legal staff. By the end of the afternoon, it was a done deal. The formalities would take a while, but these were mere details. Hi-T would go to the Boole Group Partners, an undisclosed but large amount of cash would go to Winner, and Amy Cieolara would become president and chief executive officer of Hi-T with compensation that could make her quite a wealthy woman in her own right over time.

Amy spent the evening with Diana Boole in her penthouse on Manhattan's East Side. They were joined by Diana's husband, a sculptor – somewhat accomplished – who played no role in the business, and several of the Boole Group partners. The Booles' private chef prepared dinner: a simple, yet superb coq au vin as the main course served with a magnificent Côte d'Or red burgundy. Amy allowed herself two glasses, and would have loved to have enjoyed more, but for the need to remain sharp. She slept in the Booles' guest apartment, as a light snow drifted past the bedroom windows.

The next morning, Amy got a text message from Tom:

Kids in school
Cookies delivered
Mission accomplished

When the plane returning her to Highboro touched down, she saw that Tom's Beech Baron was missing from its usual place. He was off again, who knew where, maybe on a charter, maybe just gone fishin'. She felt a pang of disappointment as she drove to the office. She grumbled silently to herself that whenever she most wanted to connect with him, he never seemed to be around. But then, she asked herself, how could she complain after she had just trusted him to be with her kids?

Back to ordinary reality in downtown Highboro, no one had any notion of what had transpired the day before. Amy was in her office, reviewing the fifty or so emails that had accumulated in her absence, when Linda came in.

"What happened in New York?" Linda asked.

"Sorry, I can't say anything for a few more hours, not until the official press release with the announcement goes out," Amy told her.

Worry instantly clouded Linda's young face.

"Is it bad news?" Linda asked. "Can you just tell me that?"

Amy stood up and wrapped her arms around her assistant, embracing her.

Then with a huge smile, Amy said, "Linda, the news this time is outstandingly, *fantastically* good."

Nearly everyone on the Hi-T leadership team – the "V Team," as Amy was calling it – remained with the company. The one exception was Kurt Konani, who accepted an offer from Winner to help turn around one of its worst operating units. It was a good opportunity for Kurt, and everyone wished the best to the Hawaiian as he departed – with Amy telling him to feel free to call any of them if he needed second opinions on anything. But Kurt moving on enabled Jayro Pepps to move up and become plant manager at Oakton, a well-deserved promotion for him. Aside from those changes, the V Team remained intact, much to Amy's relief. And she made certain that all of them had opportunities and incentives to share in the long-term success of Hi-T.

"Mr. Tom."

"Yes, Ms. Amy."

"Do you realize that both of our first names have three letters?"

"Is that a fact?"

"It *is* a fact. Amy . . . Tom . . . three letters each. And do you know what that means?"

"I have a feeling you're going to tell me."

"It means," Amy said, entwining her arm around his, "that we must be made for each other. You know, like fate. Like destiny."

Tom raised himself up and regarded her. They were slouched on the sofa at his place. An empty pizza box lay open on the kitchen table. The March Madness college basketball tournament was in progress, and in an hour the Tar Heels would be playing a televised game. Amy, with no particular guile, but fortified by a couple glasses of zinfandel, had decided it was now or never – time to at least plant the seed.

"Where is this going?" Tom asked.

"Well, let's put it this way: do you realize we've been going together now for three years?"

"And what? You'd like to try for four years? Great, so would I."

"No, Tom, I'd like to try to make it for life!"

"Oh, good Lord."

"That's right. I am bringing up the 'M' word."

"Why? How is marriage going to improve what we already have?"

"Let me count the ways. For one thing, we could share a house and a bedroom together."

"We could do that now, Amy."

"No, not with me. I have a reputation; I have responsibilities. I am a straight arrow. It has to be legitimate."

"Amy, come on. We have a great relationship! We love each other, we have fun together –"

"When we *are* together."

"That's as much your fault as mine – if it even is a fault. I mean, yes, I have some kind of whatever it's called . . . wanderlust. But what about you? If we were to get married, would you give up traveling on business?"

"Well, I couldn't."

"And yet you would expect me to give up things I really enjoy, things that make me happy?"

"Now, wait a minute. I'm not saying, 'give them up.' I'm saying –"

"Right. You're saying, hand in your freedom."

"I am not!"

"Amy, you are a smart, witty, green-eyed beauty of a woman, who is a workaholic, too responsible, and usually too tired to stay awake past nine thirty. You won't go or can't go to even half the places I want to go, or do all the things I want to do. So why don't we just *leave it* the way it is, and enjoy each other when we're together?"

"Because – you want to know the truth? It's not good enough for me."

"Oh! Not good enough! Well!"

"Tom, I'll tell you who you are. You are a funny, handsome, good-hearted man, who has some kind of moth-to-flame addiction to adventure, possibly has a death wish, and is too independent and way too competitive. And you won't commit. Just what I want in a husband. Actually, why am I even interested in you?"

"Wait a minute. What do you mean I won't commit? I committed to the Marines! I committed to my first wife – who left me, who was miserable!"

"All right, I take it back. You can commit. You just can't commit to me."

"I am committed to you. I love you. It's just that we're . . . you

know, different people. And I know what's going to happen. You're
going to want me to stay home and putter around the house or something, and I'm going to want you to take off work and fly to the Keys
or something and you'll have some quarterly report that has to go
out. And, you know what? We'll be at each other's throats."

Amy felt tears welling up – because she knew there was truth in
what he said.

"I won't try to change you," she said, fighting the urge to break
down.

"I just don't believe you," he said.

"Well, I guess it's over then," she said.

"I guess it is. I want my flight jacket back."

"You can have it back. No problem."

She stood up.

"Good-bye."

"Be seeing you," he said.

"No, I don't think so."

Amy strode toward the door. She opened it. She hesitated. She almost looked back. Then she stepped outside into the rainy evening.
And then she stopped.

His arms enveloped her from behind, lifted her in a bear hug, so
she could not move. She kicked backward at his shins, but he just held
her there.

"Just let me go," she said.

"Not a chance," said Tom, his lips on her hair, next to her ear.
"Some way, some how."

"Some way," Amy allowed. "Some how."

The wedding was three months later, a June wedding in a small cha-
pel in the mountain foothills on a day blessed with gentle breezes and
blue skies.

On the bride's side of the aisle was of course Amy's personal fam-
ily. But everyone else was, well, the Hi-T family: Clarence "Murphy"
Maguire, Wayne Reese, Elaine Eisenway, Jayro Pepps, and Garth
Quincy – and their spouses: Coreen, Teresa, Bill, Ellie, and Fanny.

On the groom's side, Tom's family had come in from Alaska, and
just about everyone else was from his other family, the United States
Marine Corps, approximately evenly divided between active duty
and retired.

As there were two cases of champagne on chill at the reception
pavilion nearby – one a case of Dom Pérignon, courtesy of the

Booles, who had sent their regrets; the other a case of Veuve Cliquot Ponsardin sent by Nigel Furst, who had sent it as a warm gesture of goodwill – it would prove to be a many-storied evening to come.

In the meantime, on that wedding day in June, the bride was as all brides are, beautiful and perfect. As the wedding march played, and Amy Cieolara – soon to be Amy Cieolara Dawson – in her white gown looked down the aisle, she saw in their places the members of the wedding party:

Linda, as matron of honor, and her daughter Michelle and Sarah Schwick as bridesmaids.

And there was Tom in his tuxedo, hands clasped, smiling patiently. Her own son Ben, asked by Tom to be the best man, looked serious and nervous. And as groomsman, Tom's former squadron leader, still active, wearing at Tom's request his dress blues.

Amy took her father's hand, and said, "C'mon, Dad."

In a few months' time, her father would almost abruptly lose all interest in life, and in a matter of weeks he would be gone. But on *this* day, in his dark suit with the flowery outrageous tie he insisted upon wearing, Harry was high on the occasion, and he stepped forward with his daughter. He shuffled and shuffled and shuffled down the aisle, beaming proudly, and the wedding march ran out and the pianist had to start again – but they made it to the altar. Harry, now a man of ninety-one years, looked at Tom and said loudly:

"Here she is."

And taking Amy's hand, Tom whispered to him, "Thank you, sir. You and your wife, you've done a great job. Thank you."

Acknowledgments

VELOCITY, as a concept and as a book, would not exist without the efforts of many brilliant people who came before us. W. Edwards Deming, Taiichi Ohno, Shigeo Shingo, Walter Shewhart, and so many others built a wonderful framework of techniques and disciplines for the AGI-Goldratt Institute to build upon.

In particular, the authors would would like to express our deep appreciation to Dr. Eliyahu Goldratt, who developed the Theory of Constraints, founded the AGI-Goldratt Institute, and authored *The Goal* with Jeff Cox, as well as many other books, to bring his thinking to the world. Without Eli's genius, none of the work we do today would be possible.

In addition, this book ultimately reflects all of the hard work and motivation of the people of the AGI-Goldratt Institute to make complex systems manageable and to enable our clients to achieve self-sustaining success. Everyone at AGI feels tremendous gratitude toward the many clients and their organizations that have enabled us to continue the work we find so satisfying. Among these clients we are proud to have served are the United States Navy, the United States Marine Corps, and the United States Air Force, along with a vast array of business corporations that include Nike, Corning, Procter & Gamble, Sealed Air, ITT, Northrup Grumman, Lucent, Boeing, Lockheed Martin, Gunze, and Sumino.

Key people within AGI who were vital to developing the concept of *VELOCITY* and its various applications and tools are Dale Houle and Hugh Cole, fellow partners of Dee Jacob and Suzan Bergland. Dale has been essential to the vision, verbalization, and development of TOC since the founding of AGI. Hugh has been associated with

AGI as a client first, then a consultant, and now as a partner for many years; he ensures that we make whatever we conceive understandable to all within the organization. Finally, our many consultants, our executives and partners, and our staff ensure that the story of *VELOCITY* occurs daily through those clients we engage with, mentor, and train.

A concept or an approach that works is not so easy to turn into a readable and engaging story. Jeff Cox is our special friend and collaborator on *VELOCITY*, the book. His books demonstrate not only the gift he has for conveying concepts to others, but the flair he has for making learning about business concepts easy through a story hard to put down until you've read the very last page. Working with Jeff has helped us to see further the elegance of what we do and how we touch lives every day. We thank you, Jeff, and look forward to our next collaboration.

Finally, we would like to thank those who made the publication of this book a reality. Most of all, we thank our agent, Cathy Hemming, whose experience and knowledge guided us to certainly one of the world's finest publishers: Free Press of Simon & Schuster. There, we were happy and fortunate to work with Emily Loose, an editor blessed with both vision and sensitivity, and her greatly talented editorial staff. We, the authors, thank all of you and offer our best wishes for enduring success.

About the Authors

Dee Jacob is managing partner of the AGI-Goldratt Institute. She has been a key innovator in the development of the *VELOCITY* approach, as well as in the Theory of Constraints (TOC) methodology and the TOC Project Management Solution. Since 1991, when she joined AGI, Dee has led many successful implementations of TOC for both private sector and government clients. She is a founder and lifetime member of the Theory of Constraints International Certification Organization and holds all six TOCICO certifications. A graduate of Lafayette College, Dee now lives in Guilford, Connecticut.

Suzan Bergland is an AGI-Goldratt Institute partner and is president of its North American Group. She has extensive, direct experience in applying the *VELOCITY* approach for integrating TOC and LSS with a wide range of clients. A founder and lifetime member of the Theory of Constraints International Certification Organization, she also holds all six TOCICO certifications, as well as three certifications from the American Society for Quality (ASQ). Suzan has a master's degree in quality management from Loyola University. She currently lives in Naples, Florida.

Jeff Cox is an independent creative writer who specializes in writing novels based on business concepts. He is the co-author or author of seven previous works of business fiction: *The Goal, Zapp!, The Quadrant Solution, Heroz, The Venture, Selling the Wheel,* and *The Cure.* These have sold millions of copies and have been translated into many languages worldwide. Jeff and his family live near Pittsburgh, Pennsylvania.